I0818863

CARCHITECTURE USA

AMERICAN HOUSES WITH HORSEPOWER

Thijs Demeulemeester — Bert Voet

Lannoo

**"An automobile
is a familiar
20th-century artifact,
and is no less worthy
of being judged
for its visual appeal
than a building
or a chair.
Automobiles
are hollow,
rolling sculpture,
and the refinements
of their design
are fascinating."**

Philip Johnson, architect

CHAPTERS

ESSAYS

“The design of cars and buildings can shape our cities and impact our daily lives. They have the power to transform the way we navigate and experience our environment.”

Jean Nouvel, architect

ICONIC HOUSES

1959

Rolls-Royce Silver Cloud II Drophead Coupé

ARCHITECTURE In February 2016 the Los Angeles County Museum of Art (LACMA) was gifted a textbook example of carchitecture. James Goldstein not only donated to the museum his legendary Sheats–Goldstein Residence (1963) by American architect John Lautner, he also gave it his 1961 Rolls-Royce Silver Cloud II Drophead Coupé. The donation marked the start of an 'architecture collection' at LACMA. Originally built for Helen and Paul Sheats, the iconic home was purchased by Goldstein in 1972, barely ten years after its construction, despite its dilapidated state. Together with the architect, he continued to work on the house until his death in 1994.
Lautner (1911–1994), while not as fervent a car enthusiast as his mentor Frank Lloyd Wright, shared with him a love for projects which allowed them the latitude to conceive every last detail, right down to the carpets and furniture. This can clearly be seen in the Sheats–Goldstein Residence, which gained iconic status, not only for its underlying architectural concept—a house under a triangular canopy of concrete—but also due to its appearances in an array of mainstream films, music videos and TV series, including *The Big Lebowski*, *Charlie's Angels* and *Snowfall*.

CAR Built from 1955 to 1966, the Silver Cloud is for many the most beautiful Rolls-Royce ever designed. It was the ultimate luxury car, one that was very much at home in Hollywood—Brigitte Bardot, among others, had one—and, in the spirit of the brand at the time, this Rolls-Royce was also known for its reliability. In 1959 the inline 6-cylinder engine was replaced by an aluminium V8 inspired by Buick's, which would be improved until the 1990s. The second series we see here was very successful in the US. "At 60 miles an hour the loudest noise in this new Rolls-Royce comes from the electric clock," went the legendary slogan. The fact that Rolls-Royce always built noiseless engines makes the switch to electric power today more logical than for brands that always took pride in their distinctive sound. The convertible versions of the Silver Cloud were built at H.J. Mulliner & Co., which was acquired by Rolls-Royce in 1959.

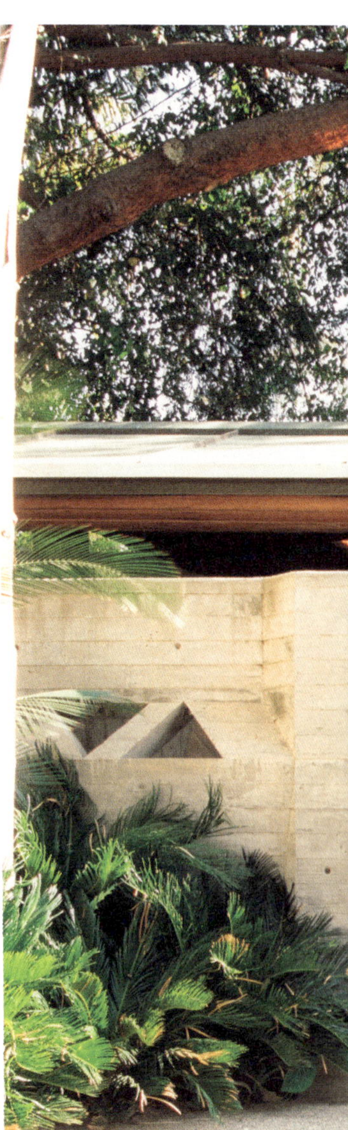

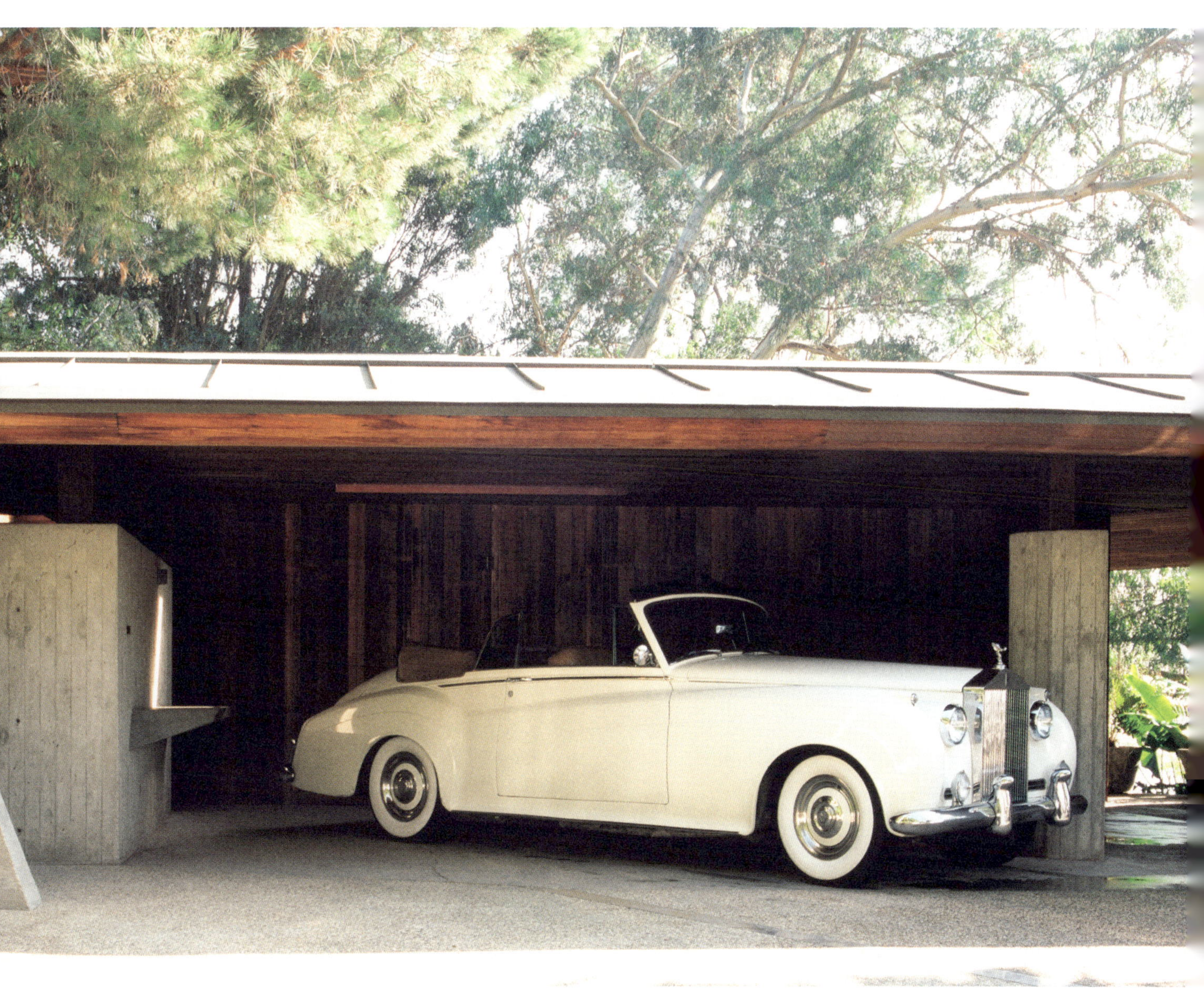

Ford Thunderbird

ARCHITECTURE Italian-American architect Pierluigi Serraino refers to the 1961 Daphne House by Craig Ellwood (1922–1992) as a 'temple of steel'. This elegant house on stilts, erected in only three days, showcases a steel skeleton supported by 32 columns. Serraino likens this icon of Californian modernism to Palladio's 16th-century Villa La Rotonda, while equally drawing paralels to the architectural heritage of ancient Greece. This makes sense since Daphne was, after all, the mythological nymph pursued by the god Apollo. "Under the southern sun, Ellwood's work exudes Apollonian beauty, akin to a Greek temple basking in the radiance of the Mediterranean light," argues Serraino. He further asserts that "Craig Ellwood harnessed cutting-edge industrial materials to build an 'architecture of nobility'". However, an "architecture of mobility" could just as fittingly describe Ellwood's ethos, as he was an automotive enthusiast. During his lifetime, he was as famous for his car collection and jet-setting lifestyle as for his modern architectural oeuvre.

CAR The Ford Thunderbird was a reaction to the Chevrolet Corvette. Between 1954 and 2005, it appeared in 11 generations. The one we see here is the first, the 1956 Classic T-Bird (1955–1957), with the spare wheel on the outside and the portholes in the roof or hardtop. The Thunderbird ushered in the age of luxury cars for the masses—though we shouldn't take that too literally. It was light and was automatically fitted with a V8 under the hood, but was geared more towards comfort than speed and was not a direct rival to the Corvette or to European sports cars. It was truly American, in other words, which also resulted in many more of them being sold—more than 16,000 Thunderbirds in the first year of production compared to fewer than 700 Corvettes.

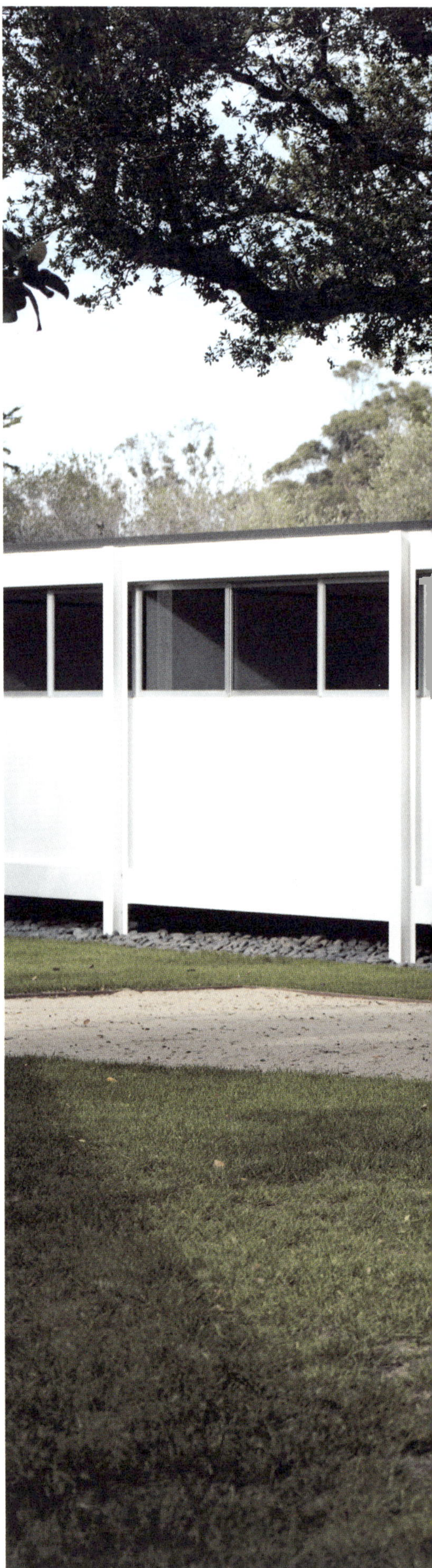

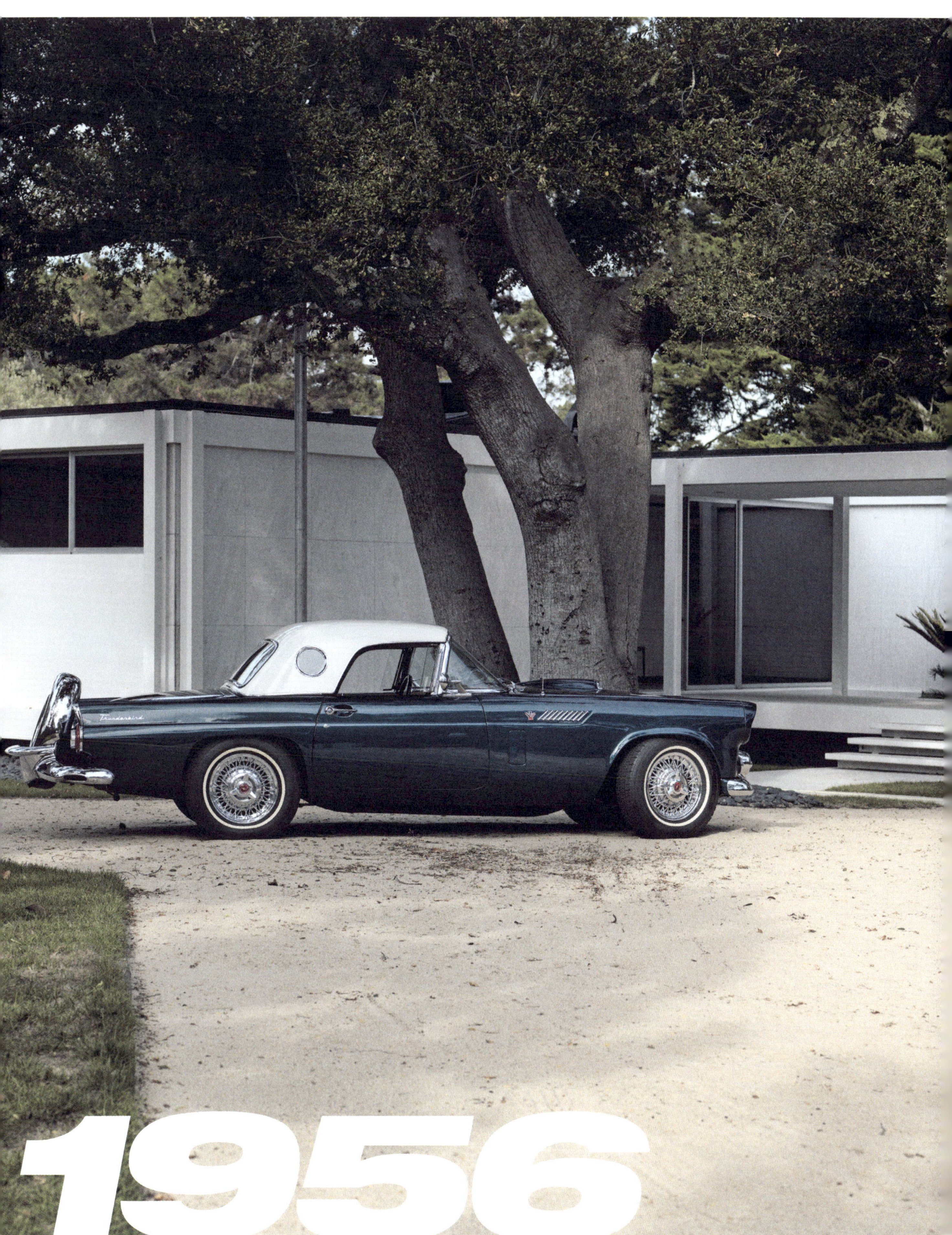

1956

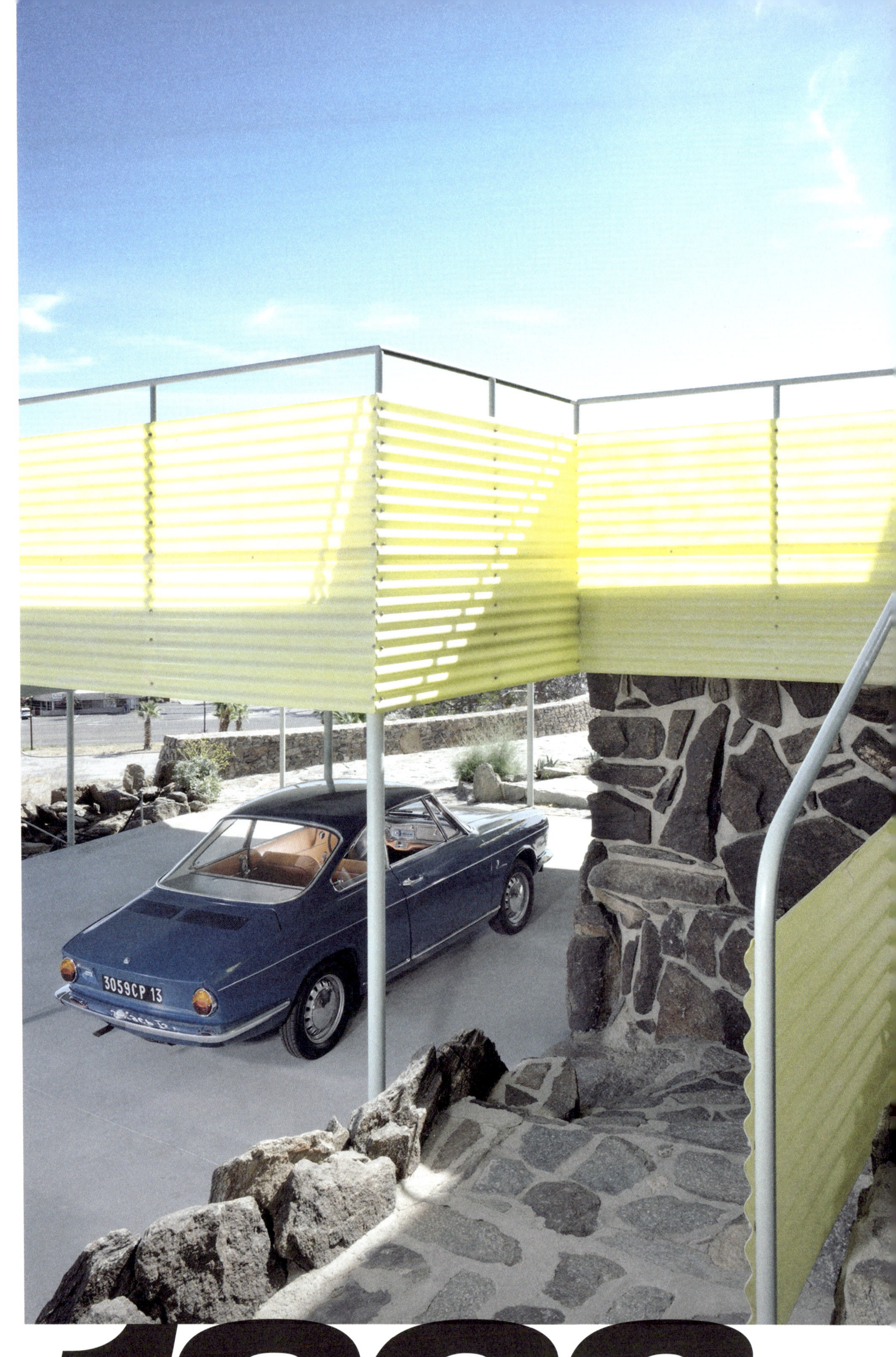

1962

Simca 1000 Coupé

ARCHITECTURE This 1955 Cree House is nicknamed 'the forgotten Frey,' not because it is inconspicuous: the private residence, instantly recognizable by its sage-green asbestos façade cladding and yellow fiberglass balustrade wrapped around the terrace, is clearly visible from Palm Canyon Drive. 'Forgotten' refers to the fact that the house, built on the border between Palm Springs and Cathedral City, long remained under the radar because the previous owners did not welcome architectural enthusiasts.
Cree House is vintage Albert Frey (1903–1998), the Swiss architect and student of Le Corbusier who is often regarded as the pioneer of Desert Modernism in California. Frey not only built several villas in the Californian desert, but also the iconic Tramway Gas Station, now the much-photographed Palm Springs Visitor Center. Raymond Cree, the original owner of the house, originally asked Frey in 1947 to build a luxury hotel on this rocky plot. The blueprints looked promising, but were never realized. At age 82, Cree commissioned Frey to build him a house on the vacant lot: a simple private home with a $40,000 budget. After Cree, the Harris family took the reins and lovingly restored the house to its former 1955 splendor. Remarkably, the original three-door wall-hanging refrigerator/freezer is still there, although, due to a lack of spare parts, Harris had a local car mechanic repaint the doors in their original color.

CAR The Simca 1000 Coupé's handsome bodywork was designed by the young Giorgetto Giugiaro at Bertone in Turin, which also produced it from 1962. The engine was in the rear, but at 944cc and 52 hp, it remained a modest source of power. With the arrival of the externally only slightly modified 1200S in 1967, the car got two carburettors, giving it 80 hp and reaching 108 mph (175 kph). Nevertheless, labels such as 'pseudo-sporty' and 'a sheep in wolf's clothing' continued to haunt it. The radiator was brought forward, as a result of which a grille appeared at the front of the hood: a visual element borrowed from the Lamborghini Miura. The 1200S remained in production until 1971. The coupés were quite successful in the Simca's native France, less so abroad.

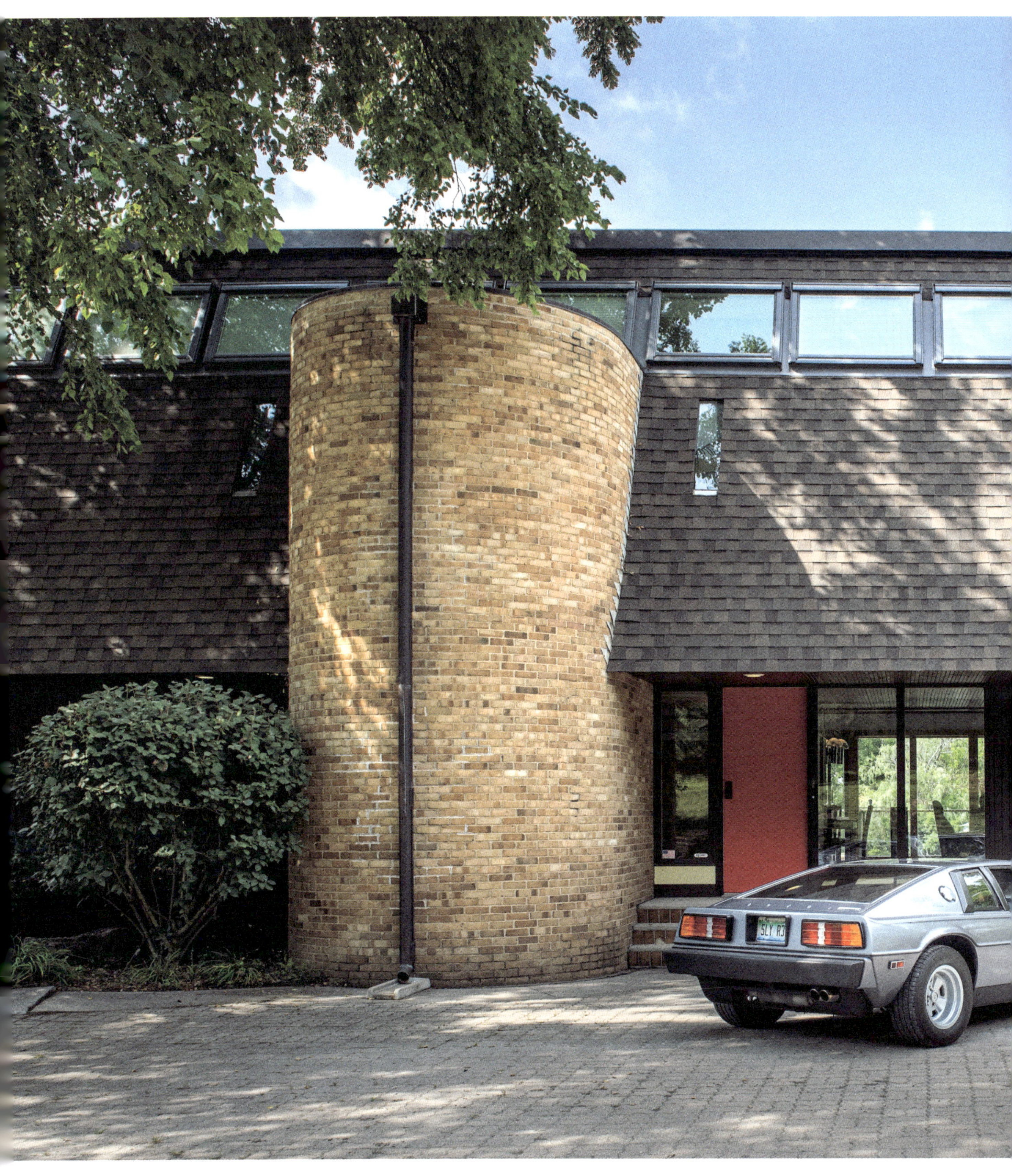

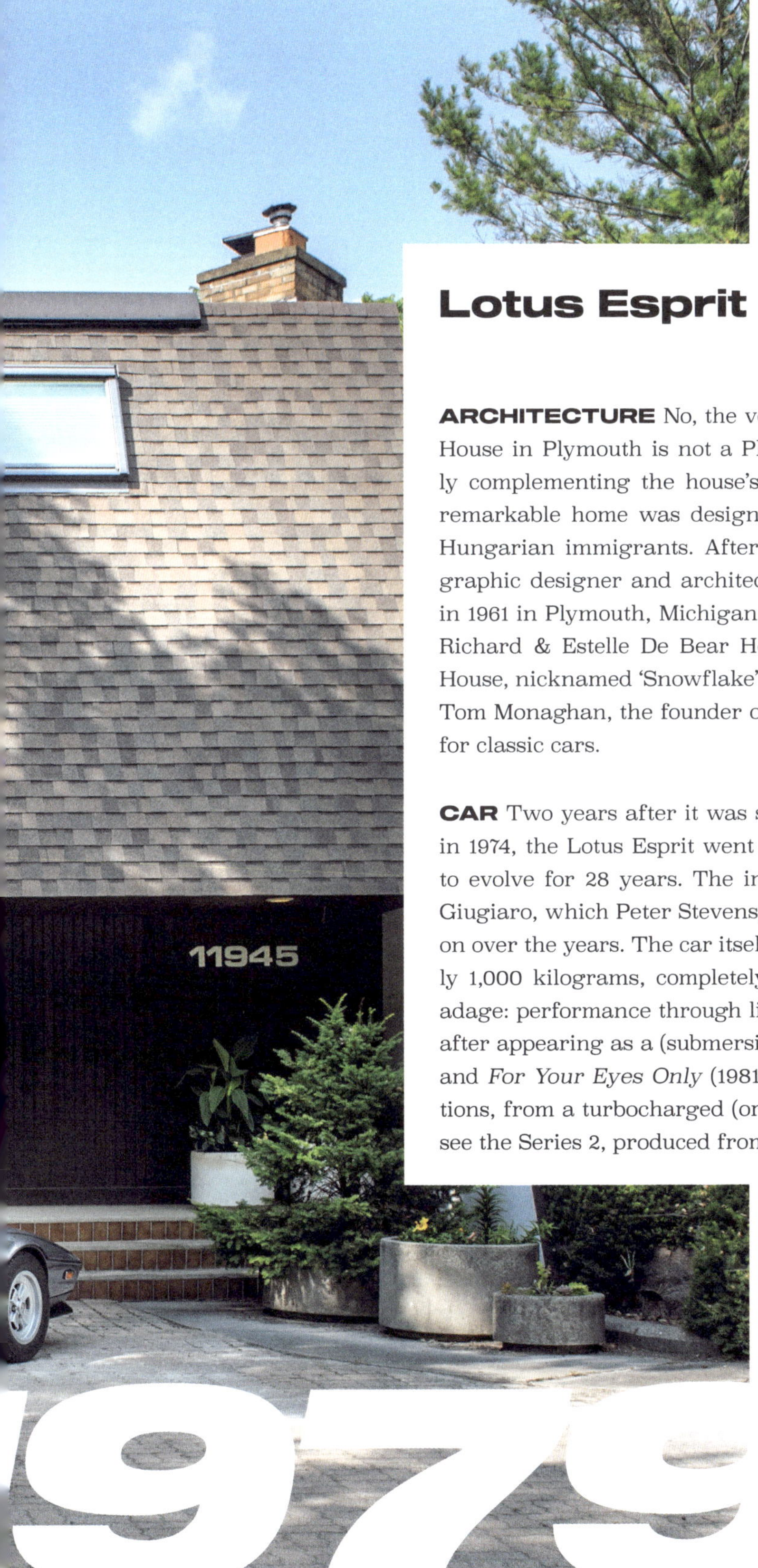

Lotus Esprit

ARCHITECTURE No, the vehicle in front of the Richard & Estelle De Bear House in Plymouth is not a Plymouth, but a Lotus Esprit from 1979, perfectly complementing the house's blend of angular and rounded volumes. The remarkable home was designed by Tivadar Balogh (1926–2006), the son of Hungarian immigrants. After his military service, he worked as a teacher, graphic designer and architect, before establishing his own private practice in 1961 in Plymouth, Michigan. There is another legendary dwelling near the Richard & Estelle De Bear House: Frank Lloyd Wright's 1941 Carlton Wall House, nicknamed 'Snowflake' for its hexagonal design. It was once owned by Tom Monaghan, the founder of Domino's Pizza, who shared Wright's passion for classic cars.

CAR Two years after it was shown as a prototype at the Turin Motor Show in 1974, the Lotus Esprit went into production, after which it would continue to evolve for 28 years. The initial, highly original design was by Giorgetto Giugiaro, which Peter Stevens, Julian Thomson and Russell Carr would build on over the years. The car itself was particularly agile and weighed in at barely 1,000 kilograms, completely in line with Lotus founder Colin Chapman's adage: performance through lightweight. The Esprit also gained iconic allure after appearing as a (submersible) Bond car in *The Spy Who Loved Me* (1977) and *For Your Eyes Only* (1981). It came in numerous versions and motorizations, from a turbocharged (or not) 2-litre 4-cylinder to a 3.5 V8. Here we can see the Series 2, produced from 1978 to 1980.

Jaguar XKE Roadster Series 3

ARCHITECTURE Rosen House on Oakmont Drive in Los Angeles is a textbook example of Craig Ellwood's (1922–92) Californian modernism. Built in 1961 for Gerald and Arlene Rosen, this steel pile house clearly echoes the formal aesthetics of Mies van der Rohe's Farnsworth House (1945–51). However, as a patio house, it is conceptually akin to Ellwood's own Daphne House (also covered in this chapter). In automotive terms, it appears as though both houses were built on the same chassis but finished at separate car body shops. While Rosen House was undoubtedly a milestone in the work of Ellwood, its realization also led to a turning point in his career, due to Ellwood's oversight in adequately acknowledging his close associate, Jerrold Lomax, in the communication surrounding this project. As a result, Lomax left Ellwood's design office in 1962, disgruntled. This was a significant loss, considering that between 1953 and 1961, Lomax had been the creative mastermind behind some of the design studio's key creations, including the three Case Study Houses which propelled Ellwood's career forward.

CAR Launched in 1961, the Jaguar XKE, known outside the US as the E-Type, is revered by many as one of the most beautiful cars ever made. The design was the work of Malcolm Sayer, although the co-founder of Jaguar, Sir William Lyons, added the final touches. In 1971, Jaguar launched the third series of the XKE, which we see here. It features a longer wheelbase and marked the introduction of, a 5.3-liter V12 engine beneath its seemingly endless hood. In addition, the car boasted improved brakes, standard power steering and a lavish chrome trim.

Despite these enhancements, the Series 3 has not garnered the same level of demand as its predecessors, which may be attributed to its slightly less streamlined design. Furthermore, when compared to Series 1 and 2, it is more like a refined cruiser than a road racer. After a 13-year production run, the curtain finally closed on the XKE in June 1974.

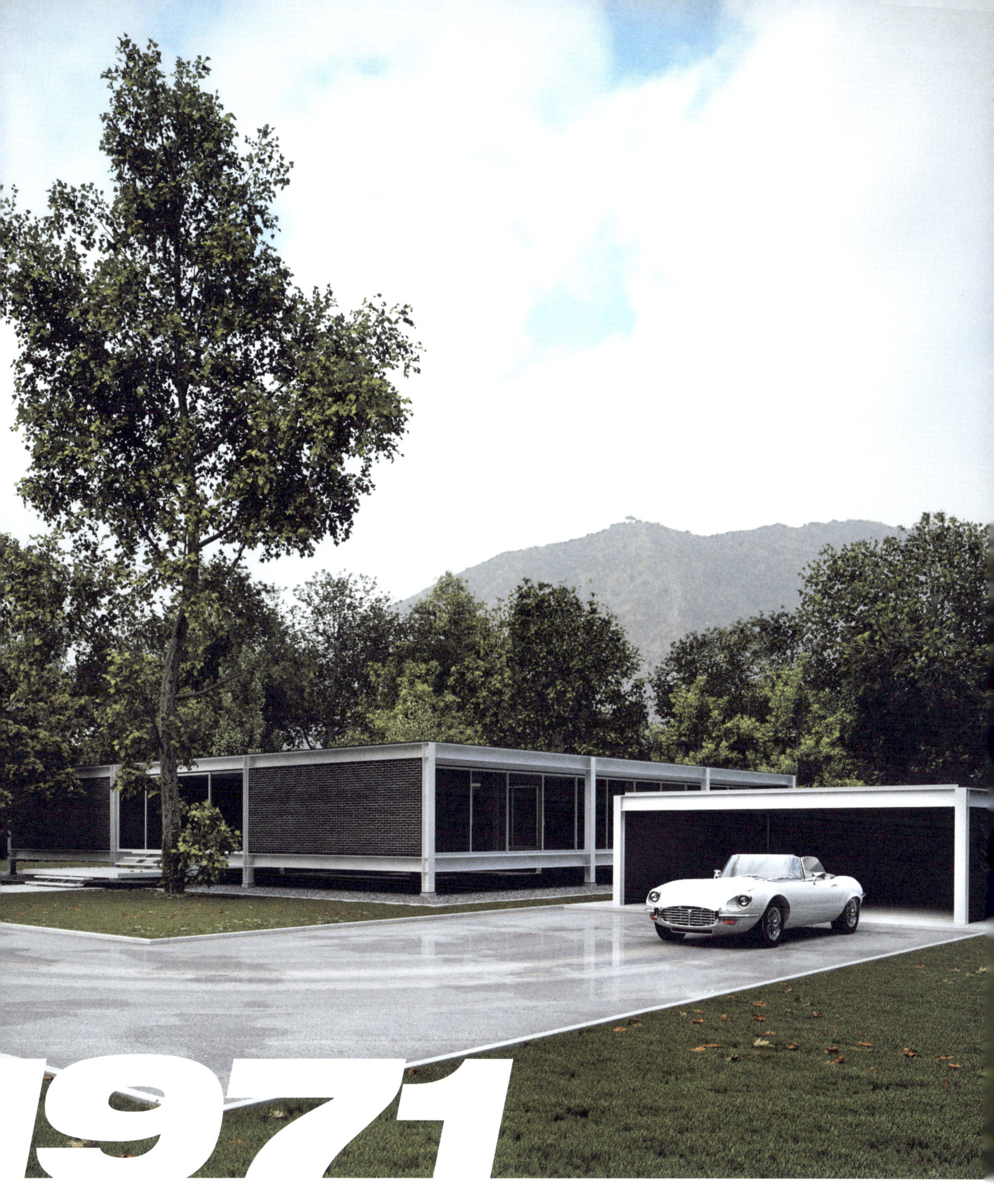

1971

Rolls-Royce Silver Shadow II

ARCHITECTURE Designed by Robert 'Bob' Wolfson in 1979 for John Mellen, this house in Bloomfield Hills, Michigan, is complemented by a sleek 1977 Rolls-Royce, echoing its vintage elegance. Bloomfield Hills was not only home to soul legend Aretha Franklin and architect Eero Saarinen, but also to iconic figures from the car world. Including John DeLorean, Philip Caldwell, the first CEO of the Ford Motor Company who was not a member of the Ford family, and Lee Iacocca, who eventually became CEO of Chrysler after his successful career at Ford.

CAR In 1965 the Rolls-Royce Silver Cloud, which had graced roads for a decade, was replaced by the Silver Shadow, a model that would remain in production until 1985. Both cars were the brainchild of London-based designer John Polwhele Blatchley (1913–2008), whose passion for automative design was ignited during his long convalescence from rheumatic fever at the age of 12. It was during this period of enforced rest that Blatchley honed his skills.

The introduction of the Silver Shadow marked a significant departure for Rolls-Royce, signaling a radical modernization aimed at dispelling criticism of stagnation and overreliance on tradition. Under Blatchley's guidance, the car was given a self-supporting chassis and independent rear suspension, representing a departure from the brand's established norms. The hydro-pneumatic suspension, borrowed from Citroën, ensured a consistent ride regardless of road conditions, and providing a superb level of comfort for passengers.

In 1977, Rolls-Royce introduced the Silver Shadow II, showcasing several enhancements, This iteration further refined Blatchley's original design, epitomising luxury and sophistication. Subsequently, following BMW's acquisition of Rolls-Royce, the venerable designer was consulted on new designs. While only one of his proposals resonated with Blatchley, it ultimately evolved into the Rolls-Royce Phantom, a modern icon that debuted in 2003, thus cementing Blatchley's enduring legacy in automative design.

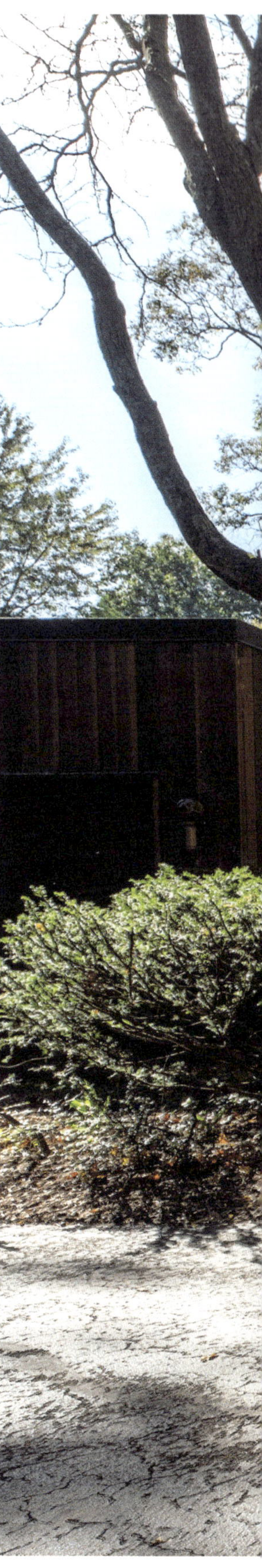

1977

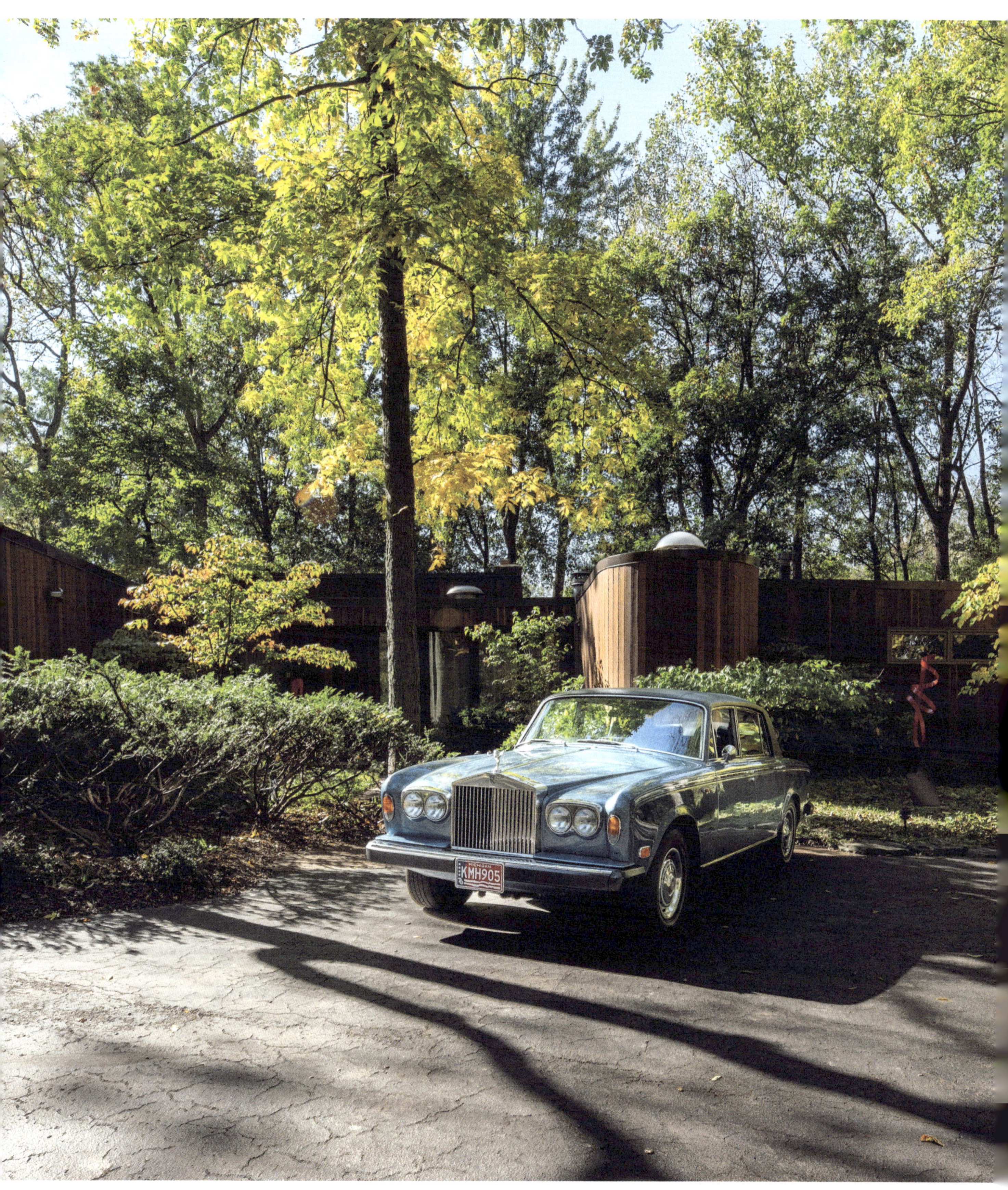
KMH905

Porsche 911 SC

ARCHITECTURE A 1978 Porsche 911 SC stands proudly alongside the Louis DesRosiers home in Franklin, Michigan, designed in 1978 and owned by Robert & Arnette Warren. The house exudes dynamism and openness, with seamless transitions between spaces, and despite its cedar ceilings, an abundance of natural light. Surprisingly, there is no XL garage on the lower level for a car collection. However, according to the architect, the indoor pool provides the perfect at-home getaway to relax and unwind in.

CAR Anyone with money for a sports car, who wants a reliable specimen that will retain its value and will provide a lifetime of pleasure on and off the track, will buy a Porsche 911. The timeless icon was launched in 1964 as the successor to the 356. The design, by Ferdinand 'Butzi' Alexander Porsche, the grandson of brand founder and Beetle designer Ferdinand Porsche, has continued to evolve steadily to this day. When the 'rear-' mounted air-cooled 6-cylinder engine gave way in the 1990s to a water-cooled variant, many called it a sacrilege. It only made the oldies more desirable, even though as many as 400,000 were produced.

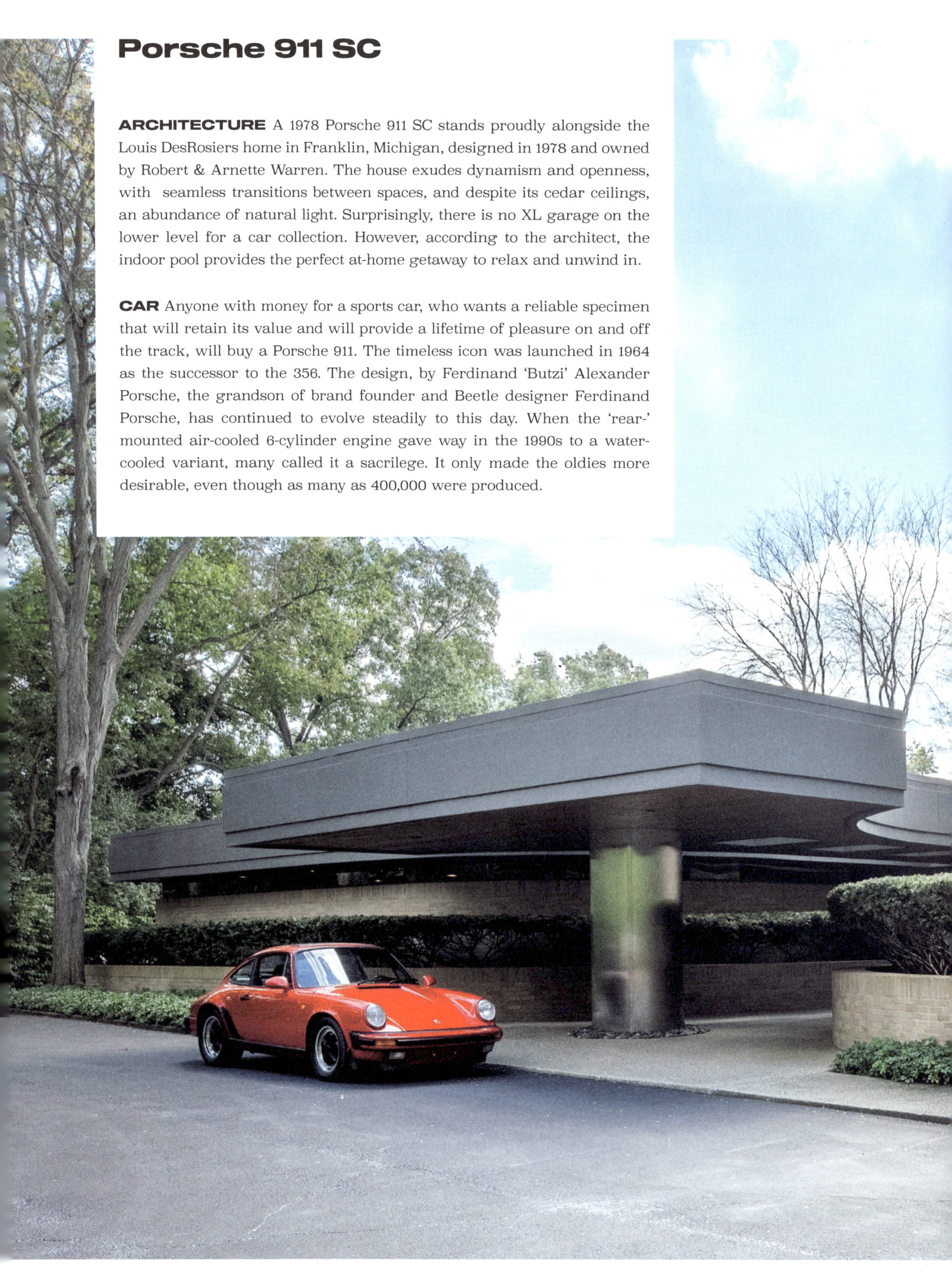

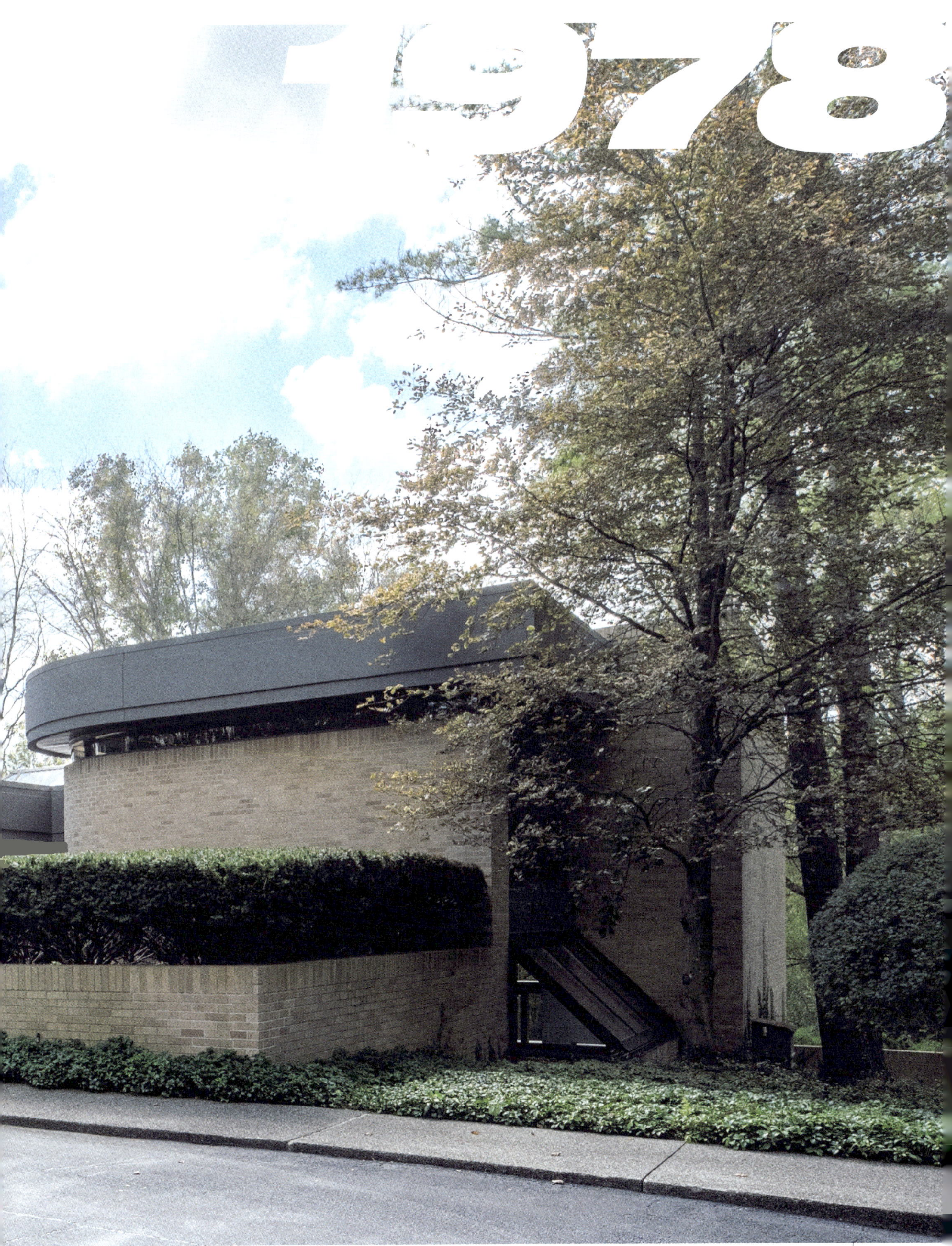
1978

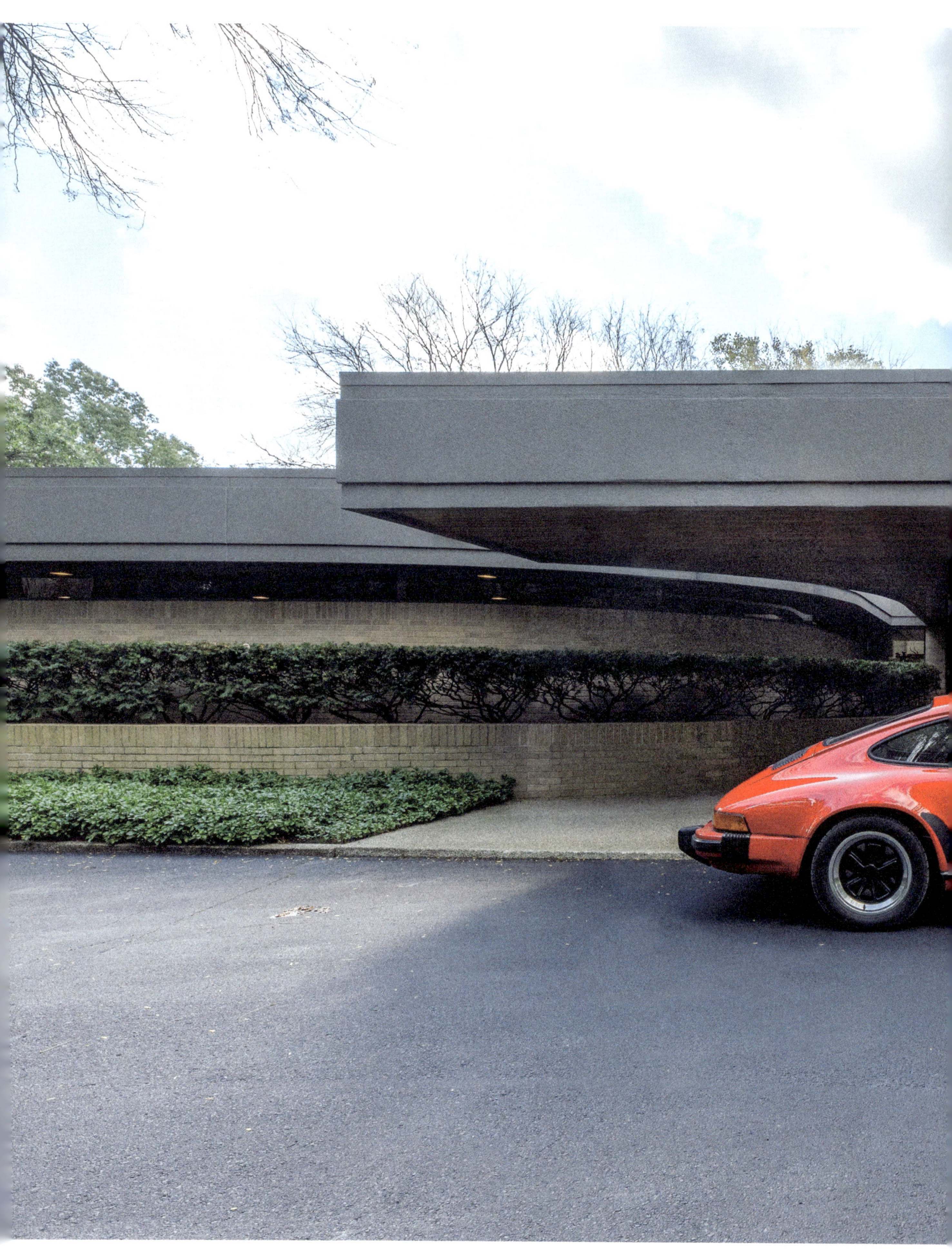

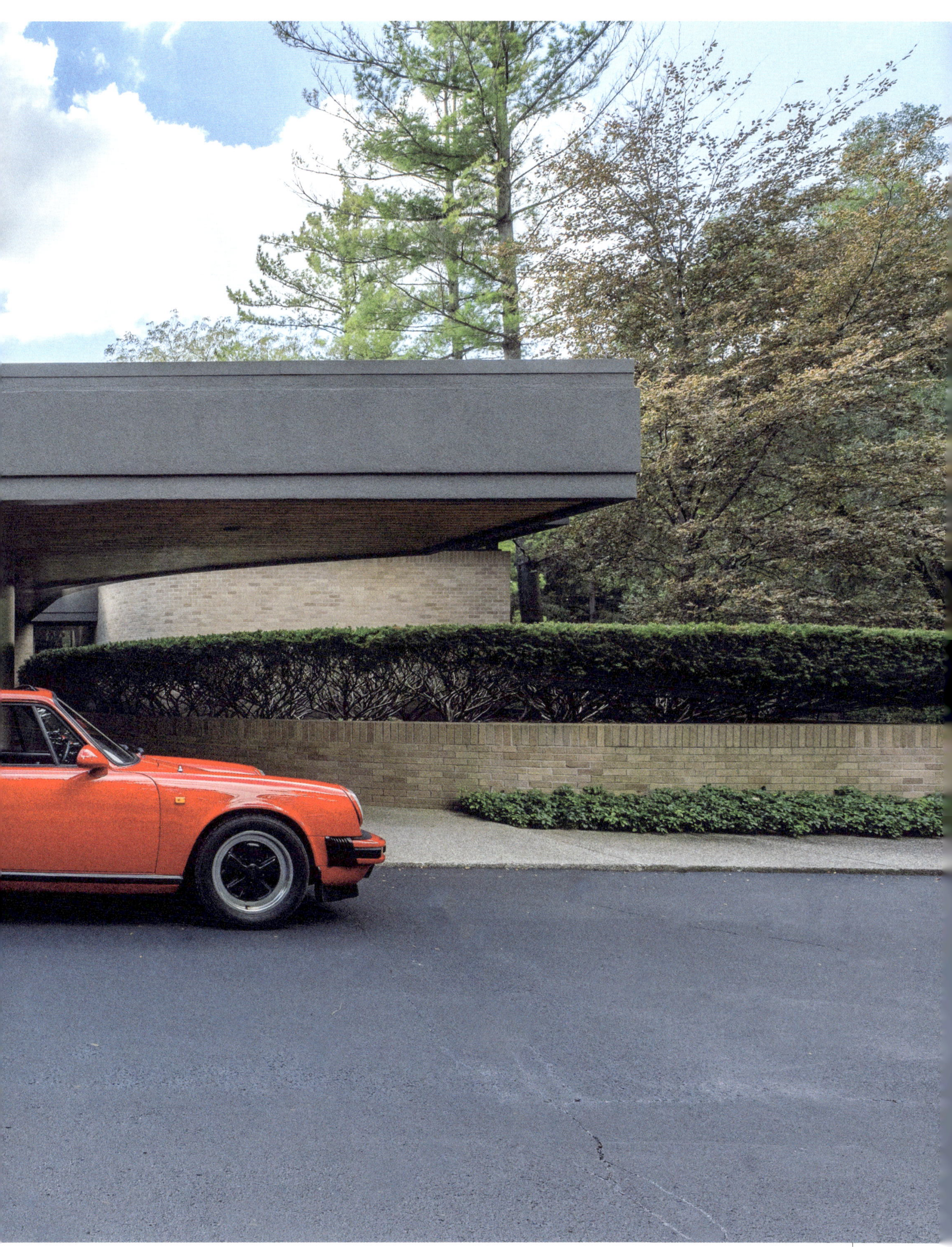

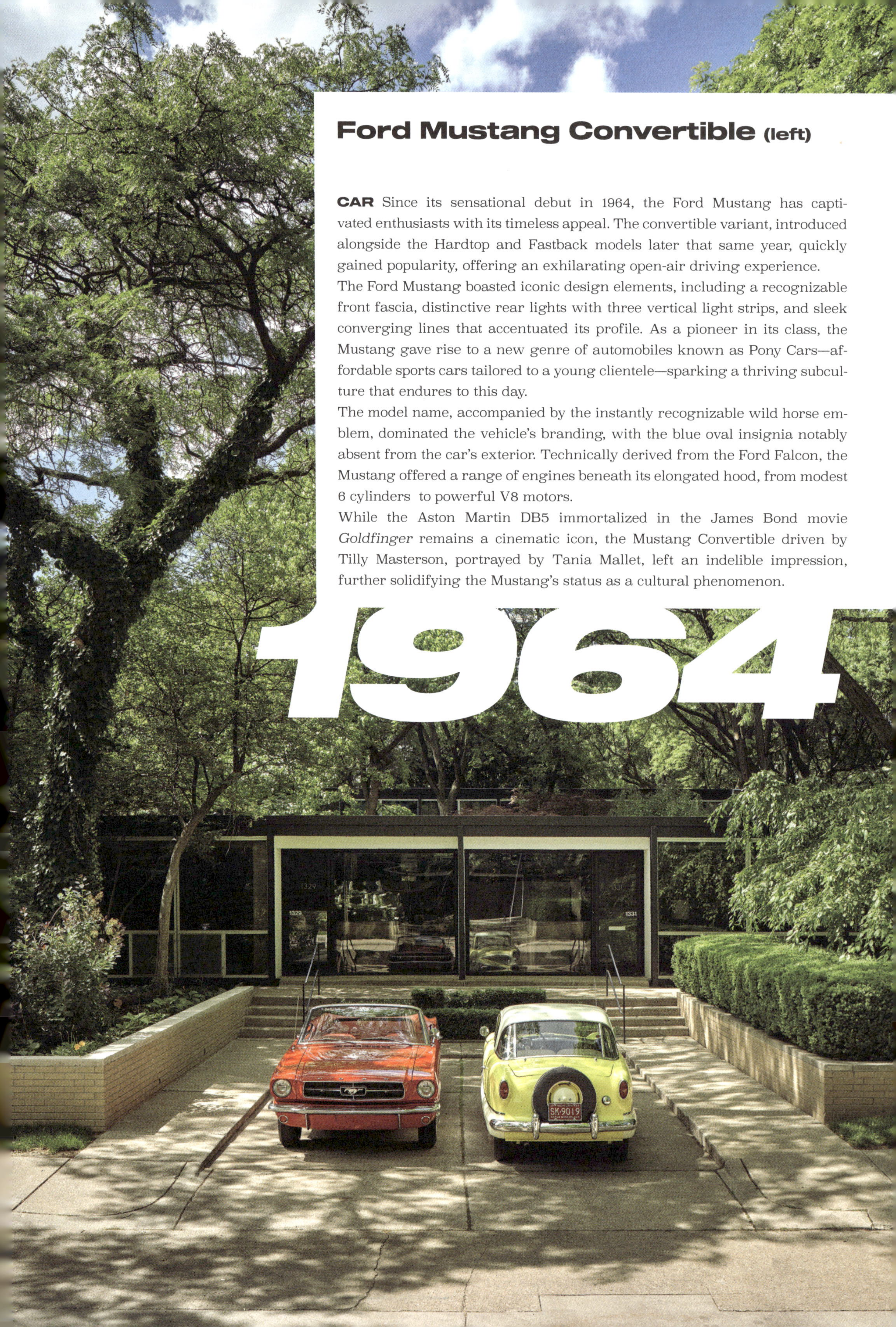

Ford Mustang Convertible (left)

CAR Since its sensational debut in 1964, the Ford Mustang has captivated enthusiasts with its timeless appeal. The convertible variant, introduced alongside the Hardtop and Fastback models later that same year, quickly gained popularity, offering an exhilarating open-air driving experience.

The Ford Mustang boasted iconic design elements, including a recognizable front fascia, distinctive rear lights with three vertical light strips, and sleek converging lines that accentuated its profile. As a pioneer in its class, the Mustang gave rise to a new genre of automobiles known as Pony Cars—affordable sports cars tailored to a young clientele—sparking a thriving subculture that endures to this day.

The model name, accompanied by the instantly recognizable wild horse emblem, dominated the vehicle's branding, with the blue oval insignia notably absent from the car's exterior. Technically derived from the Ford Falcon, the Mustang offered a range of engines beneath its elongated hood, from modest 6 cylinders to powerful V8 motors.

While the Aston Martin DB5 immortalized in the James Bond movie *Goldfinger* remains a cinematic icon, the Mustang Convertible driven by Tilly Masterson, portrayed by Tania Mallet, left an indelible impression, further solidifying the Mustang's status as a cultural phenomenon.

1964

Nash Metropolitan (right)

ARCHITECTURE Lafayette Park in Detroit is home to the largest cluster of Ludwig Mies Van der Rohe (1886–1969) buildings in the world. Following the Nazi regime's closure of the Bauhaus, where he served as the last director, Van der Rohe emigrated to the US in 1937, leaving an indelible mark on modernist architecture. After the war, he built countless steel and glass towers in the States, such as the famous Seagram Building in New York. But his legend lives on in the iconic Farnsworth House, probably the most renowned stilt house in the world. Between 1956 and 1959, Van der Rohe developed a modernist model neighborhood in Lafayette Park, featuring a mix of residential towers and blocks of one-story rowhouses. Although primarily associated with Van der Rohe, other architects, such as Ludwig Hilberseimer and Alfred Caldwell, also contributed to this long-running project.

CAR With its distinctive chrome grille, two-tone paintwork and rear-mounted spare wheel, the Nash Metropolitan is a downsized version of the quintessential American car. Marketed by George W. Mason as a second family car, ideal for errands and short trips, the Metropolitan was designed in the US but produced in England from 1953 by coachbuilder Fisher & Ludlow in collaboration with the Austin Motor Company, which provided the bulk of the engineering.

The Metropolitan enjoyed a cult following and garnered attention from notable figures such as Princess Margaret, musicians Phil Collins and Elvis Presley, actor Paul Newman, and automative enthusiast Jay Leno. Available as both as a hardtop and a convertible, more than 100,000 units were sold under various brands, including Hudson, Nash, Rambler, AMC, Austin and Metropolitan.

The car featured here belongs to the fourth and final series, introduced in 1959 and distinguished by the addition of a rear boot lid. Production continued until 1962, marking the end of an era for this beloved classic automobile.

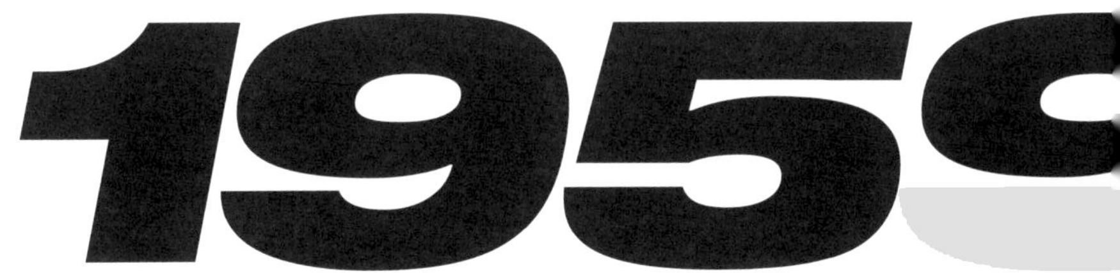

Ford Thunderbird

ARCHITECTURE Frank Sinatra is often praised for his sense of timing as a singer, and his appreciation for beautiful cars was no less impressive. The Rat Pack member's car collection included a 1942 Chrysler Convertible, a 1958 Cadillac Eldorado Brougham, a 1962 Dual Ghia L6.4 and a 1969 Lamborghini Miura. For Sinatra, cars and women were intimately entwined. He gifted his Miura to one of the women in his life and gave his final wife a Rolls-Royce Silver Shadow painted in the color of his Ol' Blue Eyes. Legend has it that he also drove a Studebaker Avanti, the angular 'supercar' designed by Raymond Loewy. Both Sinatra and Loewy lived in Palm Springs: Loewy in a house designed by architect Albert Frey, Sinatra in a villa designed by E. Stewart Williams (1909–2005), a former employee of Loewy's. Sinatra is said to have strolled into William's office on May 1, 1947 with an ice cream in his hand and a sailor's cap on his head. He promptly expressed his desire for a retro mansion in Georgian style to be ready by Christmas. The architect managed to sway the crooner towards a contemporary design. Sinatra lived in his Twin Palms villa from 1948 to 1957, hosting many parties around his piano-shaped swimming pool. Twin Palms Estates was an early housing project by the Alexander Construction Company. In 1957, the year Sinatra left, the subdivision was still called Smoke Tree Valley Estates. However, because each plot contained two palm trees, it was renamed Twin Palms. The rest is history.

CAR During World War II, American soldiers stationed in Europe had the opportunity to admire the beauty of Italian, German, French and English sports cars, and some of them were lucky enough to bring one home. American manufacturers soon began producing their own sports cars, albeit tailored to their unique standards. The Ford Thunderbird was the brainchild of industrial designer and vice-president George Walker and former GM executive Louis D. Crusoe. They proposed that the Ford Motor Company needed a sports car to compete with Chevrolet's Corvette. Inspiration struck when the two viewed European models at the Grand Palais motor show in Paris in 1951. The design of the Thunderbird was executed by William P. Boyer under the supervision of Frank Hershey. Boyer assumed the role of manager of Thunderbird Studio in 1955, which allowed him to influence the design of future generations of this iconic car. The image presented here shows an 'Early Bird' from the first generation, while ten more iterations would follow in the years to come.

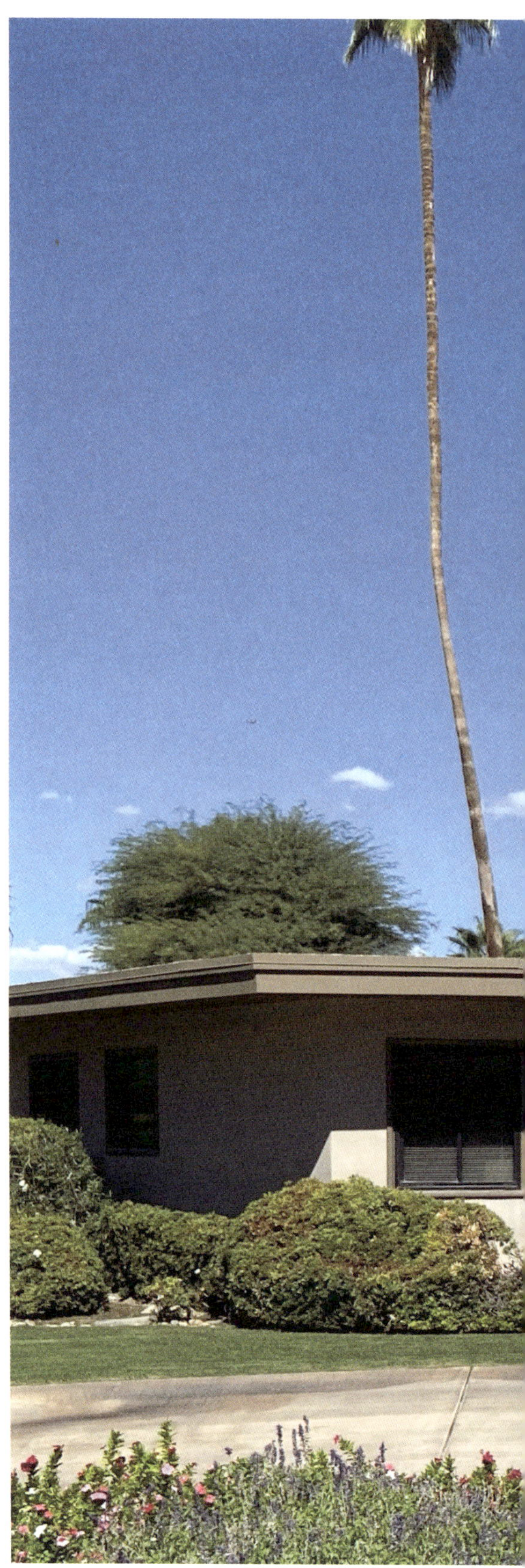

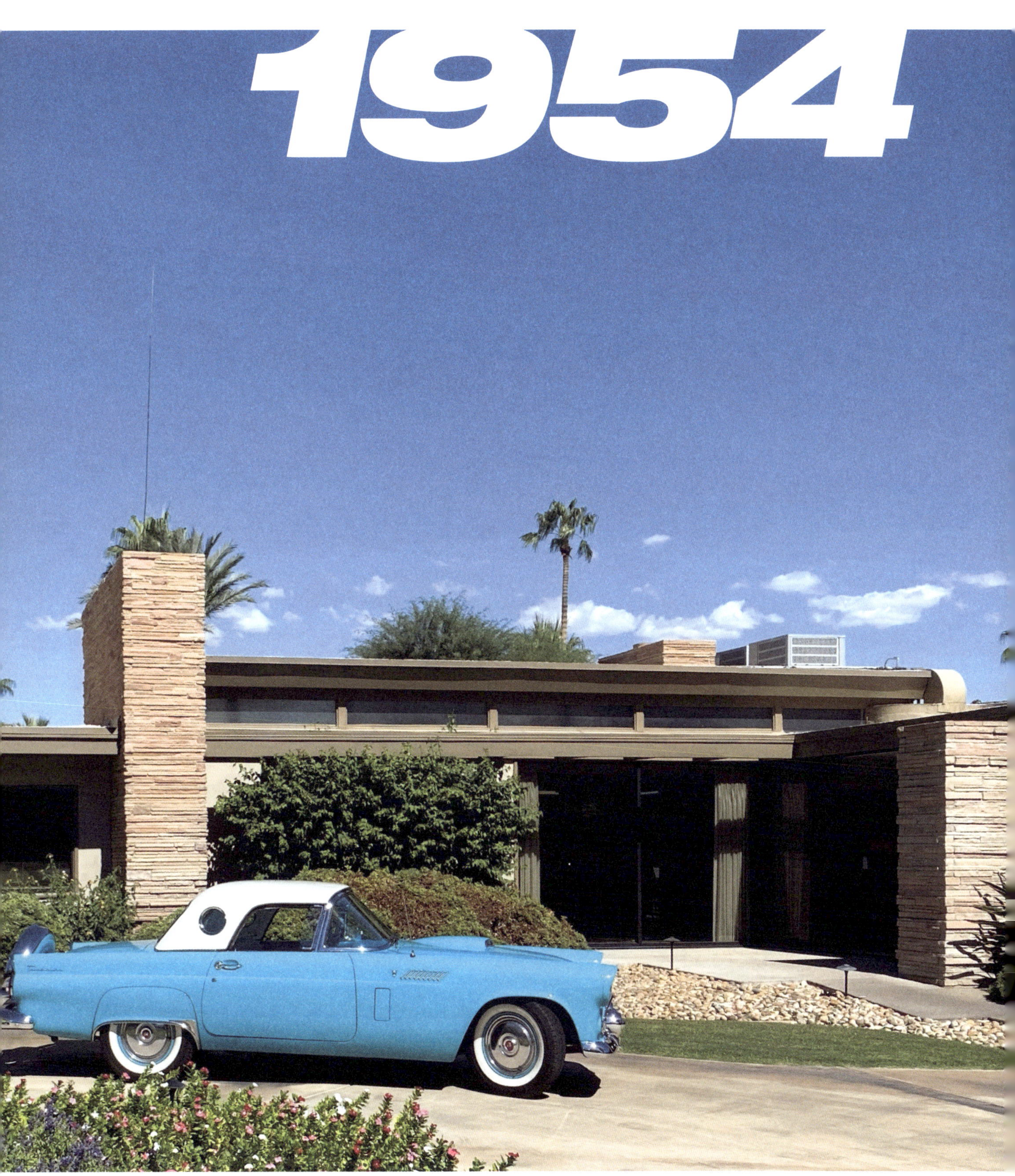
1954

Porsche 356 A 1600

ARCHITECTURE Mark Haddawy, the American founder of Resurrection Vintage, is the epitome of carchitecture, with his knack for both iconic homes and collectible cars. Before he bought this Harpel House (1956) by architect John Lautner (1911–1994), he lived in Pierre Koenig's Case Study House #21: the world-famous 1959 Bailey House, which you can also admire in this book. Haddawy traded the stark steel-glass box for a Lautner villa with more texture and warmth, perched high in the Hollywood Hills. However, Harpel House presented a challenge; it had been horribly disfigured after its original owner, radio producer Willis Harpel, sold it. Haddawy undertook an architectural 'rescue operation' and painstakingly turned back the clock, based on original blueprints and photographic documentation. Harpel House is more of a pavilion than a house: it has no real front or back. Lautner's honeycomb concept, manifested through hexagonal elements in both the pergola and the supporting structure, underpins the design. The restoration required enormous effort, but the result is stunning: this vintage masterpiece is ready to face the next 50 years. "It was never intended to be a perfect house", says Haddawy. "There's a lot of texture and movement in a way that's very sympathetic to the house sort of aging and taking on its own character over time".

CAR The first production car bearing the Porsche name was introduced in 1948. Over the decades, a fierce debate has raged over who was the real designer of the 356 model, which established the typical Porsche lineage we see today. The contenders in this debate are Ferry Porsche, Ferdinand Porsche's son, and his chief designer, the Austrian Erwin Komenda. It appears that the latter played the more significant role in its design. Additionally, another Austrian engineer, Béla Barényi, has claimed his place in automotive history as the inventor of the Volkswagen Beetle, a car that Porsche helped develop and shared many parts with, including the air-cooled boxer engine. In the initial 356 model, this engine had a 1.1-liter capacity and produced 35 hp. The car depicted here is a 356 A 1600 from the 1956 model year, which already featured engines with 60 or 75 hp. By the time the 356 was withdrawn from production in 1965, after more than 75,000 cars were produced, the most powerful engine in the 356 C 2000 GS Carrera generated 130 hp. The 356 was succeeded by the iconic Porsche 911, a design to which Erwin Komenda also collaborated.

1956

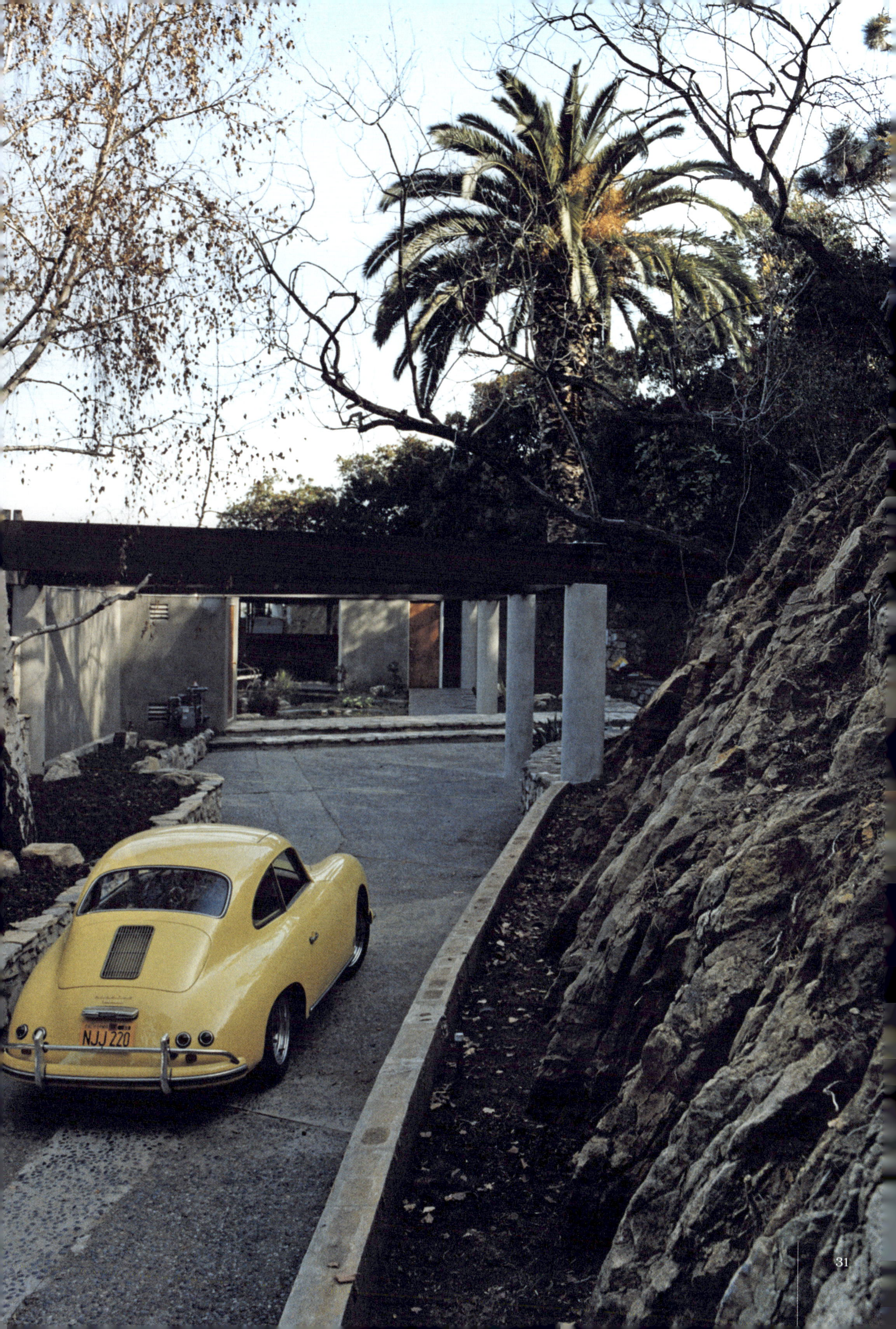
NJJ 220

DeLorean DMC-12

ARCHITECTURE That DeLorean in the driveway is not an isolated occurrence. This exceptional house, built in 1982 for the then vice chair of the Chrysler Corporation, has seen its fair share of fine automobiles. Notably, basketball legend Dennis Rodman, known for his car collection, once resided here. The villa was designed, and later restored, by Irving Tobocman, the renowned architect who tragically died in 2017 after a car crash in his Ford Thunderbird.

CAR The DeLorean DMC-12 had a phenomenal design, but was far too expensive to become a success and the factory went out of business after producing fewer than 9,000 units.

The DeLorean DMC-12 became ensnared in a web of scandal and intrigue, with allegations of a cocaine deal involving John DeLorean (of which he was acquitted) and reports of bank accounts in Panama purportedly linked to Colin Chapman and financed by John DeLorean. Additionally, conspiracy theories within the DeLorean community have speculated about John DeLorean's alleged poisoning of Colin Chapman following bankruptcy.

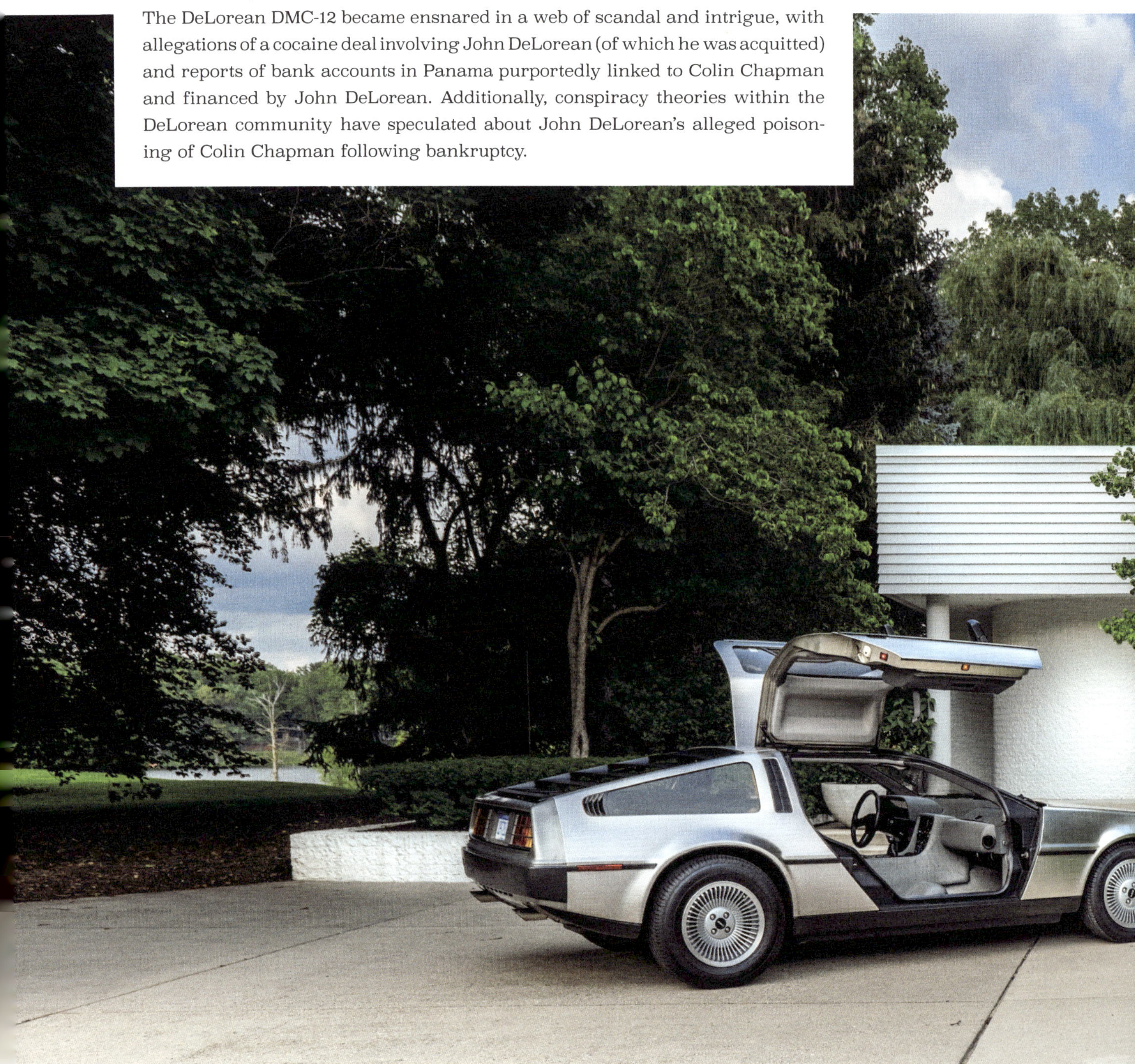

1981

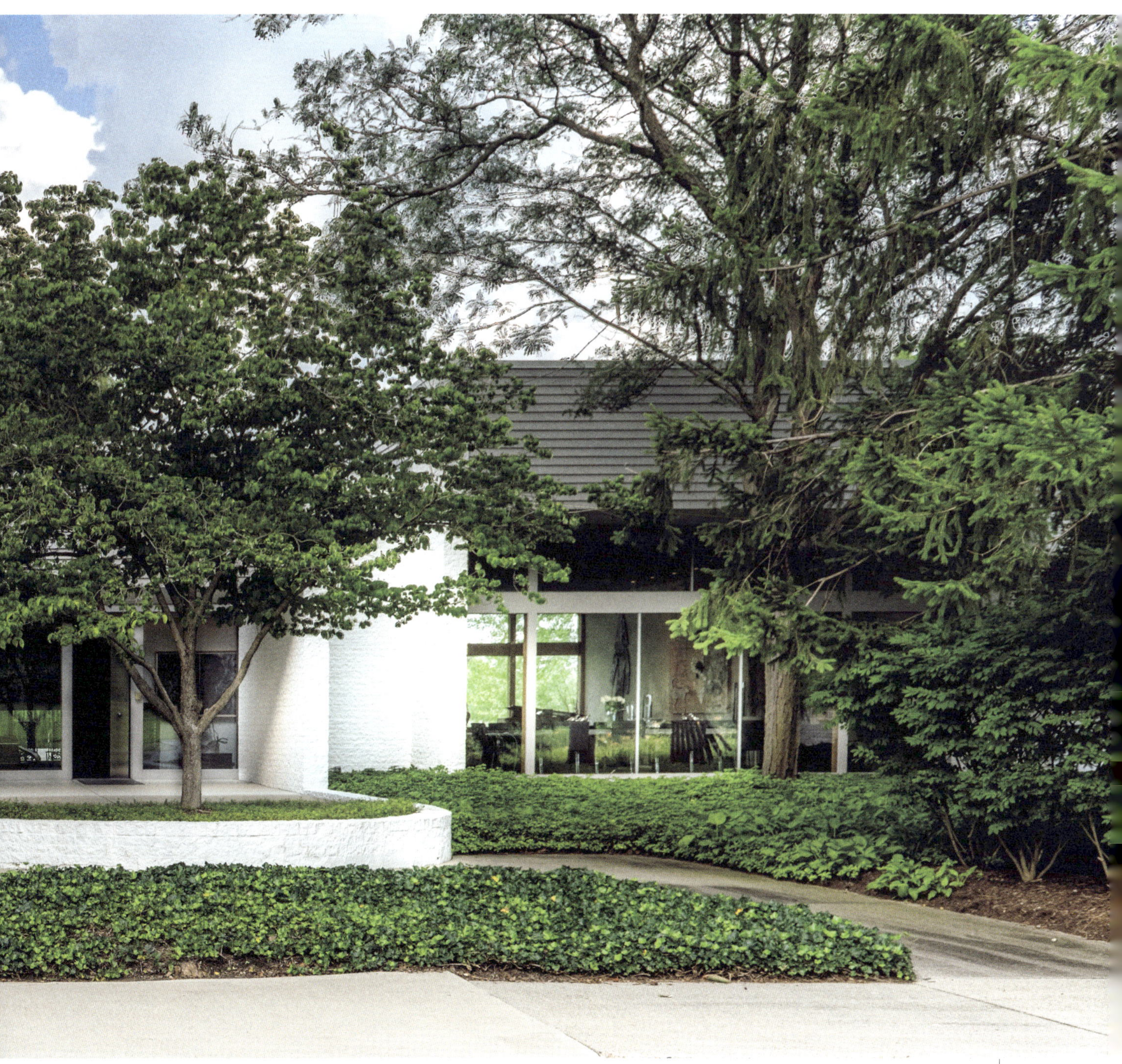

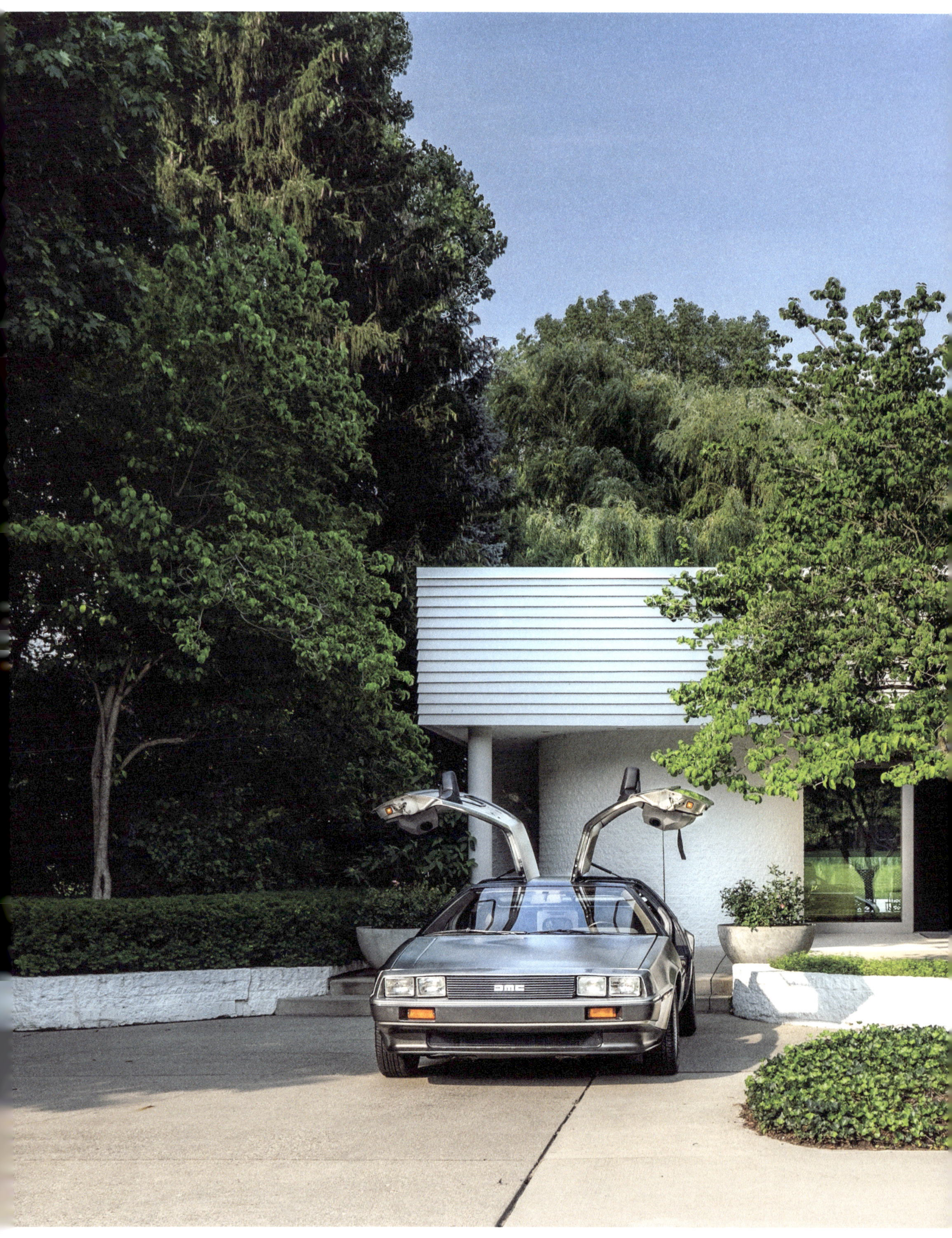
DMC

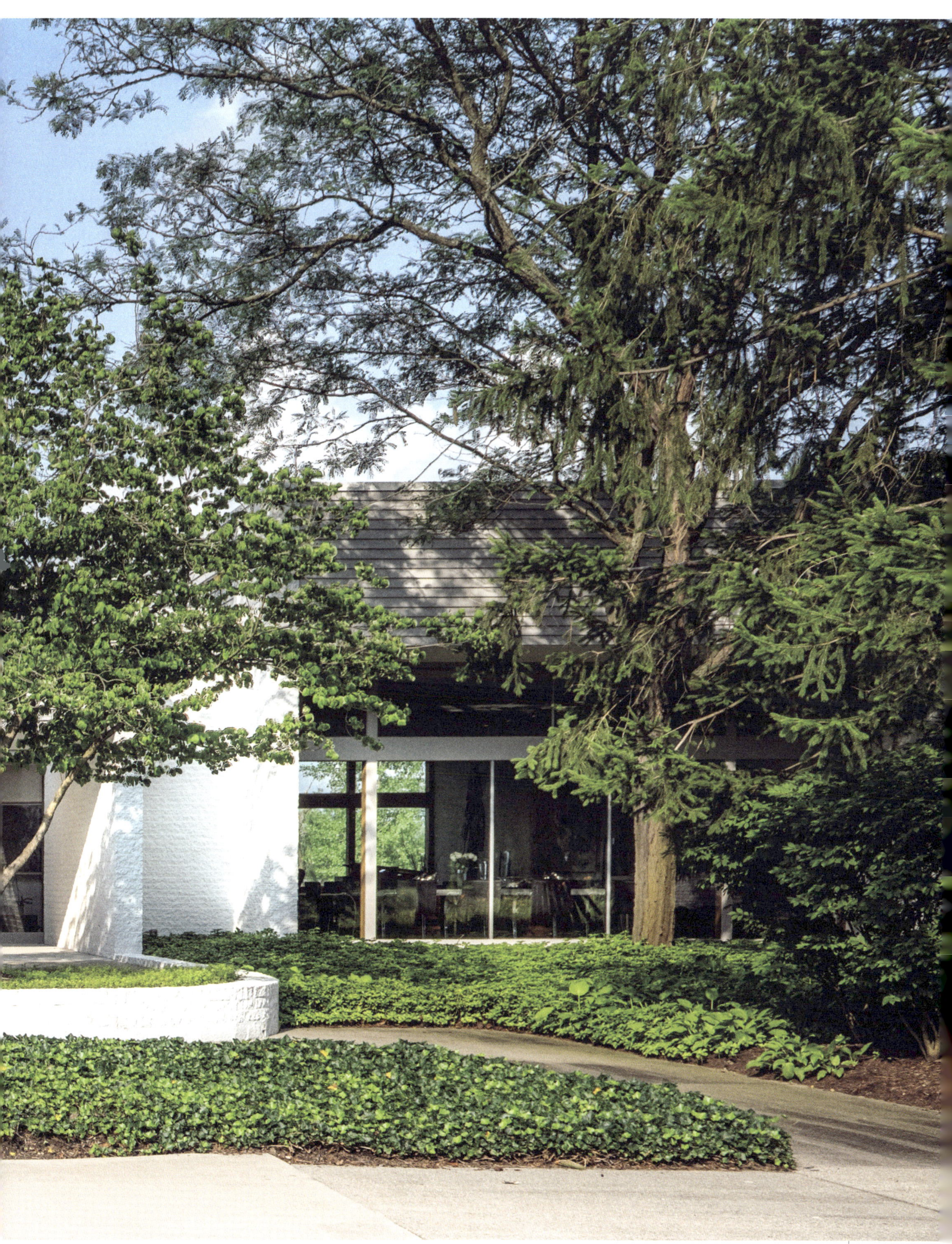

Brave New Ford: Albert Kahn, the World's First Carchitect

In the age of advanced technology, inefficiency is the sin against the Holy Ghost. A really efficient totalitarian state would be one in which the all-powerful executive of political bosses and their army of managers control a population of slaves who do not have to be coerced, because they love their servitude.
— Aldous Huxley

In his visionary novel *Brave New World* (1932), Aldous Huxley (1894–1963) employs the world of car-making as a metaphor for a standardized society. Within the narrative, Henry Ford (1863–1947) is portrayed as the architect of a totalitarian regime built upon assembly-line principles. This dystopian literary work even introduces the idea of making babies in the same manner that Ford manufactured cars. The people in *Brave New World* are portrayed as docile followers of their prophet, the high priest of mass production. In this context, Ford takes on the role of a god-like figure in a world in which crucifixes have been replaced by capital Ts (after Ford's Model T) and the 'Our Ford' chant is used in place of 'Our Lord'.

Huxley drew inspiration for his novel from Ford's industrial and assembly-line innovations, using them symbolically to represent the dehumanizing consequences of mass production and efficiency-driven ideologies. In his satirical, yet visionary masterpiece, Huxley paints a vivid picture of a world where streamlined uniformity triumphs over individuality, technology supersedes craftsmanship and efficiency dominates aesthetics. Huxley illustrates a society that has mastered the creation of compliant individuals, preprogrammed for productivity and devoid of critical thinking. In essence, these individuals are ignorant workers who revere Ford as the equivalent of a divine figure, chanting 'Our Ford' in place of religious devotion.

THE FATHER OF MODERN FACTORY DESIGN

The true visionary behind Fordism was not Aldous Huxley, but Albert Kahn (1869–1942), an industrial architect who played a pivotal role in the development of standardized mass car production in the United States, earning himself the rightful title of the world's first and most influential carchitect. His groundbreaking innovations in factory design, particularly for companies such as Packard and Ford, left an indelible mark on Detroit, at the beginning of the 20th century.

A German-Jewish architect who immigrated to the United States in 1881, Albert Kahn was recognized as 'the father of modern factory design' during his lifetime. In 1903, he achieved a remarkable feat by constructing a groundbreaking 6,500 m² factory for the Packard Motor Company in Detroit in just 90 days. However, it was his pioneering work on the Highland

Park Ford Plant (1909) that truly revolutionized car manufacturing.

At the time, the success of the Model T's predecessor, the N Ford, had created overwhelming demand, exceeding the production capacity of the existing facility on Piquette Avenue. Urgently needing a solution, Henry Ford purchased a 24-acre plot in Highland Park, just north of Detroit, in 1906. Impressed with Kahn's innovative approach to the Packard factory, which featured a concrete skeleton and large windows, Ford sought similar concepts but on a larger scale. Kahn delivered precisely what Ford envisioned, resulting in Highland Park becoming the world's largest automobile factory and the first to incorporate a moving assembly line for the Ford Model T.
Adjacent to the huge factory, Kahn designed a sprawling workshop, connected to the production hall by a 850-foot (260 meter)-long glass corridor. Highland Park's success established Kahn as America's leading industrial architect, solidifying his legacy in the field.

BLACK AS THE MOST EFFICIENT COLOR

The new factory marked a pivotal moment for Henry Ford, offering the scalability he needed. In late 1909 he relocated production from Piquette Avenue to Highland Park, where 15 million Model T cars rolled off its assembly line. The Model T was designed to be the ultimate family car, accessible to everyone. Ford articulated his vision: 'To manufacture a motor vehicle for everyone, it must be so economic that even a person with modest income can buy one and enjoy with his family the blessing of hours of happiness in the open spaces of Our Lord.' With this goal in mind, Ford made every effort to produce his cars as affordably and efficiently as possible.

Ford's famous slogan, 'Any customer can have a car painted any color that he wants, as long as it's black,' succinctly captured the essence of his efficiency-driven approach. Black paint was chosen because it dried faster than other colors, thus enhancing production efficiency.

Highland Park was designed with efficiency as its core principle. The factory complex earned the nickname 'Crystal Palace' due to its spectacular glass windows, accounting for 4,600 m² of glass or three quarters of the façade area. The four-story, 866-foot (264 meter) long factory was often compared to a '68-story skyscraper lying on its side', as noted by Richard Snow in his biography of Henry Ford. This architectural innovation not only added elegance to the building but also significantly improved working conditions inside the factory.
Thanks to the assembly lines, cars could be manufactured faster and more efficiently, resulting in reduced prices and labor costs. The Highland Park Ford set a new global standard for industrial car manufacturing,

while Albert Kahn's architectural contributions established his reputation as a pioneering carchitect.

RIVER ROUGE COMPLEX

Unlike his son Louis (1901–1974), Albert Kahn was not an idealistic architect keen on expressive material details. Rather, he was renowned for his pragmatic approach to architecture. He argued that "industrial buildings must deal largely with practical requirements, structural design and mechanical equipment". Recognizing the changing needs of entrepreneurs such as Henry Ford, Kahn understood that the traditional layout of factories was no longer sufficient.

Commissioned once again by Ford in 1915, Kahn began work on the River Rouge Complex, which became operational in 1923. This huge production facility in Dearborn, just outside Detroit, not only housed assembly lines, but also facilities for manufacturing steel and glass components. The most striking difference from the Highland Park Ford Plant was that the River Rouge Complex had only one story.
At River Rouge, 6,000 cars rolled off the assembly line daily. Kahn designed the plant with this standardized mass production in mind. To this day, River Rouge remains a masterpiece of efficiency and functionalism. With its large windows and lightweight supporting structure, Kahn was able to create expansive industrial spaces that allowed natural light and air to circulate freely. Ample daylight, roof lights and ventilation provided a pleasant and healthy work environment, indirectly contributing to the well-being and productivity of workers.

LE CARBUSIER

The principles of Fordism, along with Albert Kahn's innovative approach to designing and constructing factories, served as a profound source of inspiration for numerous modern architects during the interwar period. One notable figure among them was Le Corbusier (1887–1965), who, as early as the 1920s, dreamed of constructing standardized houses in factories, much like the assembly-line production at Ford. In his influential 1924 book *Toward an Architecture*, Le Corbusier wrote:

> ***If houses were built industrially, mass-produced like chassis, an aesthetic would be formed with surprising precision.***

During the 1920s, Le Corbusier designed the Maison Citrohan, a series of standardized concept houses intended for industrial-scale production. These houses can be considered the forerunner of modern modular prefab housing concepts. However, it's worth noting that the Citrohan houses were never constructed. Le Corbusier also attempted to design a car known as the Voiture Minimum, although this project also never came to fruition. Nevertheless, in November 1935, while on a study trip to the United States, Le Corbusier visited the Ford factories in Detroit and Dearborn. This visit had a profound impact on him and, in January 1936, he conveyed his Ford experience in a letter to Gordon Buehrig (1904–1990), a renowned American car designer who worked for Packard, Auburn, Cord, Duesenberg and Ford. In the letter Le Corbusier wrote:

> ***I recently visited the Ford factories in Detroit and, this time, it is the automobile that confirmed with dazzling clarity the idea I have been defending for the last ten years: that large-scale industry should be dealing with homes and should build mass production homes on an assembly line, with completely innovative production methods. Homes should be built in factories similar to those for automobiles. My trip to the United States has convinced me that this task can be carried out in your country before any other, because you are better equipped with technicians and machines than anyone else.***

In his biography of Le Corbusier, Nicolas Fox Weber provides a quotation from the Swiss architect during his visit to the River Rouge Complex: "With Ford, everything is collaboration, unity of outlook, unity of goals, perfect convergence of thought and action." This statement highlights the stark contrast between the efficient approach adopted by Ford and the less efficient practices of architecture in Europe during Le Corbusier's time.

Le Corbusier expressed his belief to *The Detroit News* that Detroit was the ideal city for the future production of prefabricated, mass-produced houses. He emphasized that it would not be architects but automobile manufacturers who would undertake the production of these innovative homes. While his prophecy has not yet materialized, the emergence of forward-looking car companies such as Tesla suggests that the future may still hold surprises. Maybe one day, Tesla will be building houses? If it's not on earth, than maybe on Mars.

“The car has become the carapace, the protective and aggressive shell, of urban and suburban man.”

Marshall McLuhan, philosopher

CALIFORNIA DREAMING

Citroën SM

ARCHITECTURE During the interwar period, Palm Springs already attracted a great many Hollywood film stars and celebrities, who were drawn to its spectacular desert and mountain landscapes. However, it wasn't until after World War II that the division and utilization of land gained momentum, fuelled by the entrepreneurial spirit of the Alexander Construction Company and the Meiselman family, among others. They built thousands of affordable mid-century-style villas, in collaboration with architects such as Donald Wexler, Dan Palmer and William Krisel. This construction frenzy turned Palm Springs into the American mecca of modernism. Designed by Palmer & Krisel, this 1958 Alexander House on 815 Camino Sur is a favorite photo spot for many architecture enthusiasts in Palm Springs. The residence is often graced with a carefully selected car parked outside the door, especially during Modernism Week. Just around the corner from this picture-perfect beauty lies Elvis Presley's so-called Honeymoon Hideaway, the Alexander family's private residence, designed in 1960 by the very same architect, William Krisel.

CAR If the Citroën DS is considered a work of art, then the SM can only be described as its superlative counterpart—a masterpiece whose very existence brings sheer joy. It was unveiled in 1970 as the epitome of a fast, comfortable travel car, or Gran Turismo—a concept that only Citroën could conceive of that way. Viewed from above, the SM takes on the shape of a teardrop, boasting a wide prow and a fine rear, contributing to its low aerodynamic drag.

The chief designer of this marvel was Robert Opron, wo died in 2021, a luminary in the world of automotive design, known for his remarkable humility. The technical team led by Jacques Né also played an indispensable role in the creation of the SM and its groundbreaking innovations. In addition to its hydropneumatic suspension with level control, it featured self-centring, speed-dependent power steering. In 1968, Citroën had taken over Maserati specifically for the developed of the V6 engine used in the SM. However, both the car and engine proved to be so intricate and delicate that even Citroën's own mechanics sometimes struggled to repair them.

After a production run of just five years, during which almost 13,000 cars were sold, production of the SM came to an end.

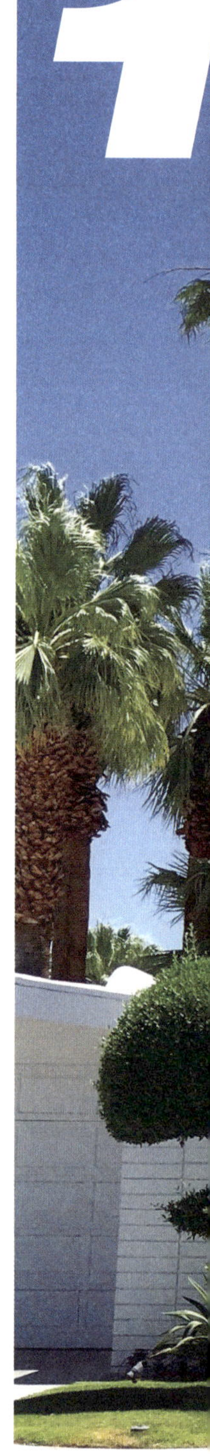

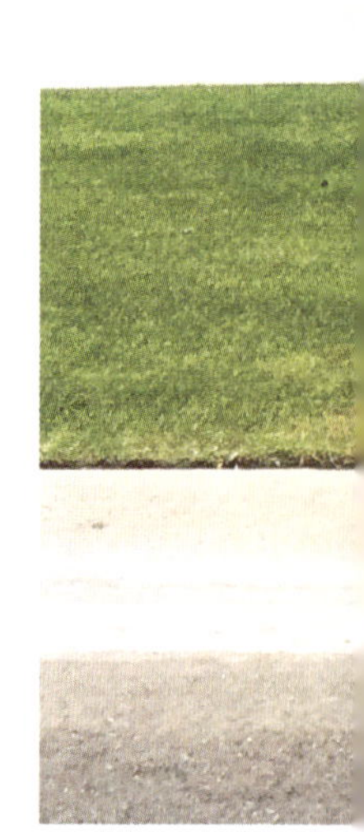

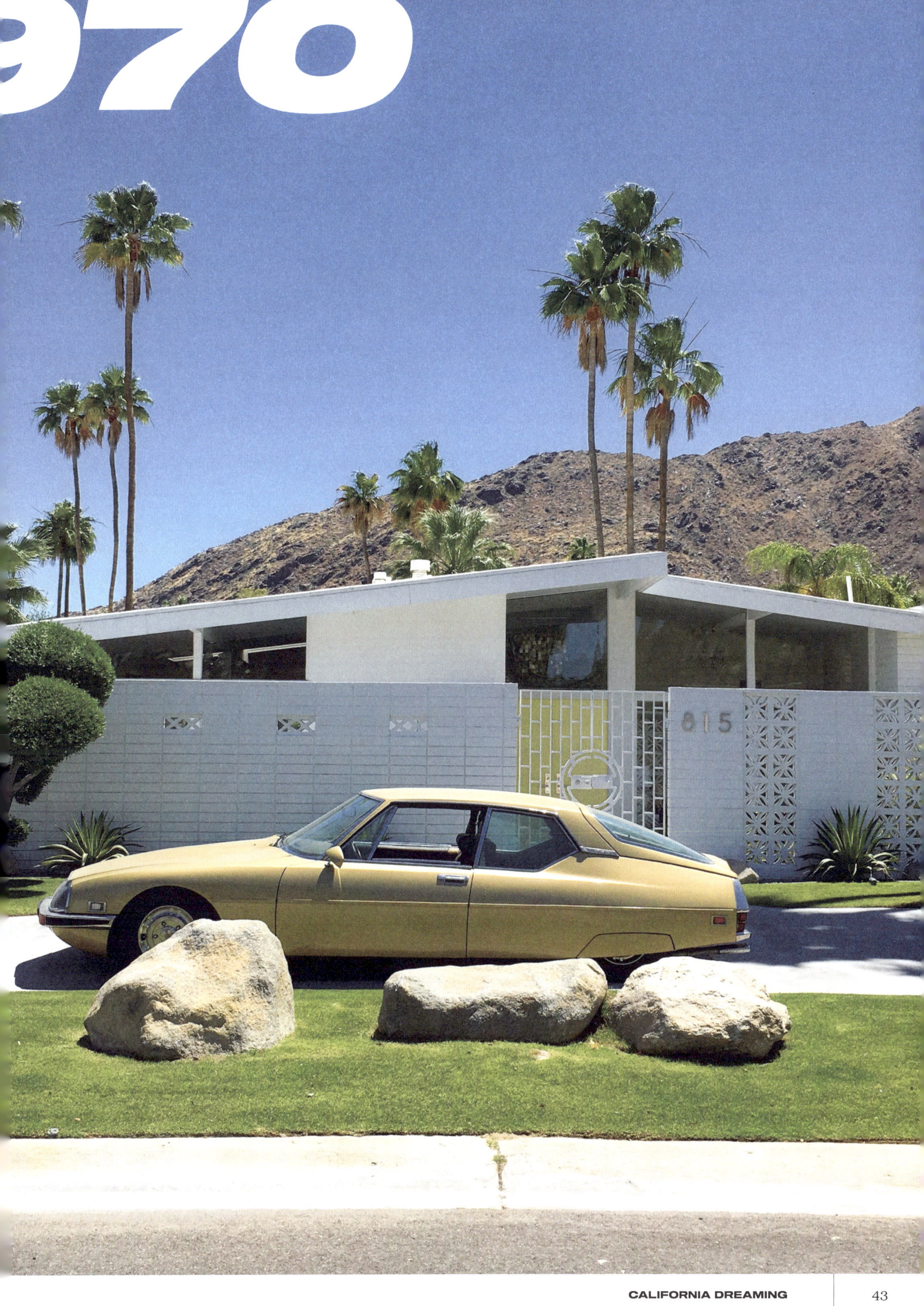
970
815

Studebaker Avanti

ARCHITECTURE From the late 1940s, mass housing projects were undertaken in Palm Springs. The aim was to create affordable holiday homes for a middle-class crowd, where the boundary between indoor and outdoor was blurred. While the homes in these subdivisions adhered to a standardized framework, the houses differed from neighborhood to neighborhood. These variations encompassed elements such as roof articulation, front gardens, lattice brick walls, the arrangement of palm trees—stylistic features denoting the architect, neighborhood or period. This house at 1111 Abrigo Road in Vista Las Palmas is a stellar example of work by architect William Krisel (1924–2017). The house is perfectly matched with a Studebaker created by Raymond Loewy, the product designer who also resided in Palm Springs. Admittedly this is no standardized holiday home, rather a villa designed by Albert Frey, next door to the Kaufmann House.

CAR The Studebaker Avanti was a unique and distinctly American creation, though it bore subtle hints of Italianate aesthetics. Fewer than 5,000 units of this car were produced in 1962 and 1963. The genesis of the Avanti can be traced back to a casual doodle made by Sherwood Egbert on the back of an envelope during a flight. The final design was crafted by the team of legendary industrial designer Raymond Loewy, known for his contributions to a wide range of products, from razor blades to the iconic Coca-Cola bottle.

The Avanti was the first mass-produced four-seater car with a fiberglass body. Its striking stylistic features included the Coca-Cola bottle waistline, a small roof and a large rear window with a built-in roll bar. The front mudguards featured sharp lines that flowed gracefully to the curved rear. The front end had a hood with an asymmetrical hump and no grille, just an air intake beneath a slender bumper.

The Avanti's interior was equally remarkable, with a dashboard reminiscent of an aircraft, and four slim bucket seats. Its V8 engine delivered 240 hp, and supercharged versions could reach up to 289 hp, propelling the car to a top speed of about 170 mph. Some even more powerful versions set numerous speed records. Notably, both Ian Fleming and singer Ricky Nelson were proud owners of Studebaker Avantis.

However, these accolades were not enough to keep the brand afloat, due to issues of scale, quality and reliability, leading to the Studebaker's demise in 1966. Subsequently, dealers Nate Altman and Leo Newman bought the rights and established the Avanti Motor Corp, where the improved Avanti II, powered by a V8 from the Corvette, was produced for years after. Following their lead, other entrepreneurs managed to keep the model in production until 2006.

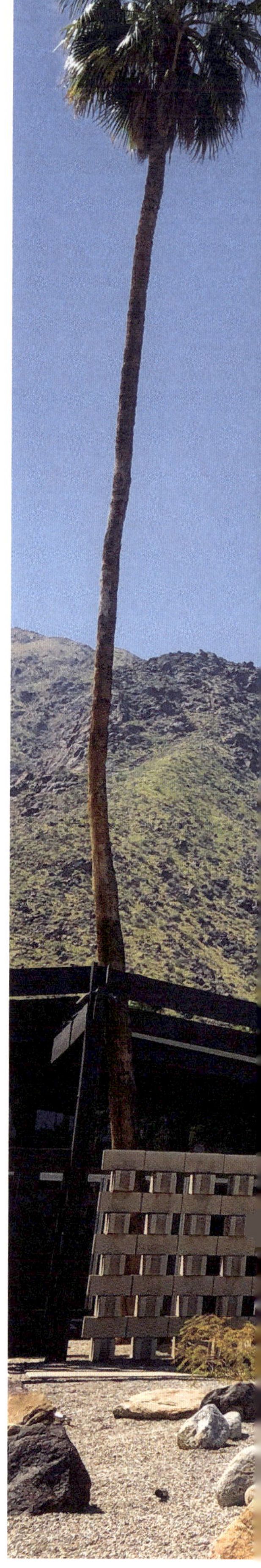

1962

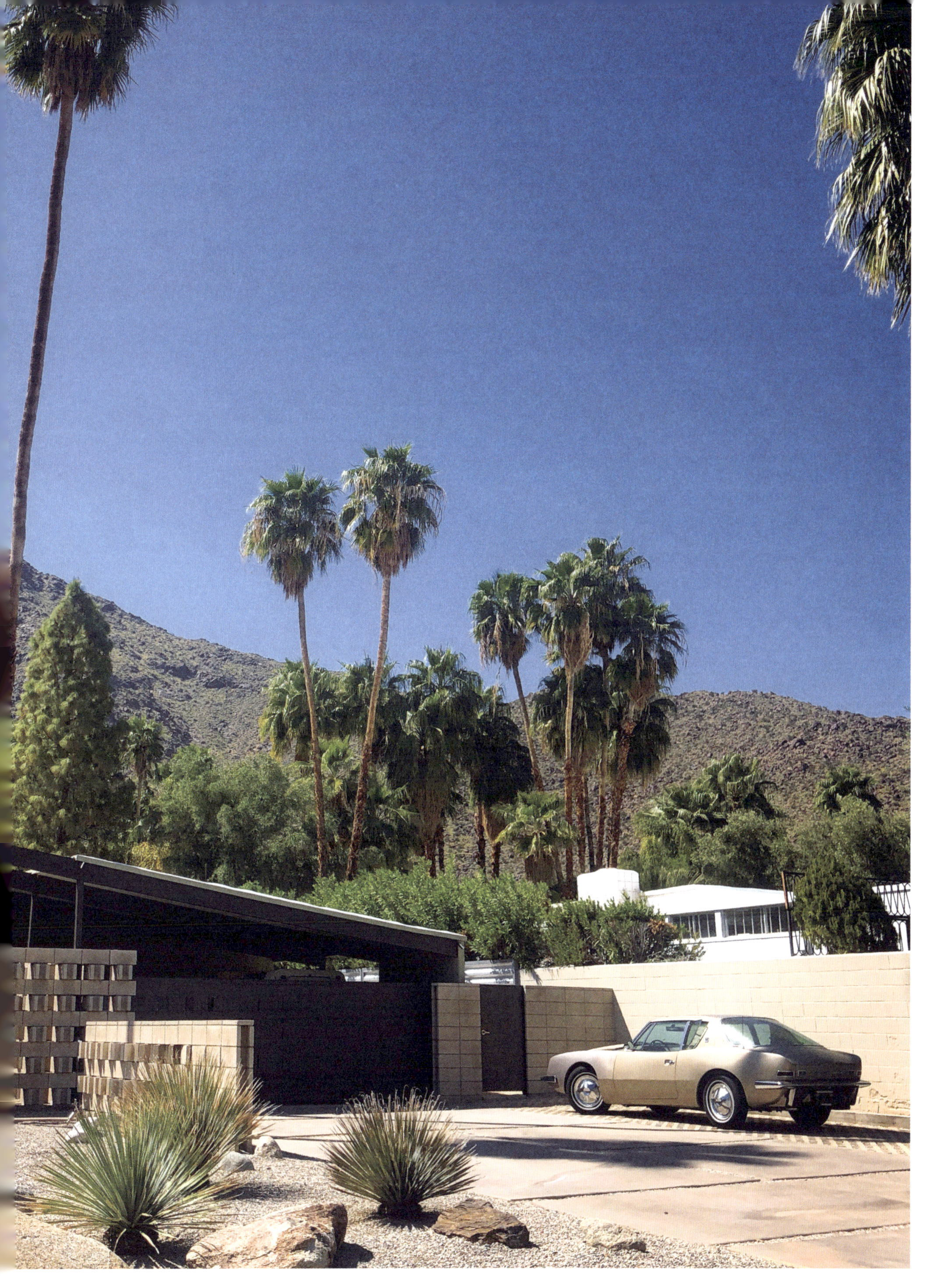

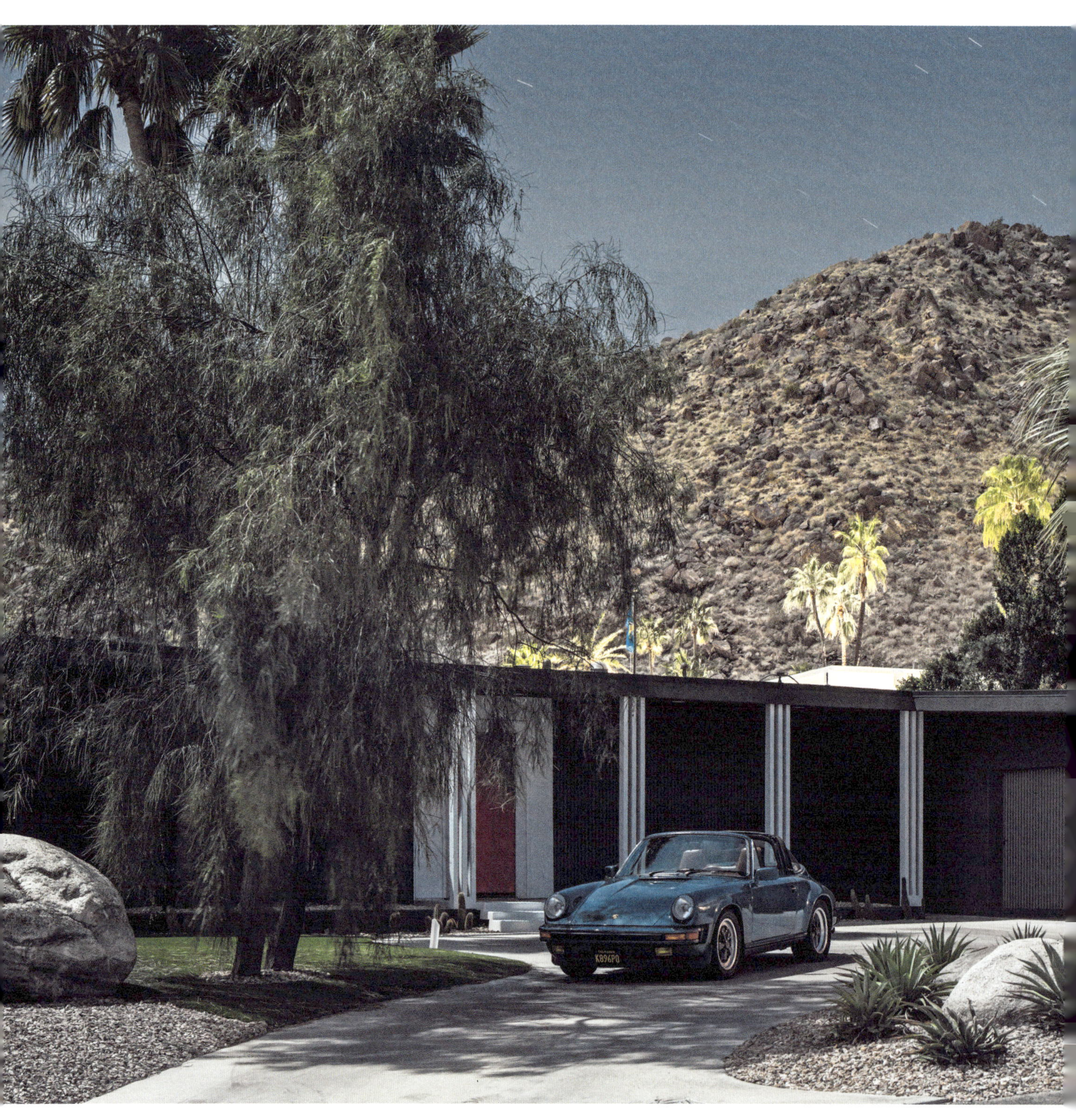
K896PO

198O

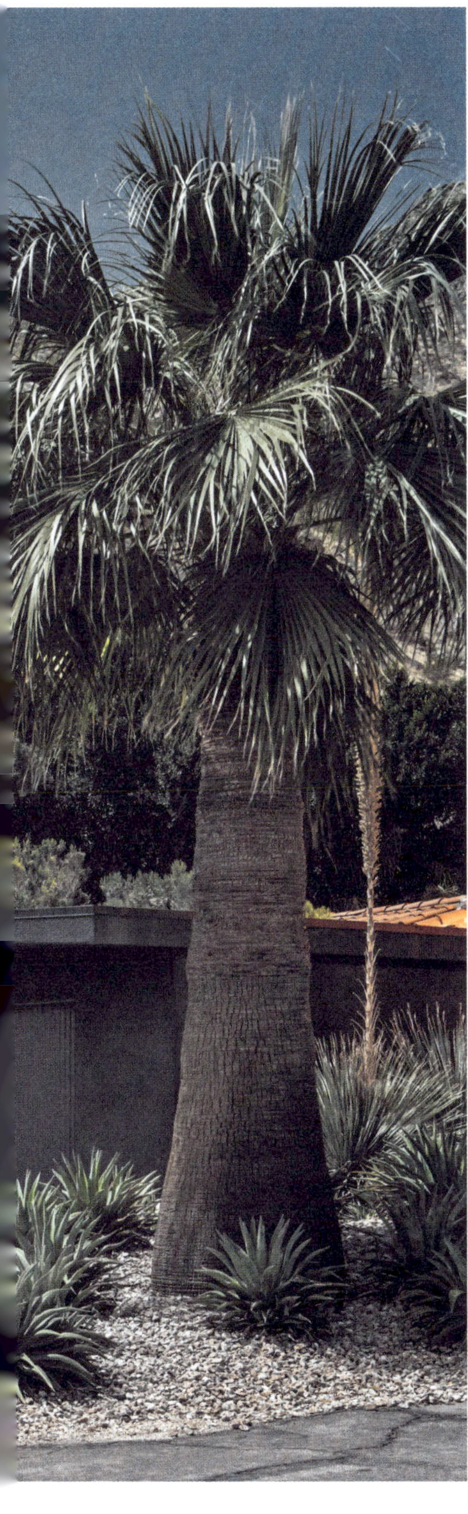

Porsche 911 SC Targa

ARCHITECTURE Architect E. Stewart Williams (1909–2005) has been immortalized on the Palm Springs Walk of Stars. And rightly so: the legacy of his iconic designs can be seen all over Palm Springs. Known as the designer of Frank Sinatra's house, he was also behind the Palm Springs Art Museum and Aerial Tramway Mountain Station, a modernist mountain refuge in the San Jacinto Mountains. That's the best place from which to admire the valley and the houses in Palm Springs. From the Aerial Tramway, it's a 15-minute drive to this stunning private villa owned by Williams on West Cielo Drive. Under the stars, its mid-century features truly resonate.

CAR Launched in 1967, the Targa is a thoroughly American variant of the Porsche 911 that enjoyed worldwide success. Fearing that convertibles would be banned in the US for safety reasons, Porsche came up with an open car with fixed roll-over bar and called it the world's first *Sicherheitscabrio*—at least, that's one version of the story. It's possible that it was simply the only way initially to build a sufficiently rigid open-body variant based on the 911. The name refers to the Targa Florio, the world's oldest racing event, in the mountains of Sicily, where Porsche often triumphed. The fact that *targa* is Italian for shield came in handy: in its advertising, Porsche called the Targa construction a safety shield.

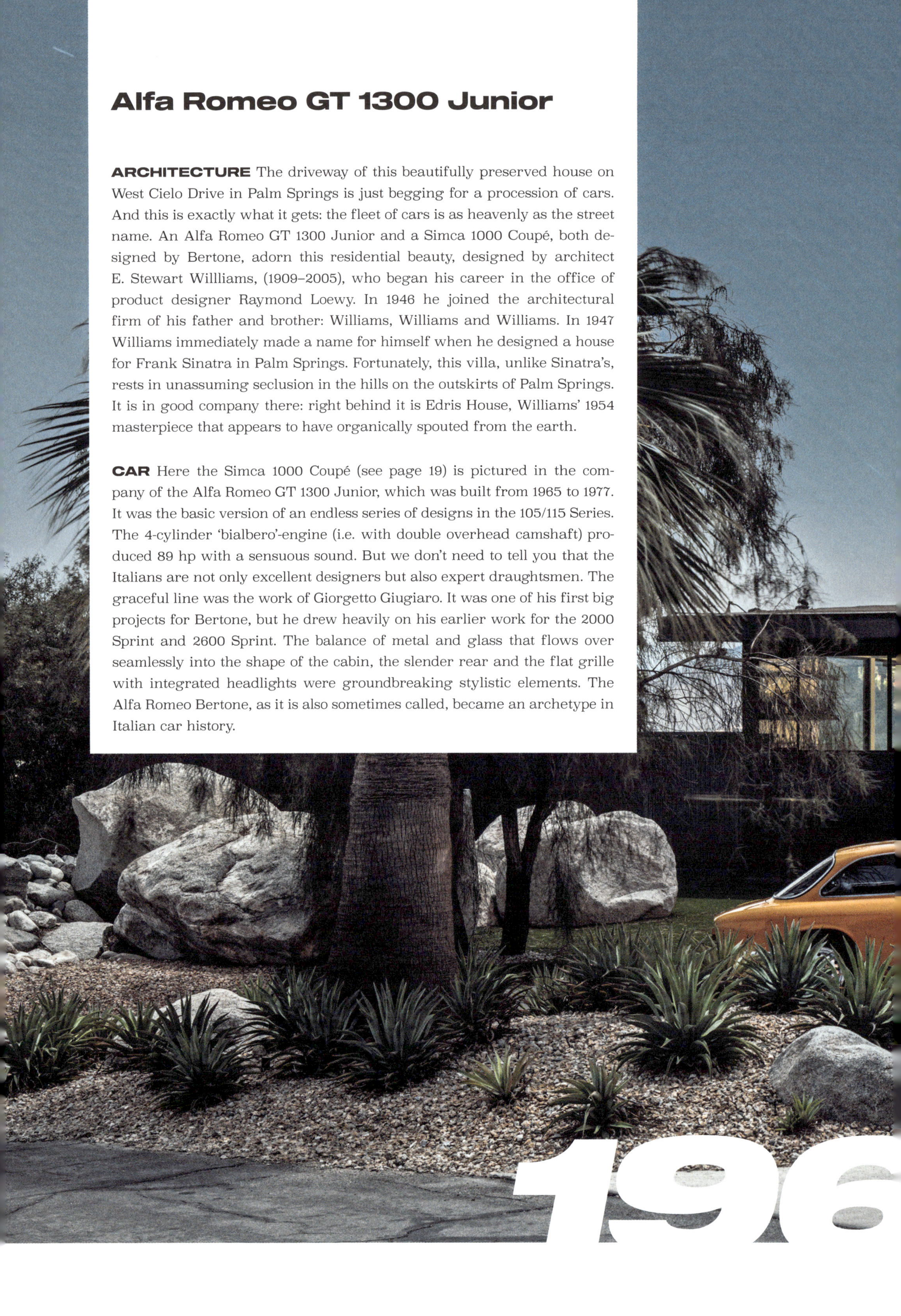

Alfa Romeo GT 1300 Junior

ARCHITECTURE The driveway of this beautifully preserved house on West Cielo Drive in Palm Springs is just begging for a procession of cars. And this is exactly what it gets: the fleet of cars is as heavenly as the street name. An Alfa Romeo GT 1300 Junior and a Simca 1000 Coupé, both designed by Bertone, adorn this residential beauty, designed by architect E. Stewart Willliams, (1909–2005), who began his career in the office of product designer Raymond Loewy. In 1946 he joined the architectural firm of his father and brother: Williams, Williams and Williams. In 1947 Williams immediately made a name for himself when he designed a house for Frank Sinatra in Palm Springs. Fortunately, this villa, unlike Sinatra's, rests in unassuming seclusion in the hills on the outskirts of Palm Springs. It is in good company there: right behind it is Edris House, Williams' 1954 masterpiece that appears to have organically spouted from the earth.

CAR Here the Simca 1000 Coupé (see page 19) is pictured in the company of the Alfa Romeo GT 1300 Junior, which was built from 1965 to 1977. It was the basic version of an endless series of designs in the 105/115 Series. The 4-cylinder 'bialbero'-engine (i.e. with double overhead camshaft) produced 89 hp with a sensuous sound. But we don't need to tell you that the Italians are not only excellent designers but also expert draughtsmen. The graceful line was the work of Giorgetto Giugiaro. It was one of his first big projects for Bertone, but he drew heavily on his earlier work for the 2000 Sprint and 2600 Sprint. The balance of metal and glass that flows over seamlessly into the shape of the cabin, the slender rear and the flat grille with integrated headlights were groundbreaking stylistic elements. The Alfa Romeo Bertone, as it is also sometimes called, became an archetype in Italian car history.

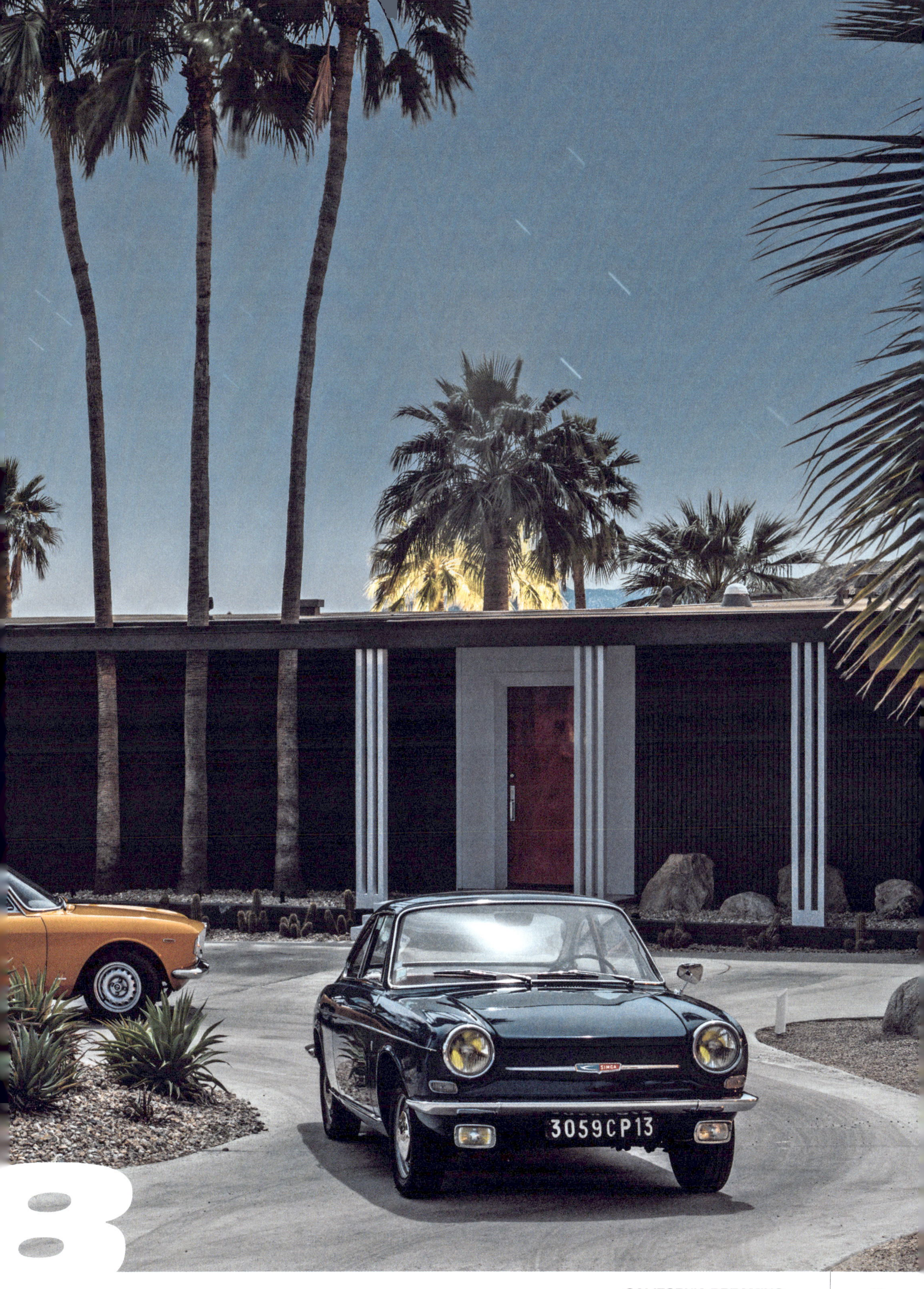
3059CP13
8

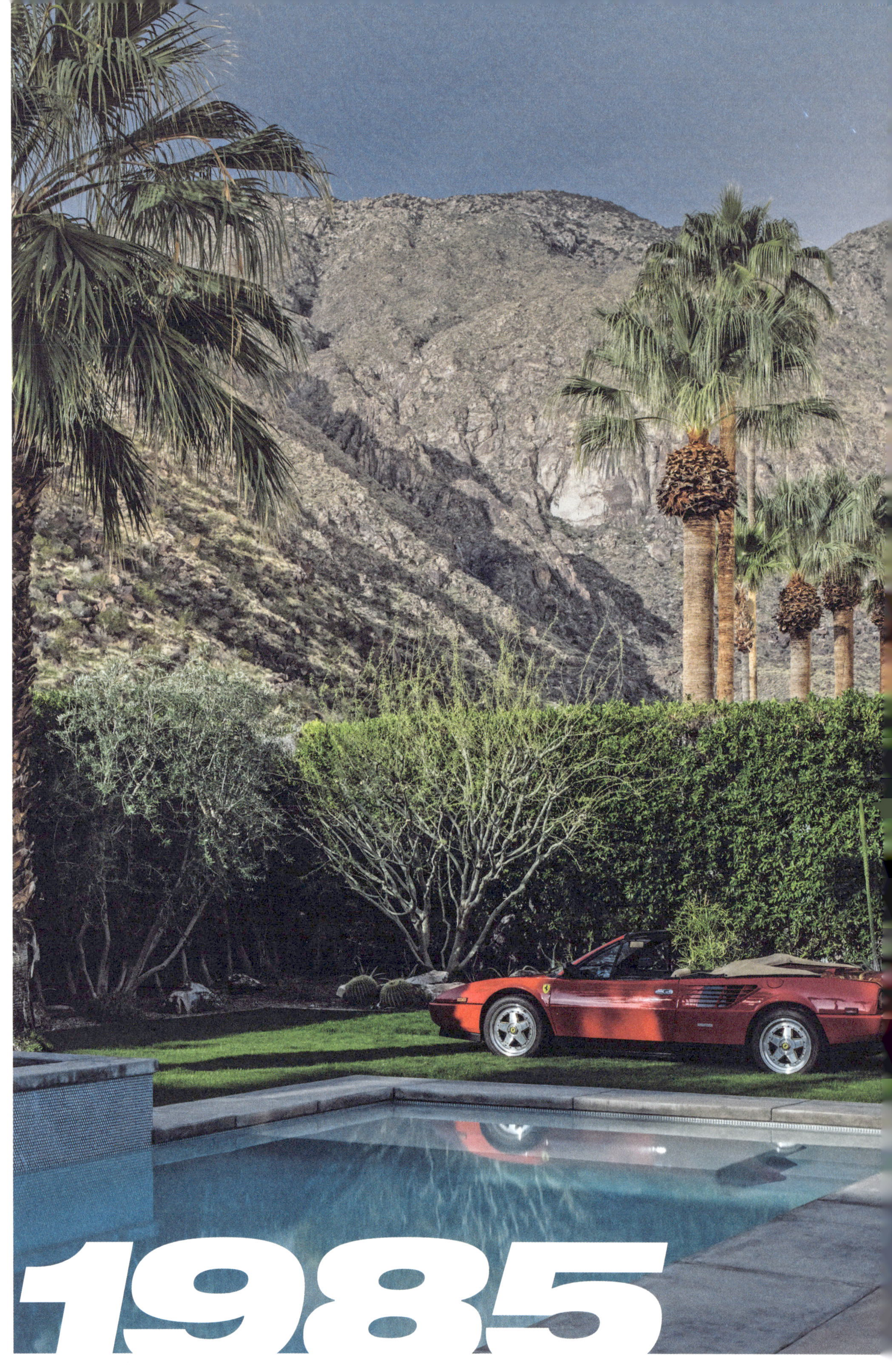

1985

Ferrari Mondial 3.2 Cabriolet

ARCHITECTURE At first glance, this is a banal swimming pool, like so many in Palm Springs. But the accompanying architecture is unique. Tom Blachford portrayed this Ferrari Mondial in the garden of a so-called 'Swiss Miss': a chalet-like bungalow, of which there are still an estimated 15 in Vista Las Palmas, a residential neighborhood of Palm Springs. These Swiss Miss houses belong to the projects of Joe Dunas and the Alexander Construction Company, although they weren't designed by their 'house architect', William Krisel. Charles Du Bois (1903–1996), a lesser-known architect, assumed the role when Krisel refused to design anything rustic. Du Bois designed romantic mid-century bungalows in chalet style, enriched with Tiki influences. With their A-frame roofs, wooden finishing and double-height living spaces, they are spatially very different from the classic open-plan bungalow concept, of which the Alexanders built thousands in Palm Springs. However, the Swiss Misses interlace with Desert Modernism, thanks to their large glass windows and seamless indoor-outdoor experience. When considering a fitting automotive companion, the choice veers away from the quintessential American muscle car toward a sightly incongruous European model that blends with Palm Springs' ethos. Picture a Ferrari Mondial.

CAR When the Ferrari Mondial 8 appeared in 1980, it was mostly met with disdain. The rather weak 8-cylinder engine was in part to blame. Pininfarina's angular design was available as a coupé and convertible; an open car with transverse mid-engine was a unique layout in the car world. The Mondial was also relatively practical for daily use. It got better and better as it evolved and would remain in production until 1993. Over 6,000 were sold but the Mondial always remained a somewhat misunderstood model, making it an altogether accessible Ferrari today.

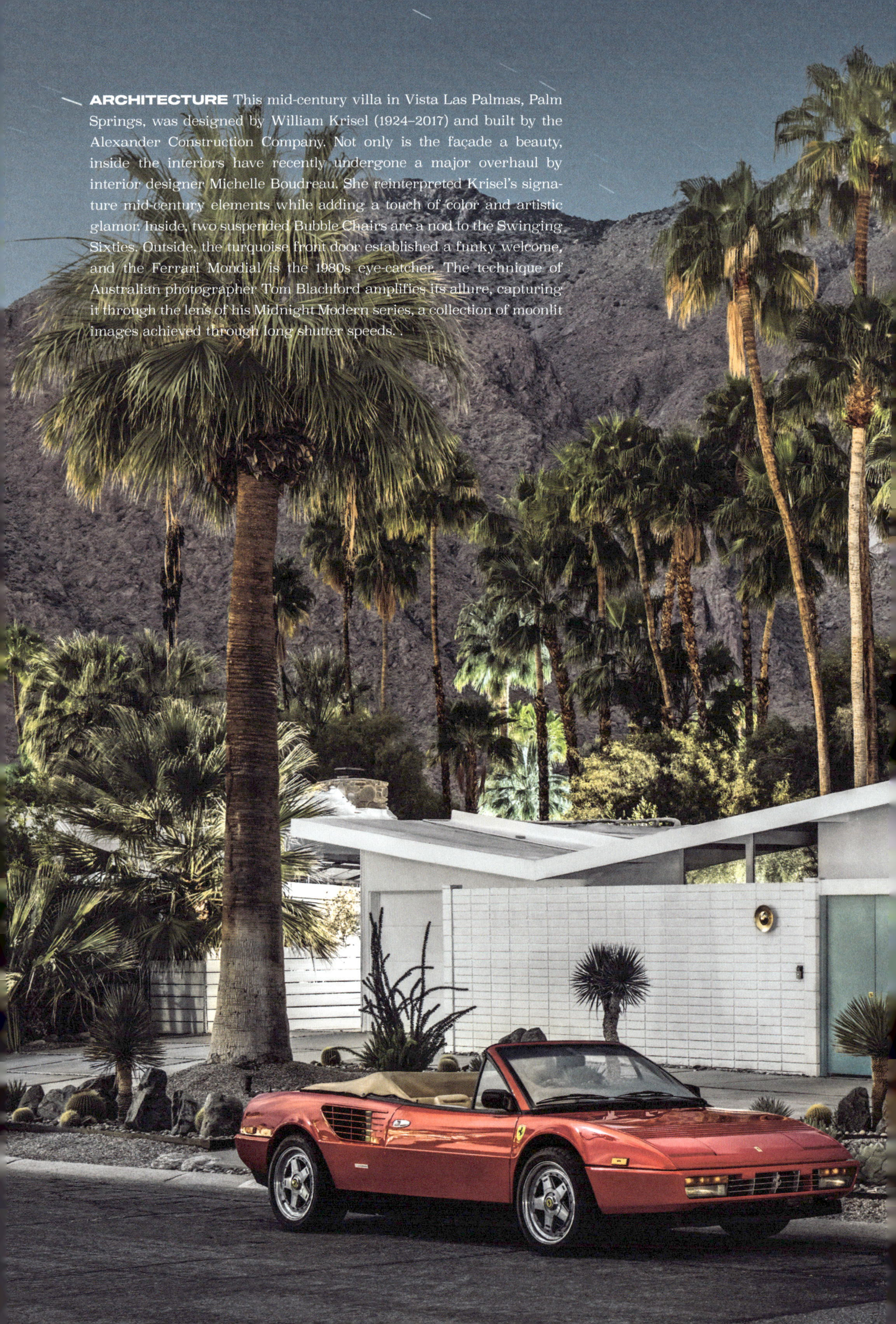

ARCHITECTURE This mid-century villa in Vista Las Palmas, Palm Springs, was designed by William Krisel (1924–2017) and built by the Alexander Construction Company. Not only is the façade a beauty, inside the interiors have recently undergone a major overhaul by interior designer Michelle Boudreau. She reinterpreted Krisel's signature mid-century elements while adding a touch of color and artistic glamor. Inside, two suspended Bubble Chairs are a nod to the Swinging Sixties. Outside, the turquoise front door established a funky welcome, and the Ferrari Mondial is the 1980s eye-catcher. The technique of Australian photographer Tom Blachford amplifies its allure, capturing it through the lens of his Midnight Modern series, a collection of moonlit images achieved through long shutter speeds. .

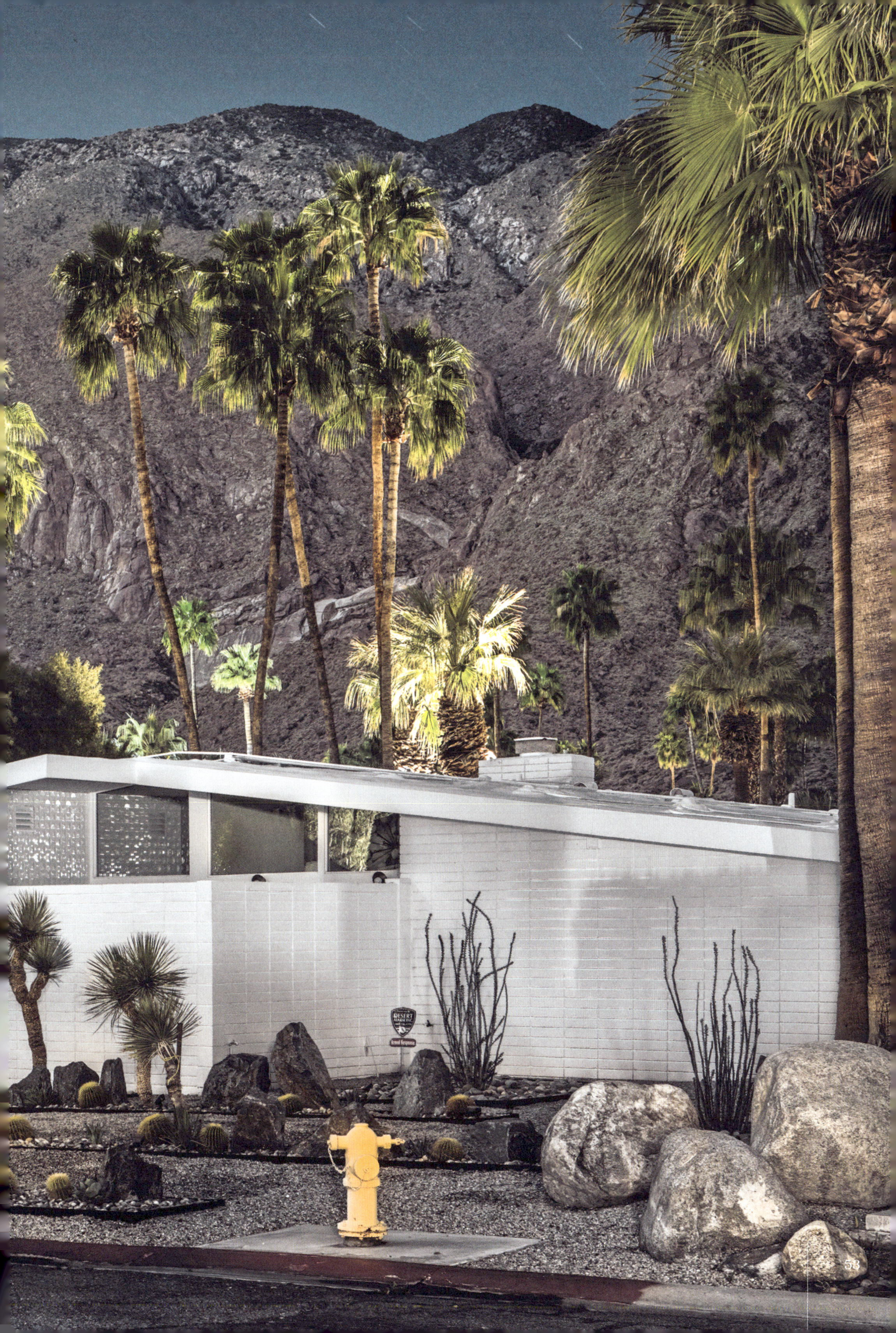

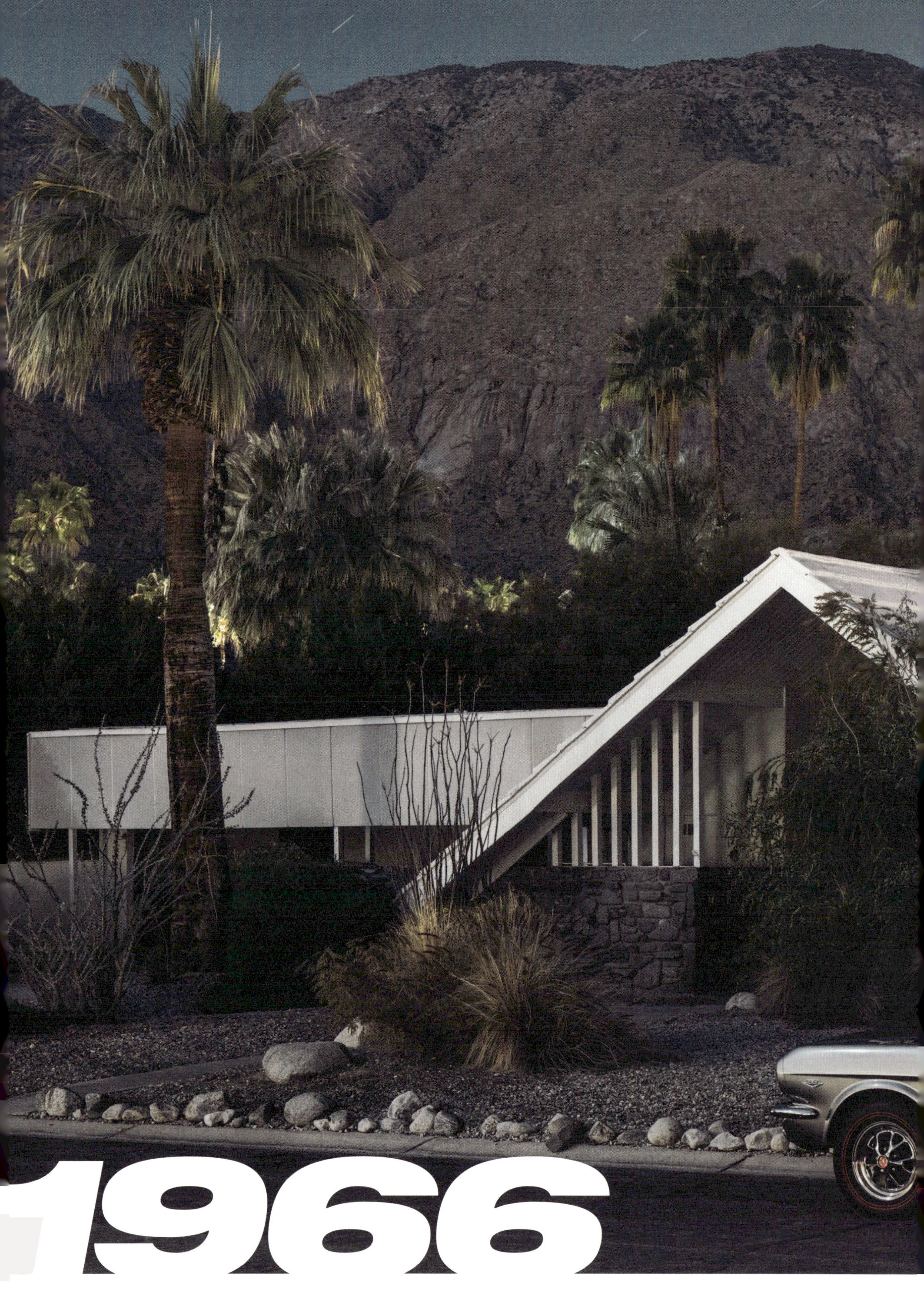

1966

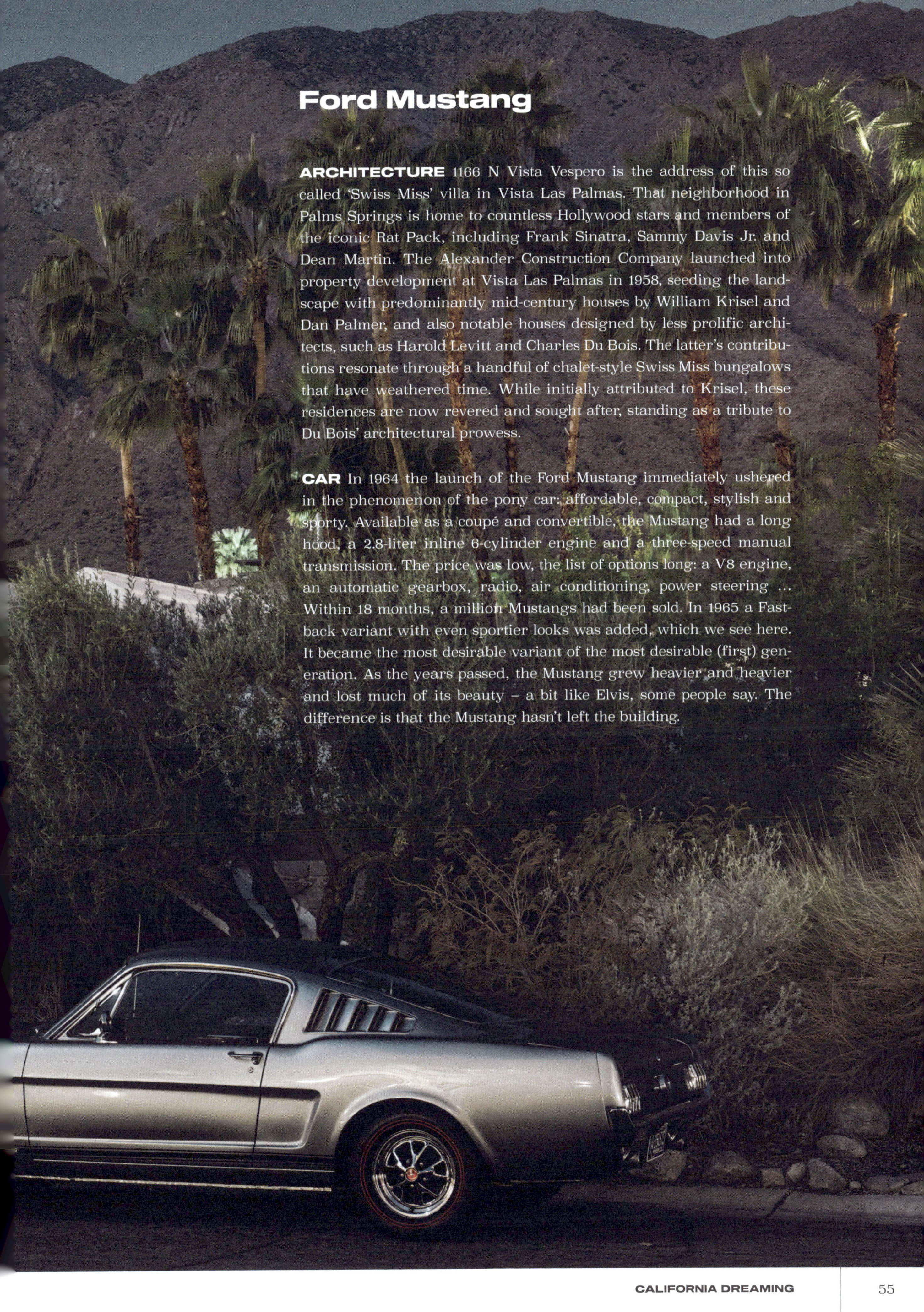

Ford Mustang

ARCHITECTURE 1166 N Vista Vespero is the address of this so called 'Swiss Miss' villa in Vista Las Palmas. That neighborhood in Palms Springs is home to countless Hollywood stars and members of the iconic Rat Pack, including Frank Sinatra, Sammy Davis Jr. and Dean Martin. The Alexander Construction Company launched into property development at Vista Las Palmas in 1958, seeding the landscape with predominantly mid-century houses by William Krisel and Dan Palmer, and also notable houses designed by less prolific architects, such as Harold Levitt and Charles Du Bois. The latter's contributions resonate through a handful of chalet-style Swiss Miss bungalows that have weathered time. While initially attributed to Krisel, these residences are now revered and sought after, standing as a tribute to Du Bois' architectural prowess.

CAR In 1964 the launch of the Ford Mustang immediately ushered in the phenomenon of the pony car: affordable, compact, stylish and sporty. Available as a coupé and convertible, the Mustang had a long hood, a 2.8-liter inline 6-cylinder engine and a three-speed manual transmission. The price was low, the list of options long: a V8 engine, an automatic gearbox, radio, air conditioning, power steering … Within 18 months, a million Mustangs had been sold. In 1965 a Fastback variant with even sportier looks was added, which we see here. It became the most desirable variant of the most desirable (first) generation. As the years passed, the Mustang grew heavier and heavier and lost much of its beauty – a bit like Elvis, some people say. The difference is that the Mustang hasn't left the building.

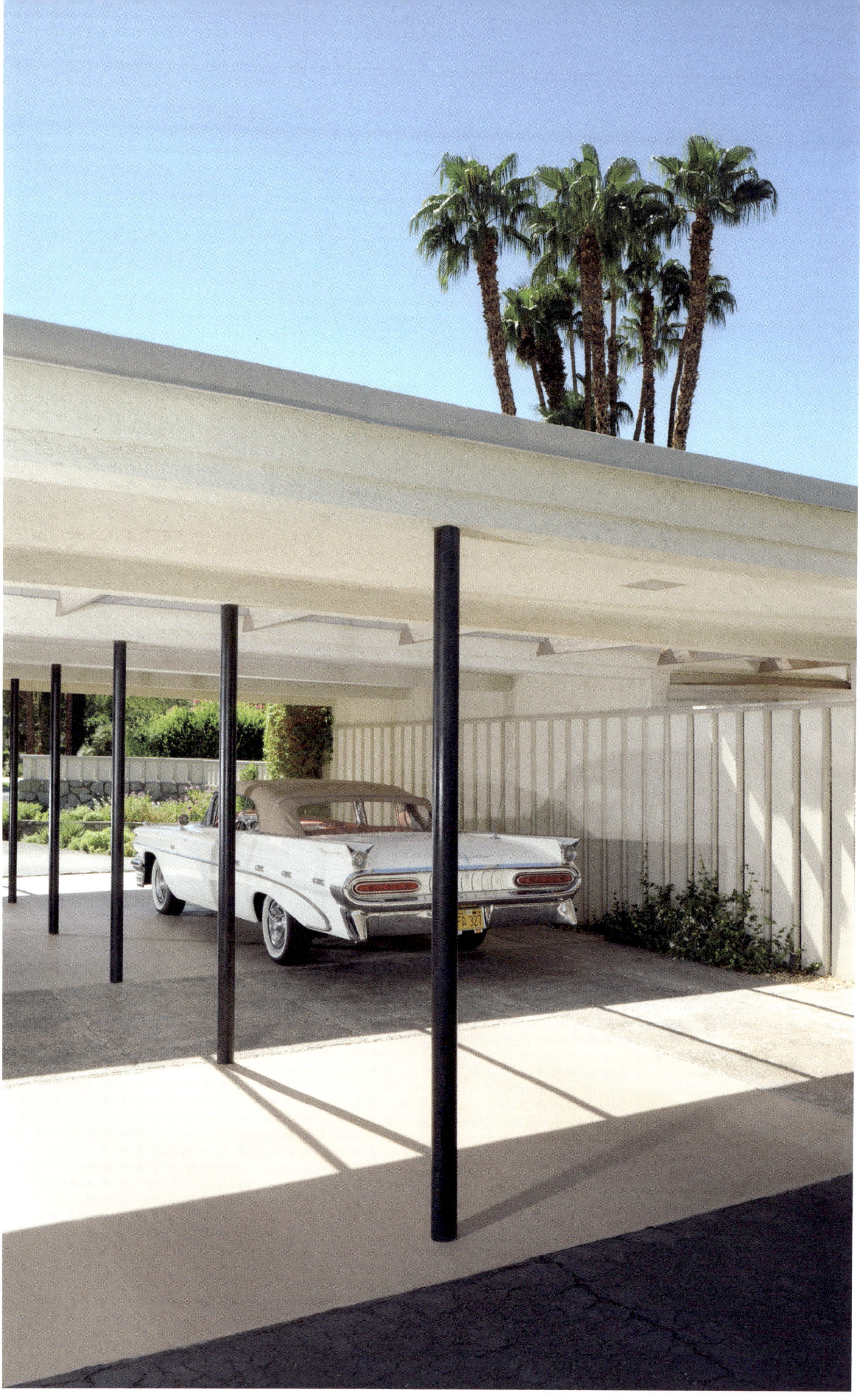

Pontiac Bonneville Convertible Coupé

ARCHITECTURE Malamut House, otherwise known as The Aubrey Pollard Simons House, is situated in Thunderbird North, Rancho Mirage. Aubrey Pollard Simons, a well-connected Texan entrepreneur and an avid golfer, was keen to live near Thunderbird Country Club, the famous golf club in Rancho Mirage. The architect of Simons' house was William Francis Cody Jr. (1916–1978), commissioned in 1950 by developer Johnny Dawson to convert the Thunderbird Dude Ranch into the Thunderbird Country Club. When it opened in 1951, it made history as the world's first 18-hole golf course around which villas were built as a real-estate project.
The venture bore fruit almost instantly, attracting stars such as Hoagy Carmichael, Lucille Ball and her then-husband Desi Arnaz, who eagerly acquired golf villas in the vicinity. William Cody drew up the master plan for the entire site. The prestigious golf club has traditionally attracted celebrities, including Bing Crosby, Bob Hope and former presidents Dwight Eisenhower, Gerald Ford and Barack Obama, all of whom were club members. The residence transitioned to new owners, Michael Lee and Barbara Malamut in 2013, which prompted the nickname 'Malamut Residence.'

CAR The Pontiac Bonneville was introduced in 1957 as a limited, muscular version of the Pontiac Star Chief, and a year later it emerged as a separate model. Pontiac took its name from the Bonneville Salt Flats in Utah, where many early car races took place and speed records were set. Along with the Grande Ville, this Pontiac was one of the biggest and heaviest ever. When it was introduced, virtually all regular options were part of the standard equipment: Pontiac's first injection system, a leather interior, electrically adjustable seats and windows, power steering and brakes, and, on this Convertible, a power-folding roof. In 1959, the Pontiac Bonneville underwent a comprehension redesign, drawing inspiration from the 1955 Strato-Star concept car, and was rendered lower and longer, featuring a split grille, twin rear fins and the iconic Wide Track stern, further enhancing its beauty and allure.

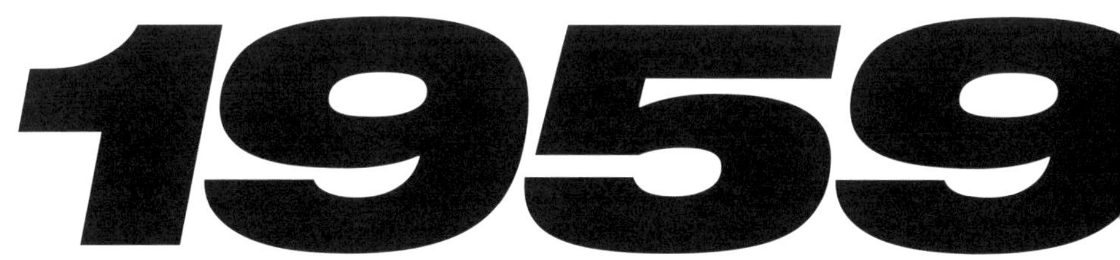

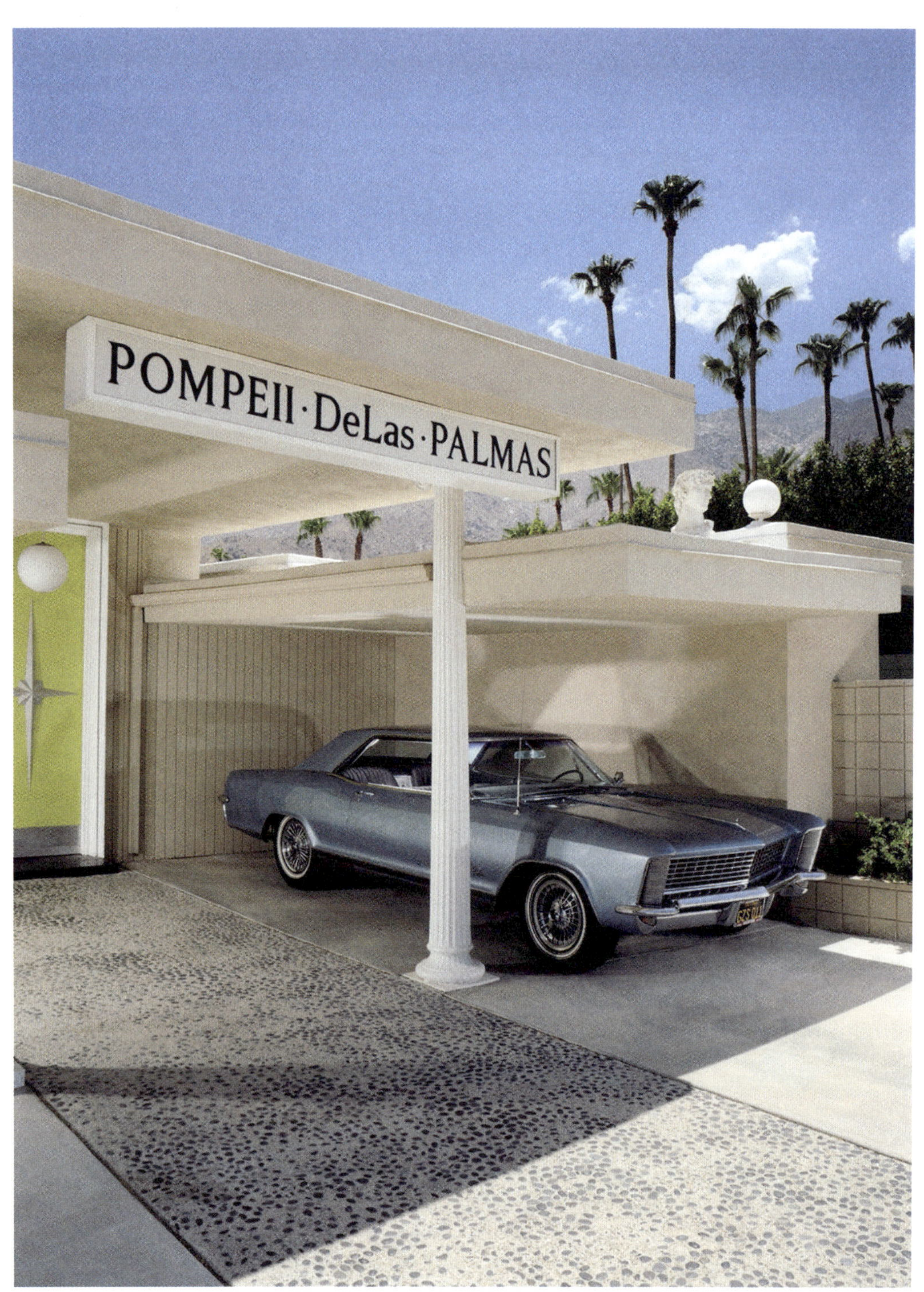

1965

Buick Riviera

ARCHITECTURE The Pompeii de Las Palmas complex comprises nine residential units in Old Las Palmas, a historic neighborhood in northern Palm Springs with a unique architectural style. The residences, built in 1964, stand as a distinct departure from conventional Desert Modernism. They are a curious blend of modernist Hollywood Regency and Roman Revival which found its way to the United States following the 1960 Olympics in Rome. With some imagination, you can see an abstract interpretation of an amphitheatre with Italianate colonnades in the grounds. While some may label this as kitsch, it was considered valuable enough in Palm Springs to earn Pompeii de Las Palmas the designation of a Class One Historic District in 2015.

CAR Although the name had previously been used to designate specific versions of other models, the Riviera emerged as a type in its own right in 1963. It was the Buick with which General Motors successfully entered the class of truly prestige cars such as the Ford Thunderbird and the Chrysler 300C. The familiar 401 and 425 cu engines delivered 325 and 340 hp respectively at its launch. Thanks to its relatively low weight, it took less than eight seconds to reach 60 mph (96 kph). The Riviera had sharp lines, a luxurious interior and unusually lively driving dynamics for the then Buick. Its angular looks were inspired by a custom-bodied Rolls-Royce that General Motors (GM) design boss Bill Mitchell had spotted in London. None other than Sergio Pininfarina magicked the Riviera into one of the most beautiful American cars ever, showing that GM had found its way back to simple design. Raymond Loewy, perhaps the most famous industrial designer of the 20th century, considered it "the most handsome American production car"—after his own Studebaker Avanti, admittedly. The first generation of the Riviera became a style icon, but as one generation followed another (there were eight in total), the car deviated more and more from the original concept.

1960

Dodge Polara

ARCHITECTURE This 1963 residence in Canyon View Estates is stunning. A retro gem, it was designed for developer Roy Fey by Palm Springs' most prolific architectural duo, Palmer & Krisel. Its location at Azul Circle, a quiet cul-de-sac, only adds to its prestige. You might recognize it as the shooting location for *Don't Worry Darling* (2022), directed by Olivia Wilde. The movie's fictitious Californian suburbs, known as 'Victory,' are portrayed against the backdrop of the very real and picturesque Palm Springs. Architecture lovers are in for a treat as the movie weaves in the architectural heritage of the region. Richard Neutra's legendary Kaufmann House and the mythical Vulcano House in the desert expanse between Los Angeles and Las Vegas, also serve as settings in the movie. "The movie is a declaration of love for mid-century architecture and design," says Wilde.

CAR The Polara, named in the midst of the space race after the Polaris star, was introduced in 1960 as the top model of the revamped Dodge range. It would remain so until the introduction of the Custom 880 two years later. That first series still had the characteristics of the 'Forward Look' style that Virgil Exners had introduced at parent group Chrysler in 1957, with jet-engine-inspired tail lights and (shortened) tail fins. The richly chrome-trimmed Polara was available as a two-door convertible, two-door hardtop, four-door hardtop sedan, four-door hardtop station wagon and a conventional four-door sedan with B-pillars, as seen here.

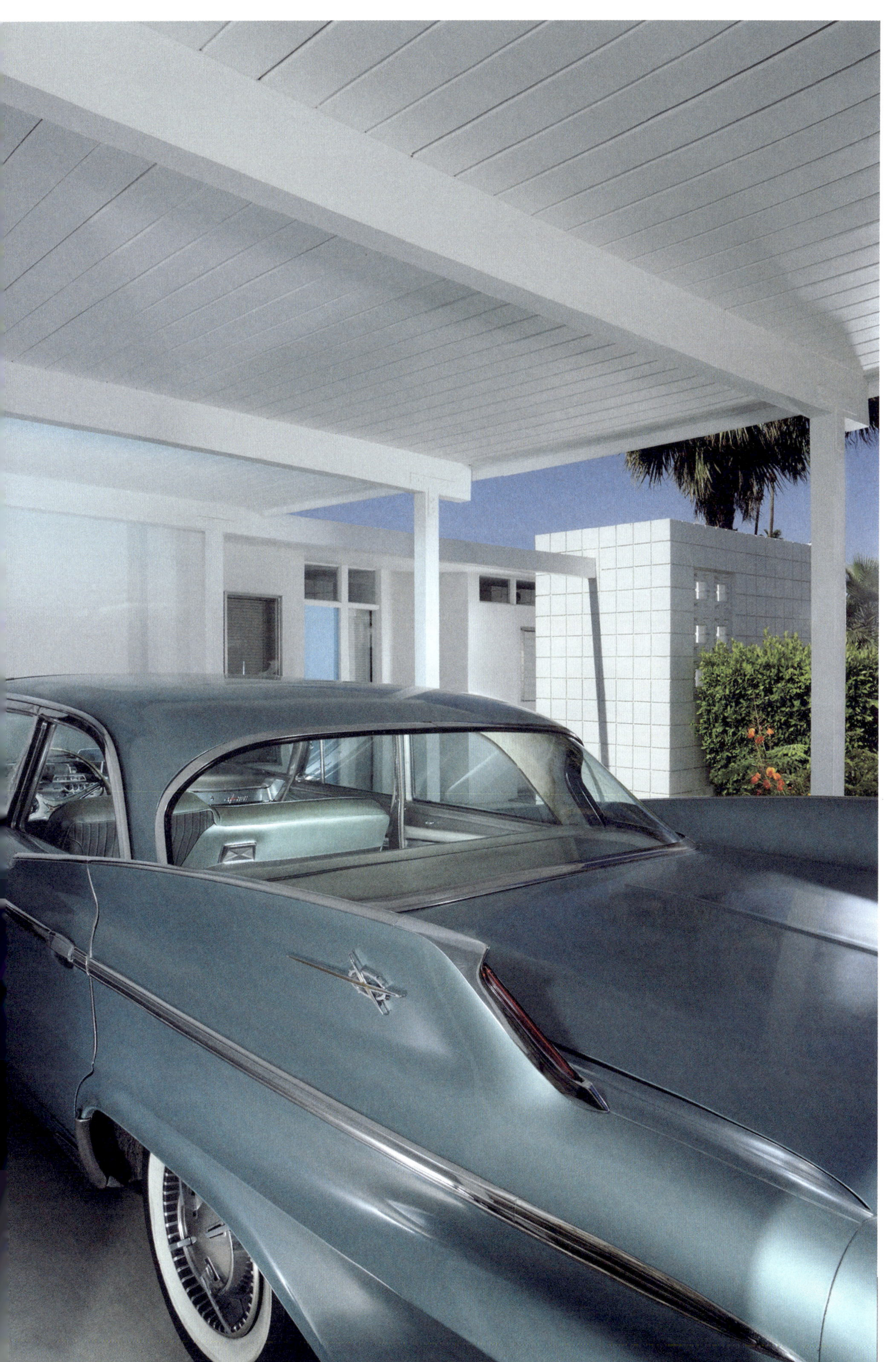

1966

Oldsmobile Toronado

ARCHITECTURE Let's not confuse A. Quincy Jones, the Los Angeles architect, with Quincy Jones, the music producer of (almost) the same name who worked for artists such as Michael Jackson, Frank Sinatra, Miles Davis, Ella Fitzgerald and Sarah Vaughan. A. Quincy Jones (1913–1979) established an architectural firm in Los Angeles after World War II. In his early career, he and his associate Frederick Emmons designed Case Study House #24. The innovative design, partly submerged and equipped with a water tank, aimed both to cool the house and provide irrigation for plants. Regrettably the revolutionary home was never constructed.
Nevertheless, Jones did bring other projects to fruition, such as the Palm Springs Tennis Club (1947), the Town & Country Restaurant (1948) and the restaurant Romanoff's On The Rocks (1950). He also designed this villa with a striking carport in 1965 on Camino Real in the Country Club Estates, a Palm Springs subdivision for which Jones had drawn up the plan.

CAR It wasn't intended as such but, when David North drew a personal and futuristic design sketch as an exercise in 1962, it was so much to the liking of GM bosses that it went into production three years later as the Oldsmobile Toronado. The car had to compete in the 'personal luxury' segment with such fine coupés as the Buick Riviera, Pontiac Grand Prix and Ford Thunderbird. When it appeared, the Toronado was the first front-wheel-drive American production car since the 1930s Cord and it would be massively emulated in the decades that followed. A big V8 and aggressive styling made the Toronado a true muscle car. With its protruding front wings, hidden headlights, robust wheel houses and a sublimely trimmed rear that finished off a smooth roofline, it became one of the most popular Oldsmobiles ever. In 1966 it was Motor Trend Car of the Year. It also won *Car Life*'s Award for Engineering Excellence and even came third in the European Car of the Year competition, a rare recognition for an American car. Jay Leno has one among his collection.

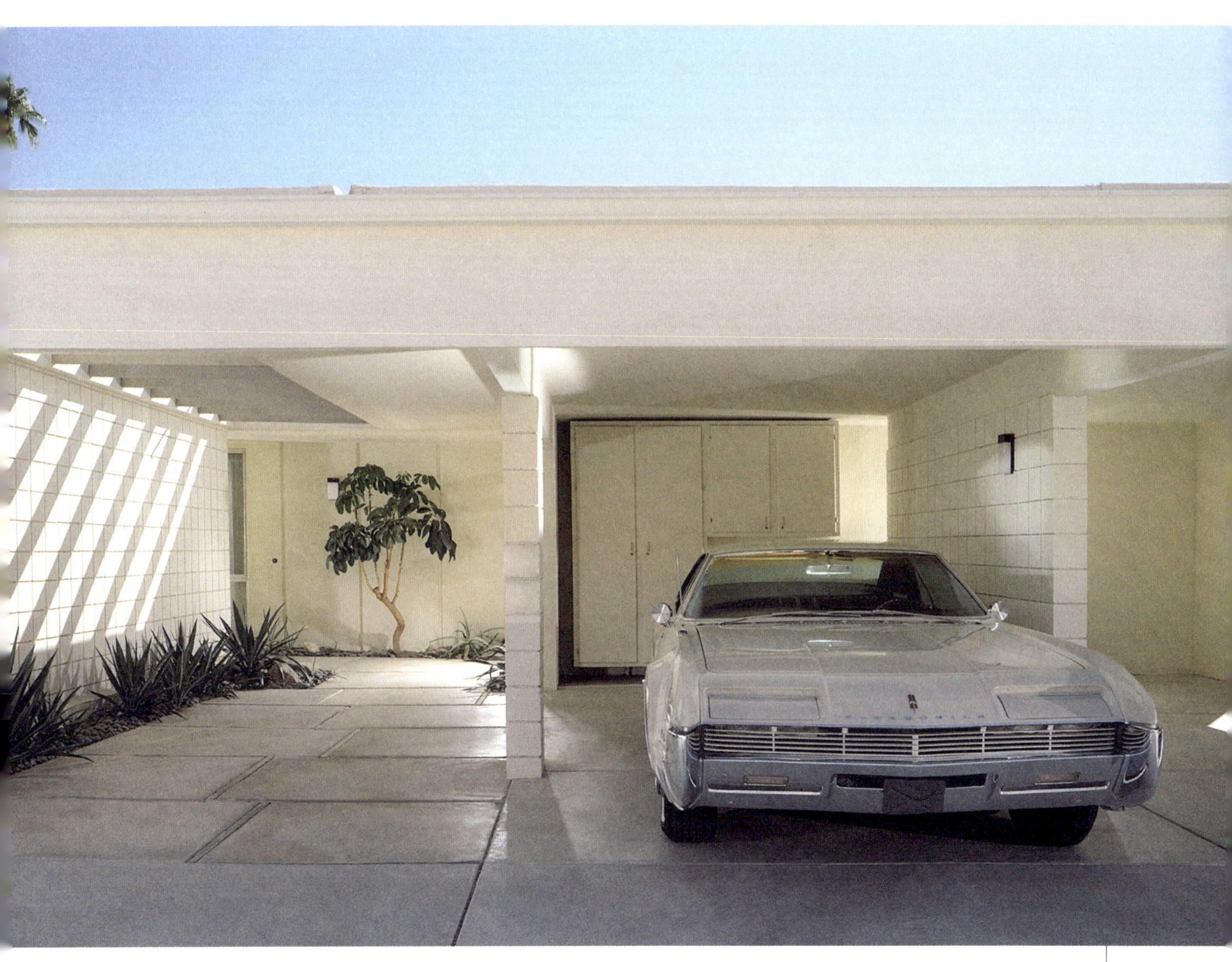

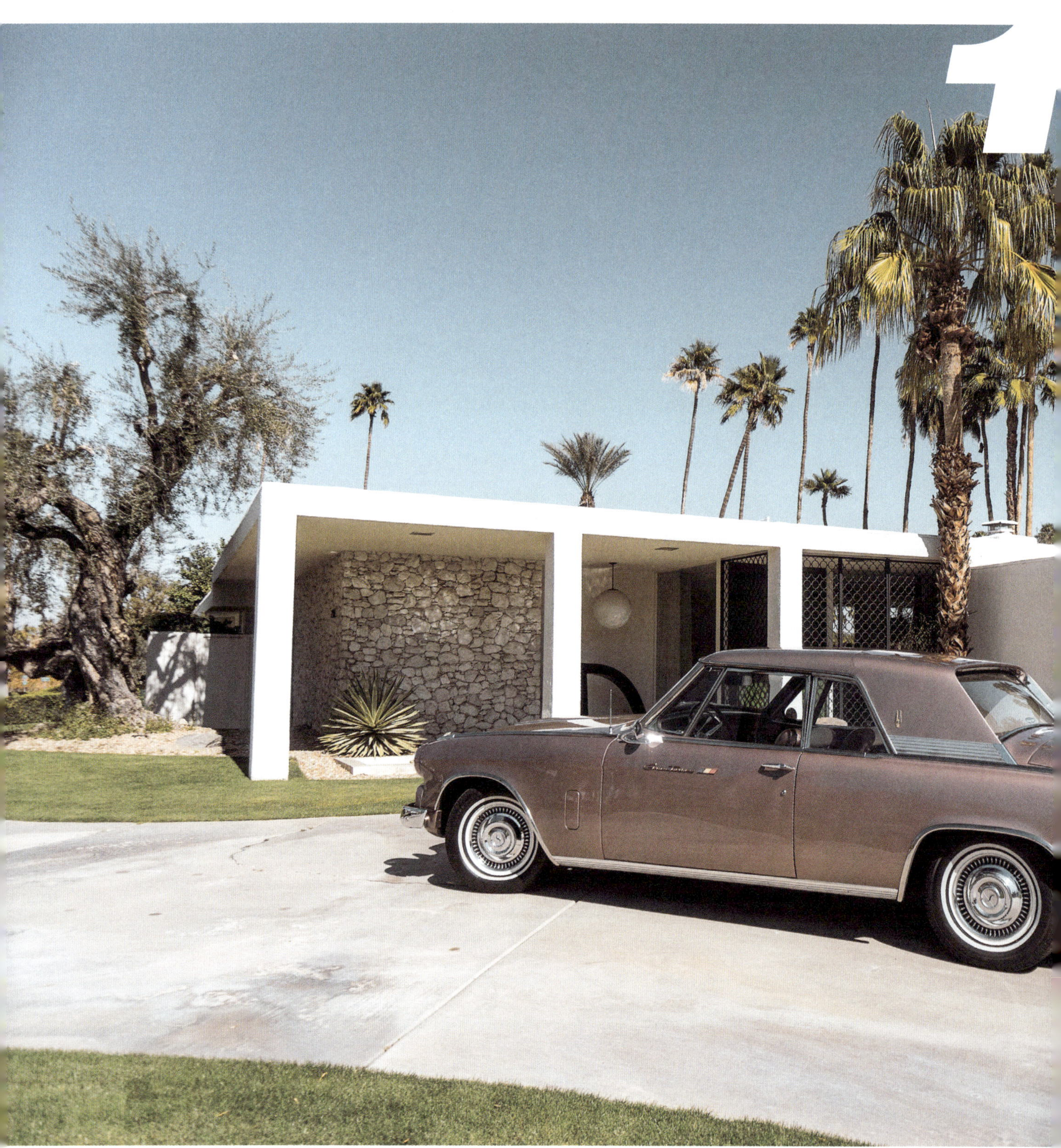

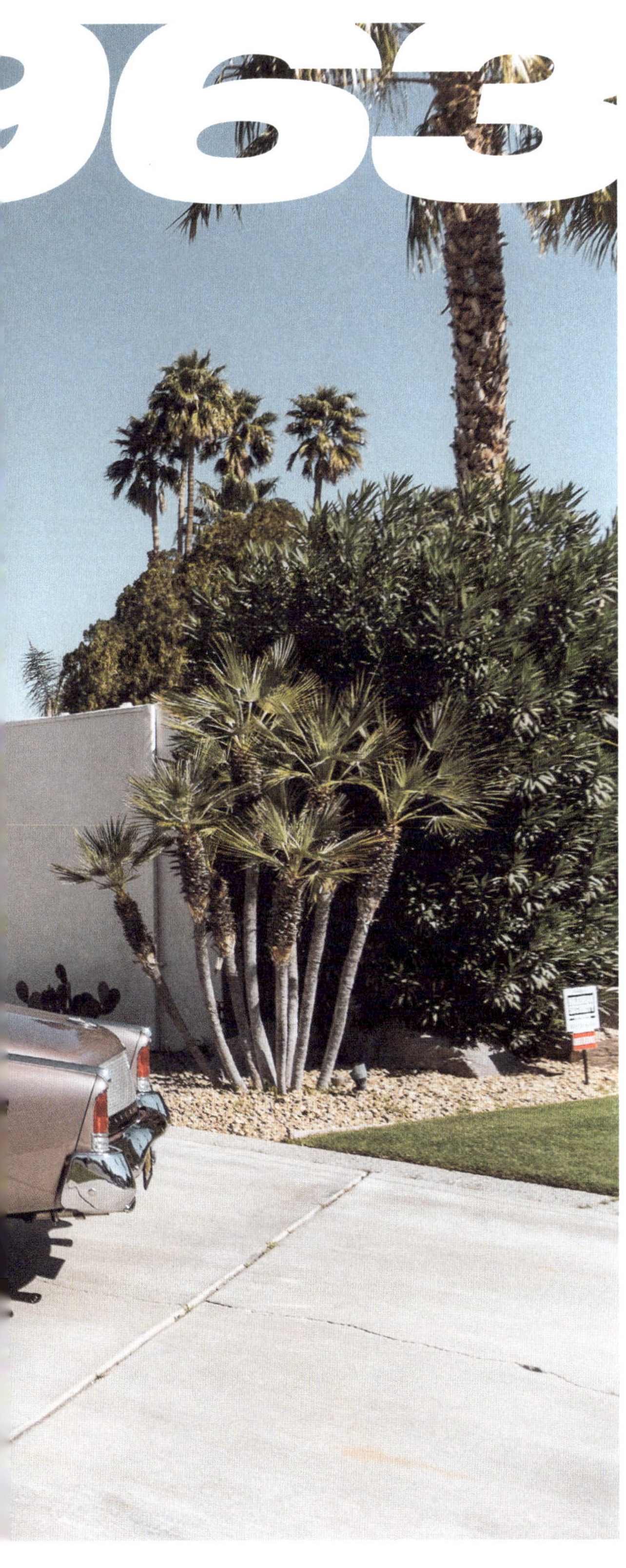

Studebaker Gran Turismo Hawk

ARCHITECTURE The Studebaker Gran Turismo Hawk in the driveway completes the mid-century vibe at this 1964 home. The villa stands in Indian Canyons, a neighborhood built in conjunction with the nearby golf course, The Canyon Country Club. Golf enthusiasts will be delighted to explore the clubhouse, a masterpiece by Donald Wexler and Richard Harrison.

Between 1963 and 1970, a trio of visionary developers—Harry Kelso, Paul Butler and Roy Fey—built a host of luxury homes around the golf course. These opulent homes were designed by William Krisel and Stan Sackley, among others. Thanks to the allure of the golf course, the holiday homes attracted golf aficionados such as Walt Disney, Tony Curtis and Jerry Lewis, each of whom owned homes there. Walt Disney even donated a fountain to the golf club, positioned between the ninth and eighteenth holes.

CAR The Studebaker Gran Turismo Hawk was a significant success for the struggling Studebaker brand, and marked the final evolution of the Hawk line, introduced in 1956. Despite working with an extremely limited budget, industrial designer and graphic artist Brooks Stevens executed a radical facelift for the 1962 model year, giving the car clean, European-inspired styling. It retained some American influences, such as the thick C-pillars inspired by the Ford Thunderbird and tail lights strongly reminiscent of Lincoln. The tail fins that had been prominent in the 1950s were removed. The GT Hawk was sold from 1962 to 1964, but with fewer than 14,000 units produced, it did not achieve commercial success.

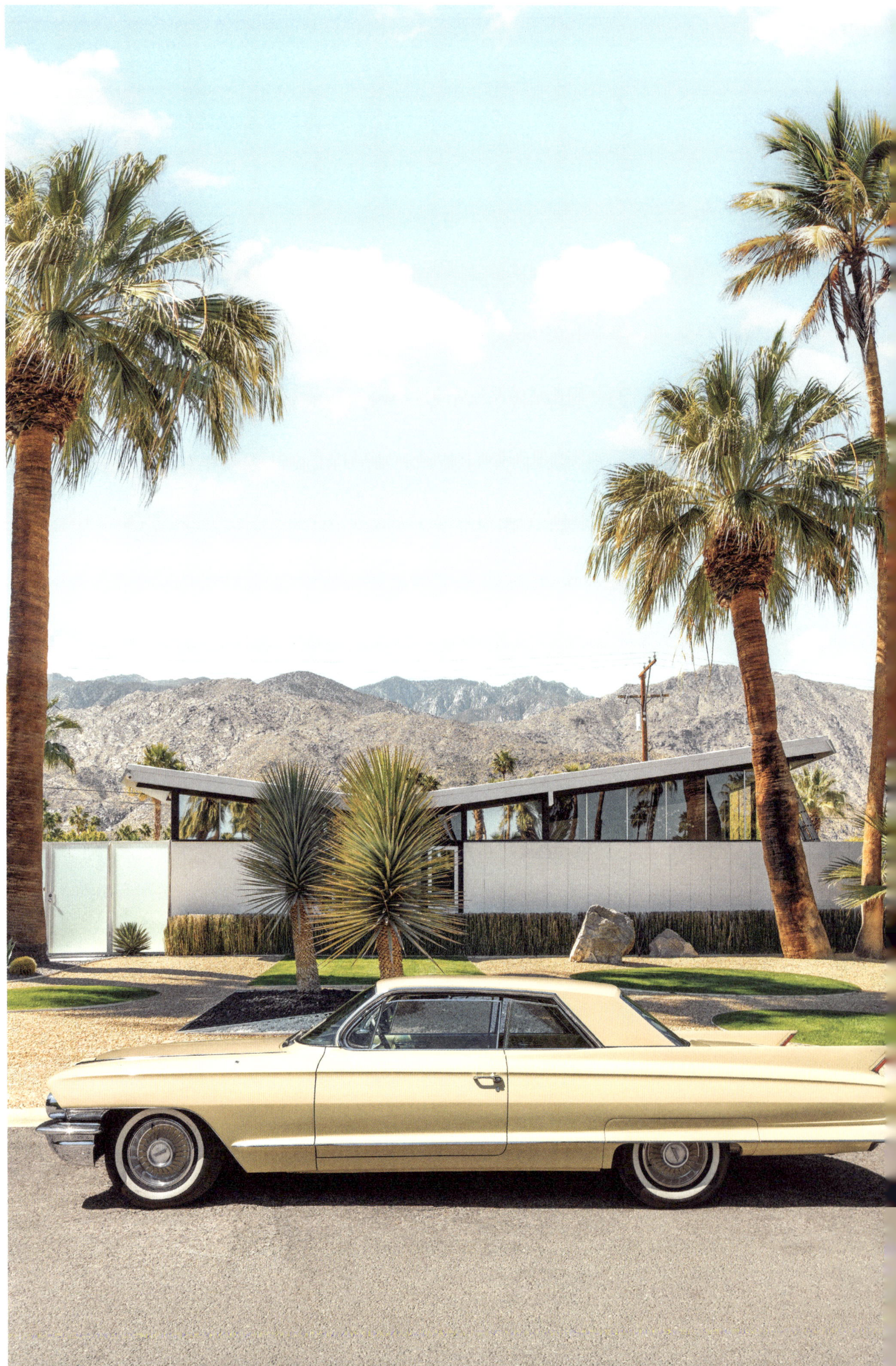

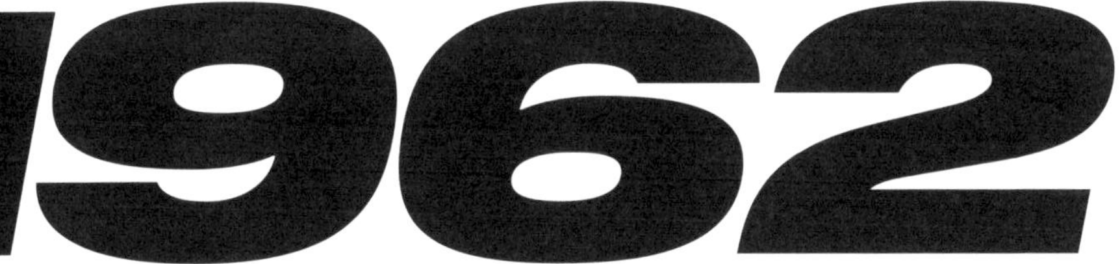

Cadillac Series 62 Two-Door Hardtop

ARCHITECTURE There's no need to ponder for long when attributing this remarkable house on Aquanetta Drive in Twin Palms to prolific architect William 'Bill' Krisel. No one has left an indelible mark on Palm Springs such as he did. This villa with a butterfly roof is a favorite photo spot for architecture enthusiasts visiting Palm Springs, thanks to its distinctive graphic roofline and the black and white yin-yang front garden. Although he only gained recognition relatively late in his career, Krisel's influence on Palm Springs is undeniable. From the 1950s, he worked with George and Robert Alexander to build the first mid-century modern homes in Twin Palms. Together with his associate Dan Palmer, he built an estimated 30,000 homes in California—a testament to their unmatched legacy.

CAR Produced from 1961 to 1964, the Cadillac Series 62 was the seventh and final generation of this model that was introduced in 1940. It incorporated various stylistic elements from the 1960 Eldorado Brougham designed by Pinin Farina. The Series 62 was available in several body styles, including four-door hardtops with four and six windows, a two-door hardtop and a convertible. Beneath the hood was a 390-cubic-inch V8 engine capable of producing 325 hp, paired with with a three-speed automatic transmission. The vehicle came well equipped with standard features such as power brakes and power steering, and there were 143 additional options available, including wool, leather or nylon-trimmed bucket seats, wood inlays and air conditioning. Major competitors of the Series 62 were the Buick Electra 225 Sport Coupé, Chrysler 300 Sport, and Imperial Southampton.

Cadillac Eldorado Convertible

ARCHITECTURE A Cadillac Eldorado in one of Palm Springs' architectural Eldorados: Victoria Park, also known as Vista Norta, the neighborhood squeezed between Raquet Club and Vista Chino. In the neighborhood, there's an abundance of modernist atomic ranches. Most of them are Alexander Houses, but you'll also encounter some realizations by the talented brothers Jack and Bernie Meiselman, like this one.

CAR The Cadillac Eldorado, introduced in 1952 as a concept car to commemorate Cadillac's 50th anniversary, made its production debut the following year. The Eldorado nameplate remained in use until 2002. Here we see a 1975 or 1976 convertible Eldorado, often jokingly referred to as 'Eldoradosaurus.' It was one of the bulkiest cars ever built by Cadillac and marked the end of the era of massive American cruisers. Powering this model was a colossal 500 cubic-inch V8 engine, making it the largest V8 ever installed in a production car. However, the car industry changed dramatically during the 1970s due to introduction of the first emissions regulations. As a result, the massive engine's output dropped from 400 to a mere 190 hp between 1970 and 1976. From then on, American cars became smaller, lighter and more fuel-efficient, while also gaining improved agility and smoother performance.

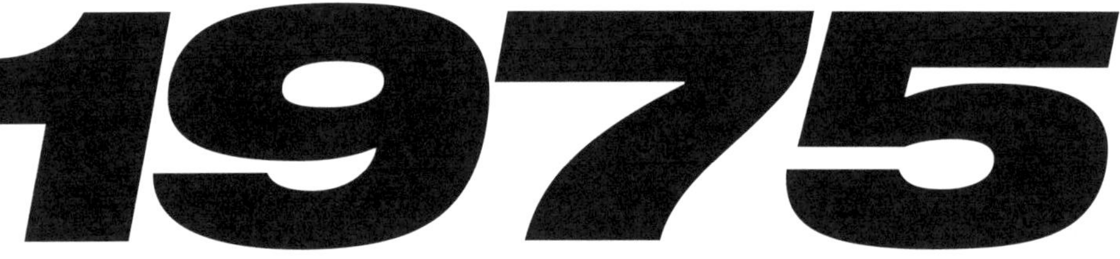

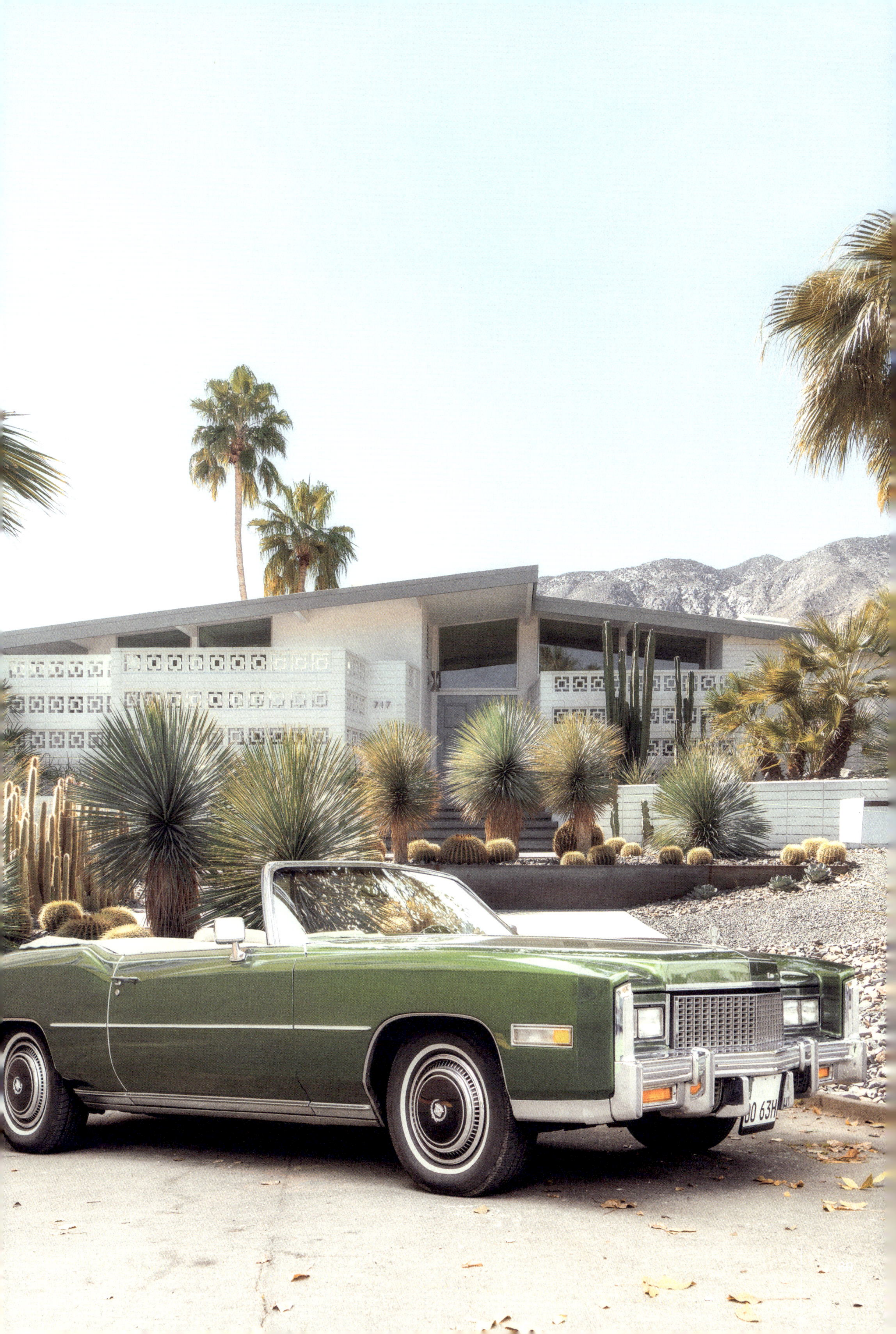
717

1961

Cadillac Sedan Deville

ARCHITECTURE The carport, an American invention, rose to prominence in the early 20th century alongside the popularity of passenger cars in America. Naturally, the surge in car ownership necessitated covered parking spaces. Although the origins of the first carport cannot be definitively traced, many credit architect Walter Burley Griffin (1876–1937) as its 'inventor.' His Prairie School-style homes, which marked the inception of a truly American architectural movement, frequently featured semi-open shelter for cars. These carports integrated well with Prairie School architecture, characterized by large canopies, ribbon windows and geometric embellishments.
Griffin worked for Frank Lloyd Wright for a while in his office in Oak Park, Illinois. During this time he fell in love with Wright's sister, although that love was not reciprocated. Despite his contributions, Griffin never became a partner in Frank Lloyd Wright's office. When wright embarked on a study trip to Japan, Griffin continued to oversee various major projects in Wright's absence, albeit in his own style. Upon his return, Wright was unhappy to learn of Griffin's independent direction, leading to the end of their professional partnership.

CAR Initially, Cadillac employed the 'de Ville' designation to signify a specific level of equipment, but starting in 1959 it evolved into an independent model line. The Sedan Deville depicted here is from the second generation. It may be challenging to imagine in today's context, but back then this car was considered rather modest. The extravagant fins and excessive use of chrome, characteristic of earlier models, were now applied more sparingly. However, a Cadillac retained its distinctive identity in every aspect, serving as a symbol that you had achieved a certain level of success and prestige.

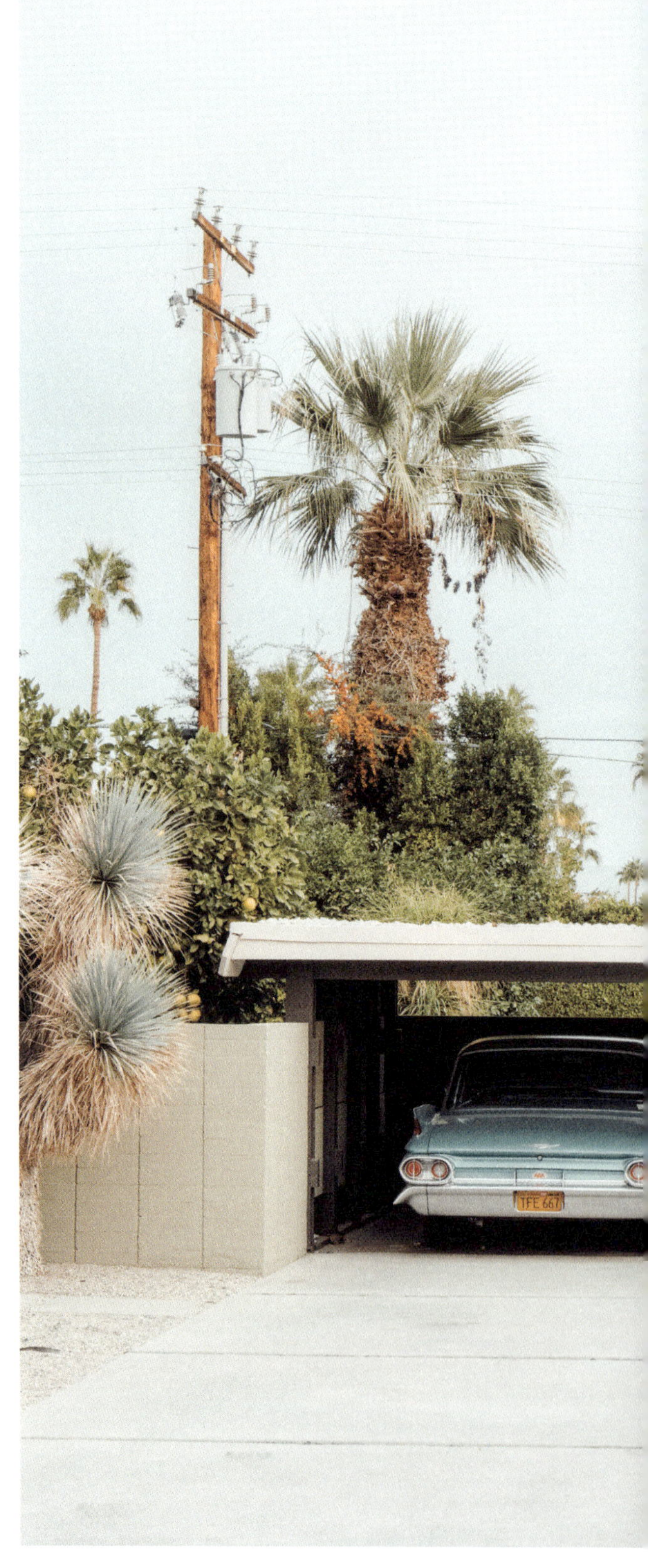

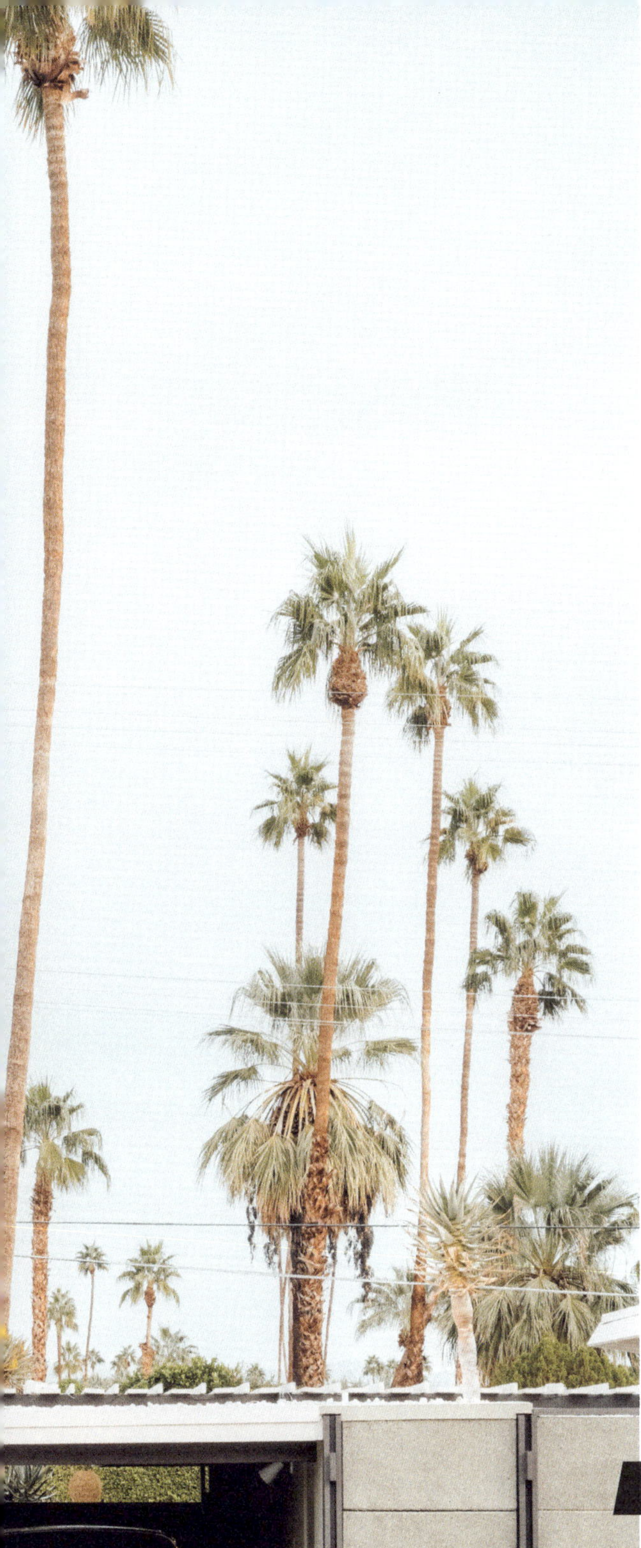

Dodge Matador/Polara

CAR In 1960 the Polara made its debut as the new flagship model in the Dodge lineup. Simultaneously, Dodge introduced the Matador, which shared the same bodywork as the Polara. Both cars were only available that year and retained the characteristics of Virgil Exner's 1957 Forward Look design, with stylized lines, tail lights inspired by jet engines, and (shortened) tail fins. An abundance of chrome adorned these models, though the Matador sported a somewhat understated interior. The Matadors were equipped with a 361 cubic-inch V8 engine, while the Polaras boasted a larger 383 cubic-inch V8 engine. Over 23,000 Matadors were sold that year, but unfortunately the model was discontinued and largely fell into obscurity.

Lincoln Continental

ARCHITECTURE Photographer Ludwig Favre can't pinpoint the exact location where he shot this breathtaking carchitecture image. What's certain is that it was in a residential area in Palm Springs; the palm trees and the backdrop of hills serve as unmistakable clues, but it's the architectural style of the villas that reveals the crime scene, so to speak. With its dense concentration of well-preserved mid-century homes, Palm Springs truly resembles a large-scale film set. Add to this Favre's cinematic photography style and you have images that convey a thousand stories, seamlessly bridging the past and the present.

CAR Between 1940 and 2020, Lincoln adopted the name 'Continental' for a wide range of equipment levels and models, from entry-level to flagship. The fourth generation depicted here was essentially the only Lincoln offering throughout the 1960s, as the company struggled with financial challenges following earlier model developments.
Interestingly, Elwood Engel originally designed this Continental proposal for the new Ford Thunderbird. At its debut, this Continental was awarded a bronze medal from the Industrial Design Institute (IDI) in New York and the Engineering Excellence award from *Car Life* magazine. Initially, the car was only available as a four-door sedan and a four-door convertible with automatic hood, both featuring distinctive 'suicide doors.' Over the course of the decade, the model underwent three facelifts.
In 1966, a two-door variant was introduced and the original V8 engine from its predecessor, the Mark V, was enlarged from 430 to 462 cubic inches, making it the largest engine ever featured in a Ford Group passenger car. It's noteworthy that the fourth-generation Lincoln Continental served as the basis for the presidential limousine in which John F. Kennedy was tragically assassinated.

1961

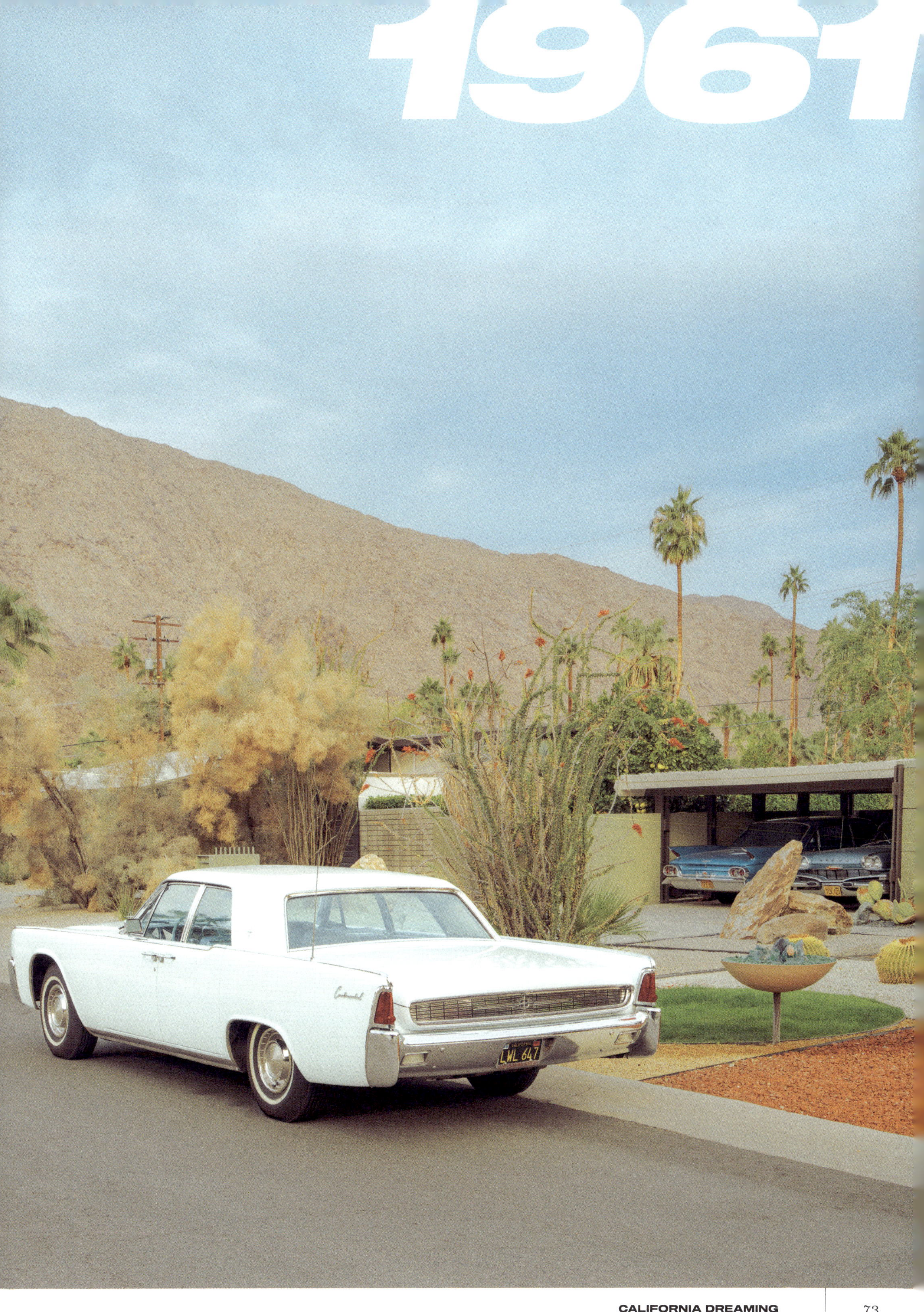

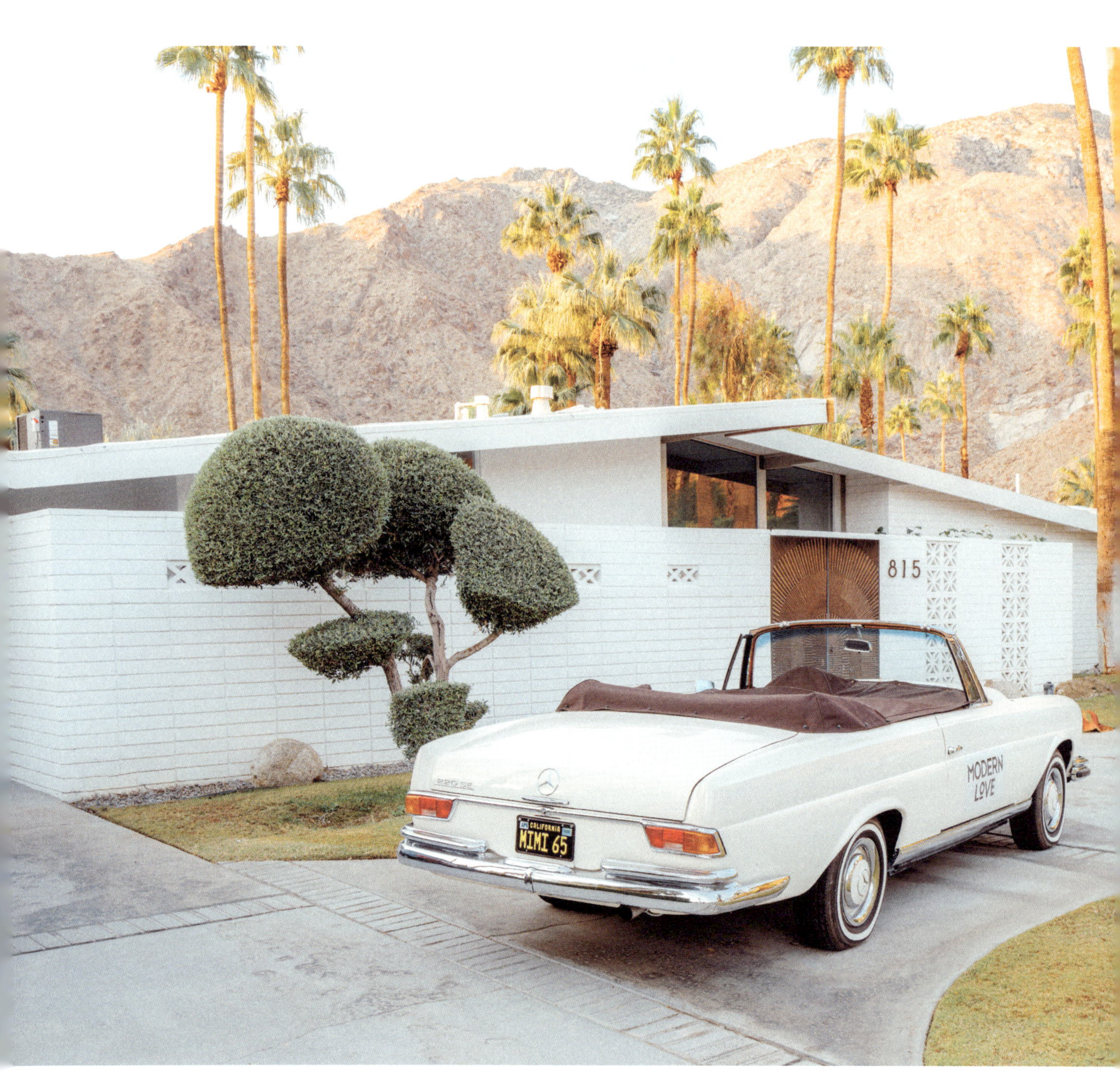
815
MODERN
LOVE
CALIFORNIA
MIMI 65

Mercedes-Benz 220 SE Cabriolet

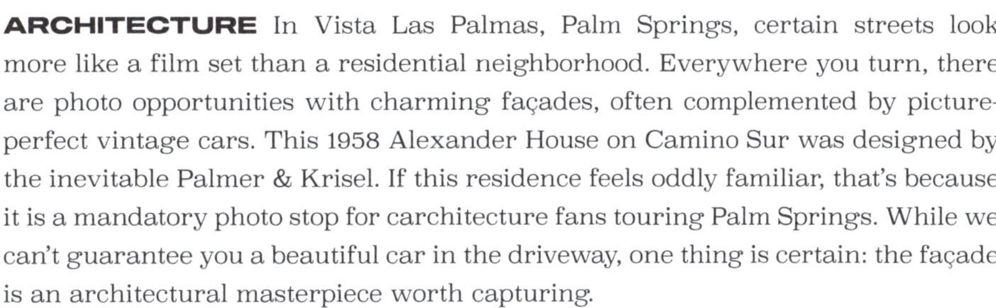

ARCHITECTURE In Vista Las Palmas, Palm Springs, certain streets look more like a film set than a residential neighborhood. Everywhere you turn, there are photo opportunities with charming façades, often complemented by picture-perfect vintage cars. This 1958 Alexander House on Camino Sur was designed by the inevitable Palmer & Krisel. If this residence feels oddly familiar, that's because it is a mandatory photo stop for carchitecture fans touring Palm Springs. While we can't guarantee you a beautiful car in the driveway, one thing is certain: the façade is an architectural masterpiece worth capturing.

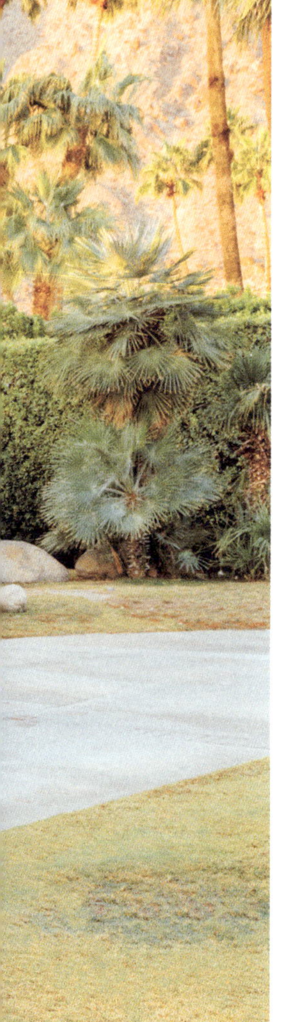

CAR The W111 series served as the precursor of today's S-Class, Mercedes-Benz's comfortable luxury limousine. It was a pioneering car in terms of passive safety, featuring a safety cage with integrated crumple zone. The vehicle's bodywork was the brainchild of the team headed by Karl Wilfert, chief designer at Daimler-Benz from 1959 to 1976.

The car became known as *Heckflosse* in German, which translates to 'fin tail,' and in English-speaking regions it was affectionately referred to as the 'Finnie.' According to Mercedes-Benz, the tail fins, while rather modest compared to their American counterparts, served as corner markers that were handy for parking purposes. Production of the convertible models within the W111 series continued until 1971, further adding to the legacy of this remarkable Mercedes-Benz lineup.

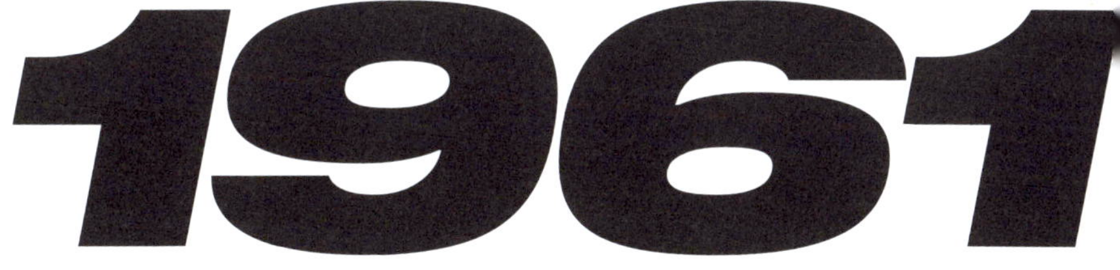

Mercedes-Benz 300 SE Coupé

ARCHITECTURE Vista Las Palmas is a neighborhood that undoubtedly deserves a star on your Google Maps. It is here that you'll discover this textbook example of an early Alexander House, envisioned by the legendary Palmer & Krisel firm in 1958. The bent roof is a captivating sight and the breeze blocks forming the lattice brick wall are characteristic of Desert Modernism. During Modernism Week, expect to find a high-end vintage car gracefully parked in front of the beautiful front door. We once had the pleasure of witnessing a light-blue Jaguar E-Type gracing the scene, but this pink Mercedes-Benz 300 SE Coupé is equally stunning.

CAR The 1961 Mercedes-Benz W112 series, part of the W111 lineup, introduced a luxury version equipped with an alloy 3-liter block alongside its 6-cylinder 2.2-liter engine. Though these vehicles shared the same chassis as their counterparts, they were set apart by distinctive features, such as chrome trims and an air suspension system, among other upgrades. The opulent interior of the W112 was fitted with extensive woodwork. Despite their limited production from 1961 to 1967, numbering only 2,419 units, they have not significantly outvalued the comparatively less progressive W111 series in the classic car market.

196

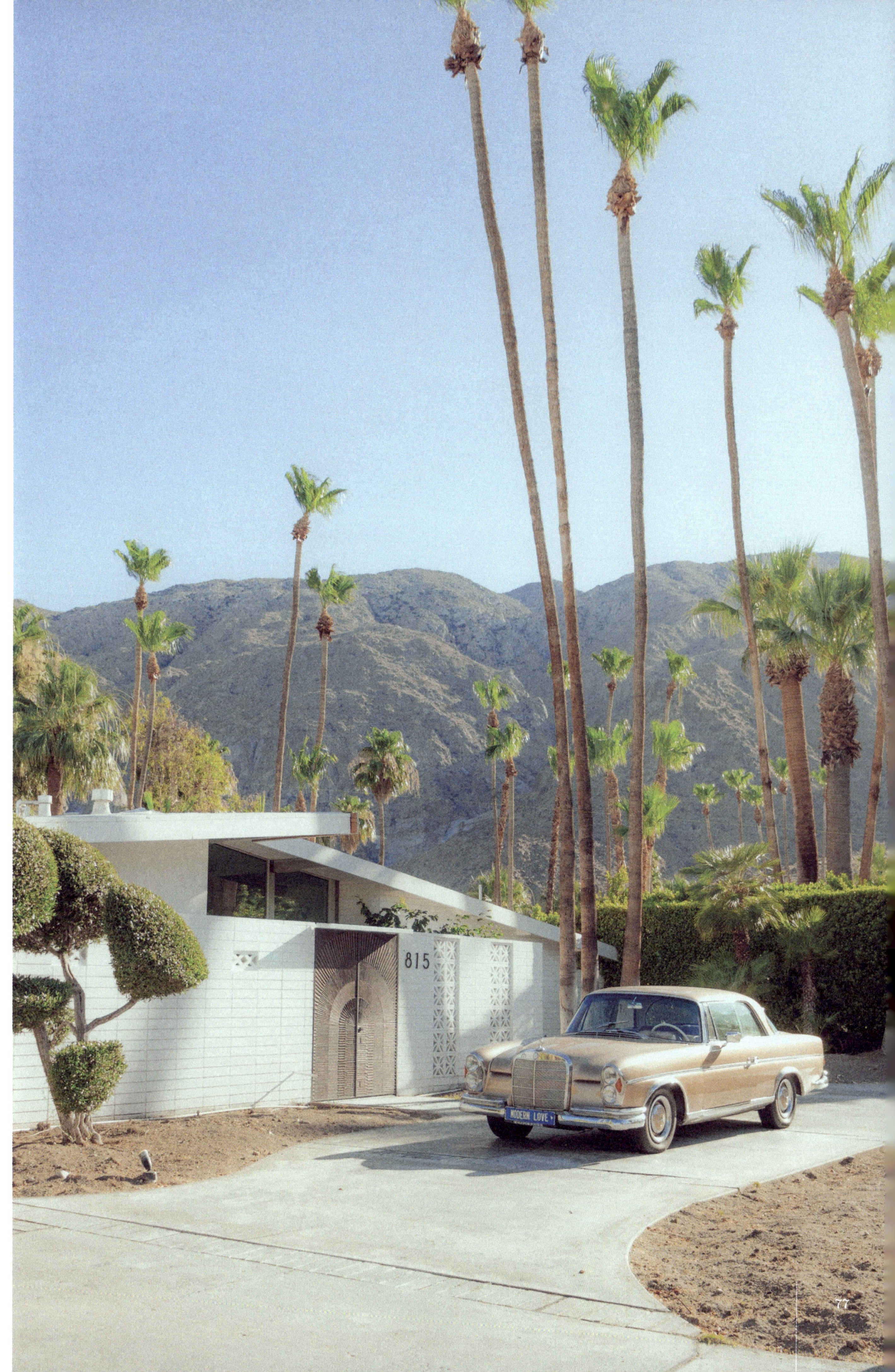
815
MODERN LOVE

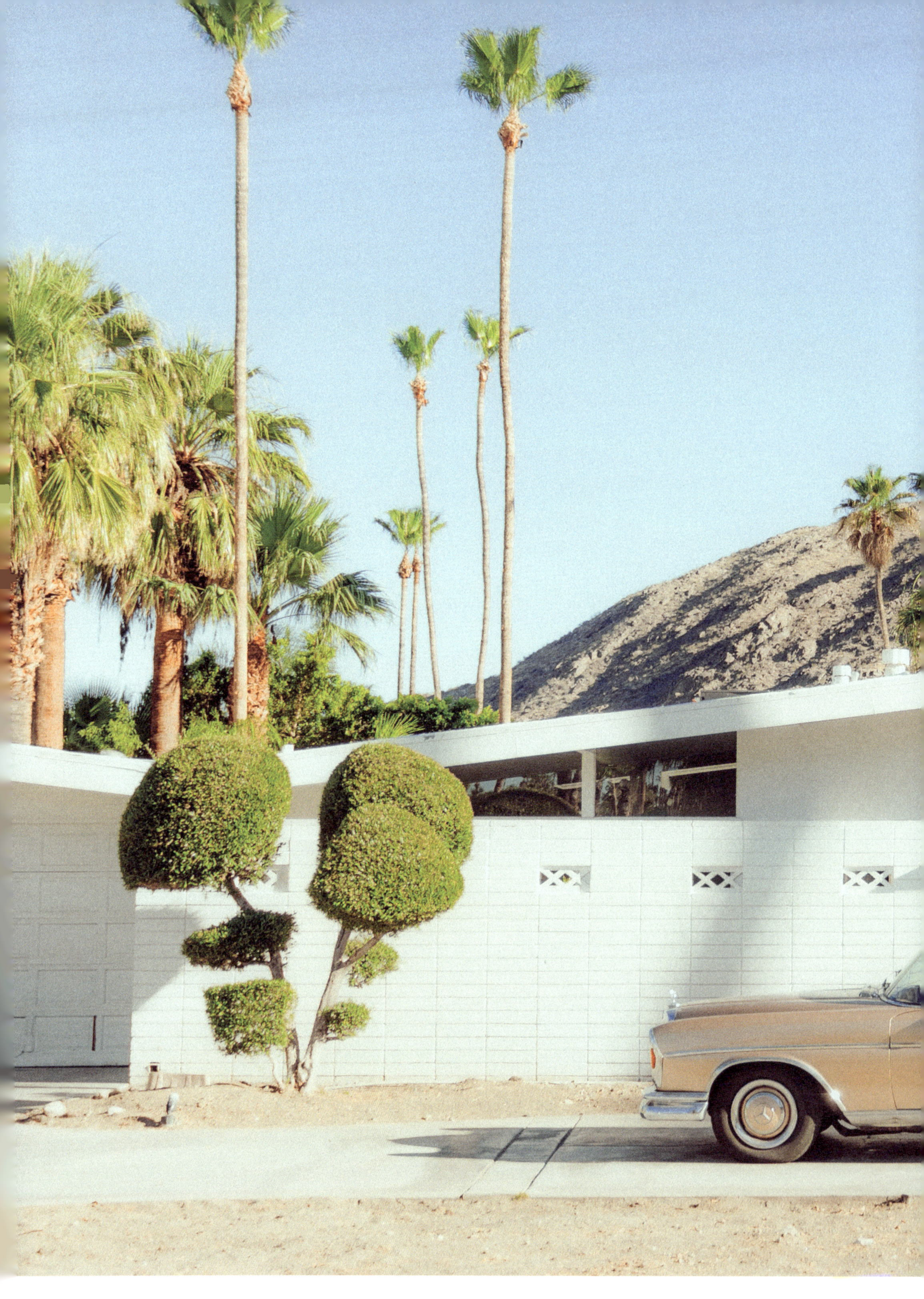

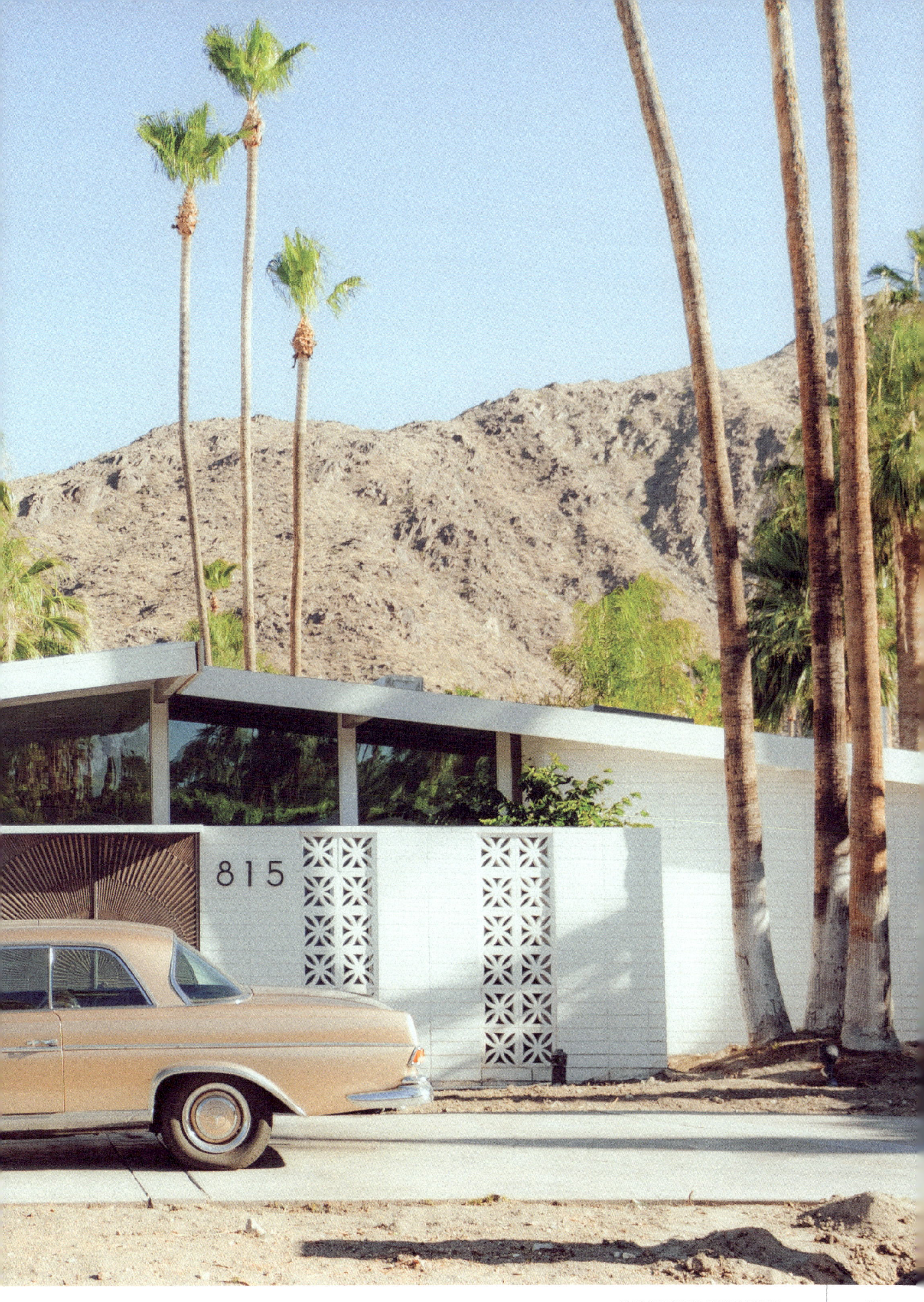
815

Chrysler New Yorker 2-door Hardtop

ARCHITECTURE Australian photographer Tom Ferguson came across this striking example of carchitecture in Sandcliff, an unusual cluster of about 40 similar homes in Palm Springs. These residences all feature characteristic concrete breeze blocks—decorative walls that ensure privacy while also filtering sunlight and blocking wind. Such breeze blocks were a typical feature of modernist architecture in Palm Springs during the 1950s and 1960s. Sandcliff itself dates back to the early 1960s, with the completion of its first house in 1960. In 1966, when another developer completed the remaining homes on the 4.5-acre plot, the project was rebranded as Garden Villas—a marketing decision aligning it with the developer's other real-estate ventures in Palm Springs, namely Villa Riviera and Villa Roma. Despite this rebranding, Sandcliff eventually reverted to its original name, and the project was designated a Class I Historic Site. Even the official nameplate underwent restoration to its original typeface, preserving the historical integrity of this architectural gem.

CAR The New Yorker nameplate made its grand entrance in 1939 and reigned as Chrysler's flagship until 1996, serving as the showpiece of Chrysler's craftsmanship. In 1960 the sixth generation New Yorker marked a significant departure from the traditional body-on-frame construction with the introduction of a unibody chassis. This iteration was available in various body styles, including sedan, two-door hardtop, four-door hardtop, convertible and Town & Country station wagon, catering to diverse preferences.

All variants boasted a robust 413 cubic-inch V8 engine, which underwent gradual improvements over time, resulting in enhanced power output. The exterior styling also evolved, initially reflecting strong influences from Virgil Exner's design ethos, known as the 'Forward Look,' before transitioning towards a more angular aesthetic.

Inside the new Yorker is the iconic and futuristic AstraDome instrument cluster adorned with an electroluminescent lighting system, complemented by an abundance of ornamental detailing in chrome and stainless steel.

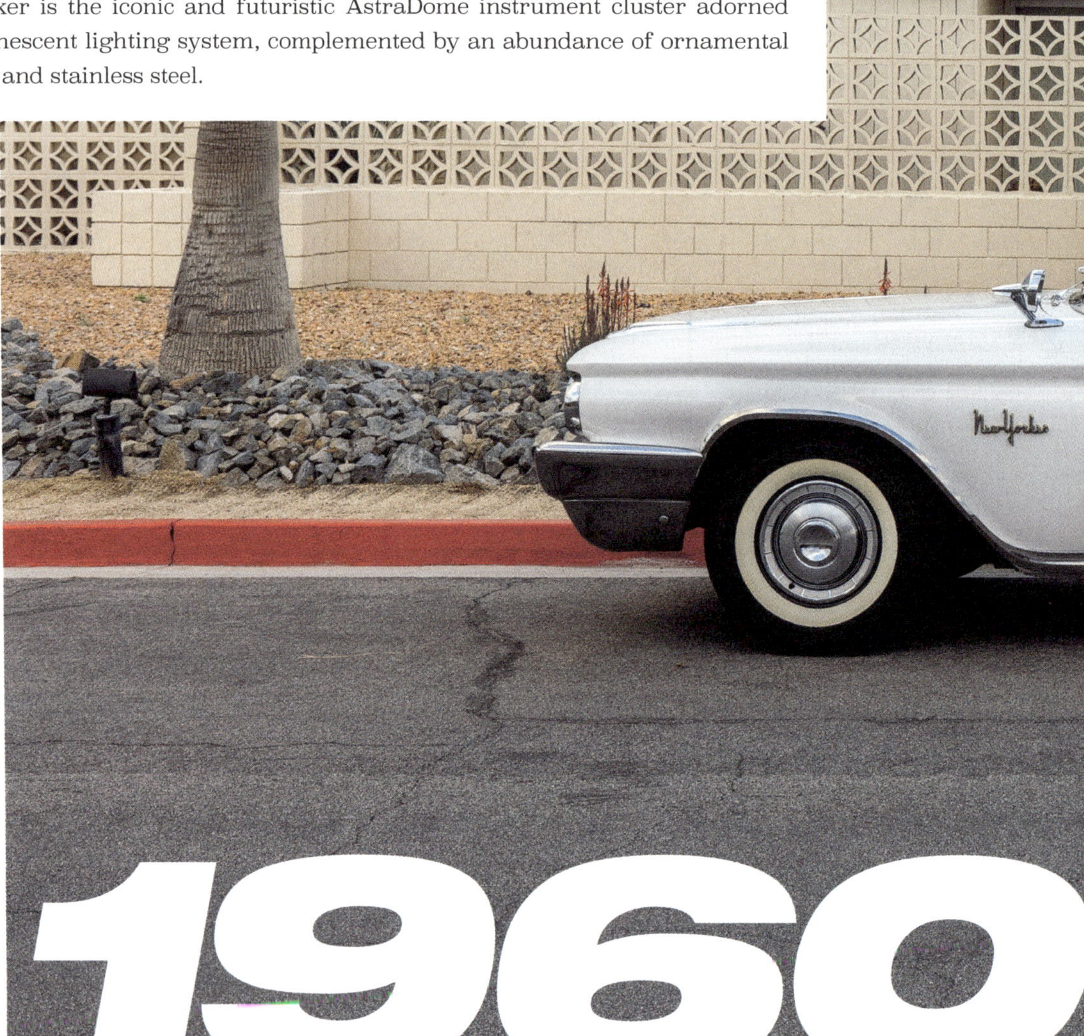

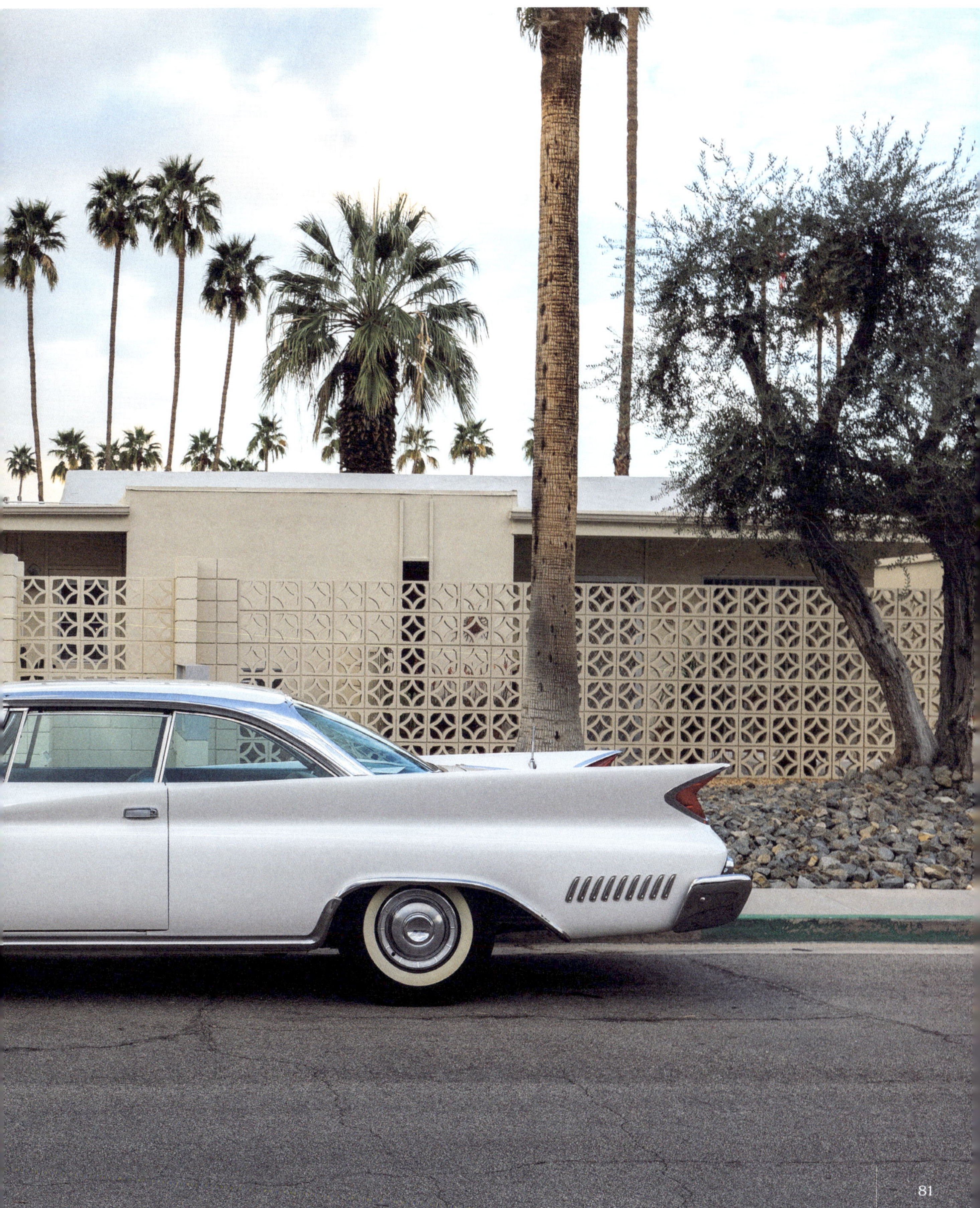

Oldsmobile Super 88 Holiday Sport Sedan

ARCHITECTURE Palm Springs was the 'Desert Utopia' of the Hollywood elite, boasting an oasis of modernist gems meticulously crafted over three decades by enterprising developers, including Roy Fey and his son Robert. Roy Fey moved from Chicago to Palm Springs in 1956 with the sole intention of erecting the Desert Skies Hotel. However, his trajectory took a different turn, and he emerged as an iconic real-estate developer who shaped the region's architectural tapestry. One of the best-known projects of the father–son duo was Canyon View Estates, the setting of this residence. An advertisement from 1965 touted it as 'prestige homes for people of prestige, who appreciate the very best.' This cluster of airy homes, recognizable by their stacked-brick façade, was designed by the renowned firm Palmer & Krisel in the early 1960s. Initially slated for 225 houses, 45 were eventually scrapped in favor of public green space.

CAR In 1959, Oldsmobile presented three distinct series: the Dynamic 88, the high-performance Super 88 and the ultra-luxurious Ninety-Eight. Following the trend set by its counterparts in other GM divisions, these models were lower, longer and had wider designs. Embracing the 'Linear Look' concept, Oldsmobile introduced vehicles featuring expansive hoods, roof sand boots, along with 'vista-panoramic' windscreens.

The exterior design boasted long flowing lines and sculpted sheet metal, exemplified by the Sport sedan's unique, unobstructed roofline devoid of a B pillar and an elegant wrap-around rear window, providing passengers with exceptional views of the surroundings. Unlike many contemporaneous models with prominent and angular fins, Oldsmobile opted for relatively subdued oval variants, and compared to its 1958 predecessor, featured significantly less chrome embellishment, resulting in a cleaner aesthetic that emphasized the car's refined lines.

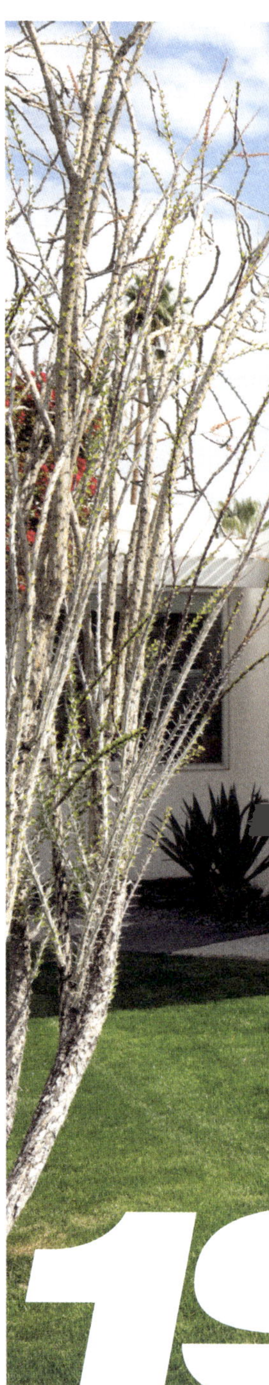

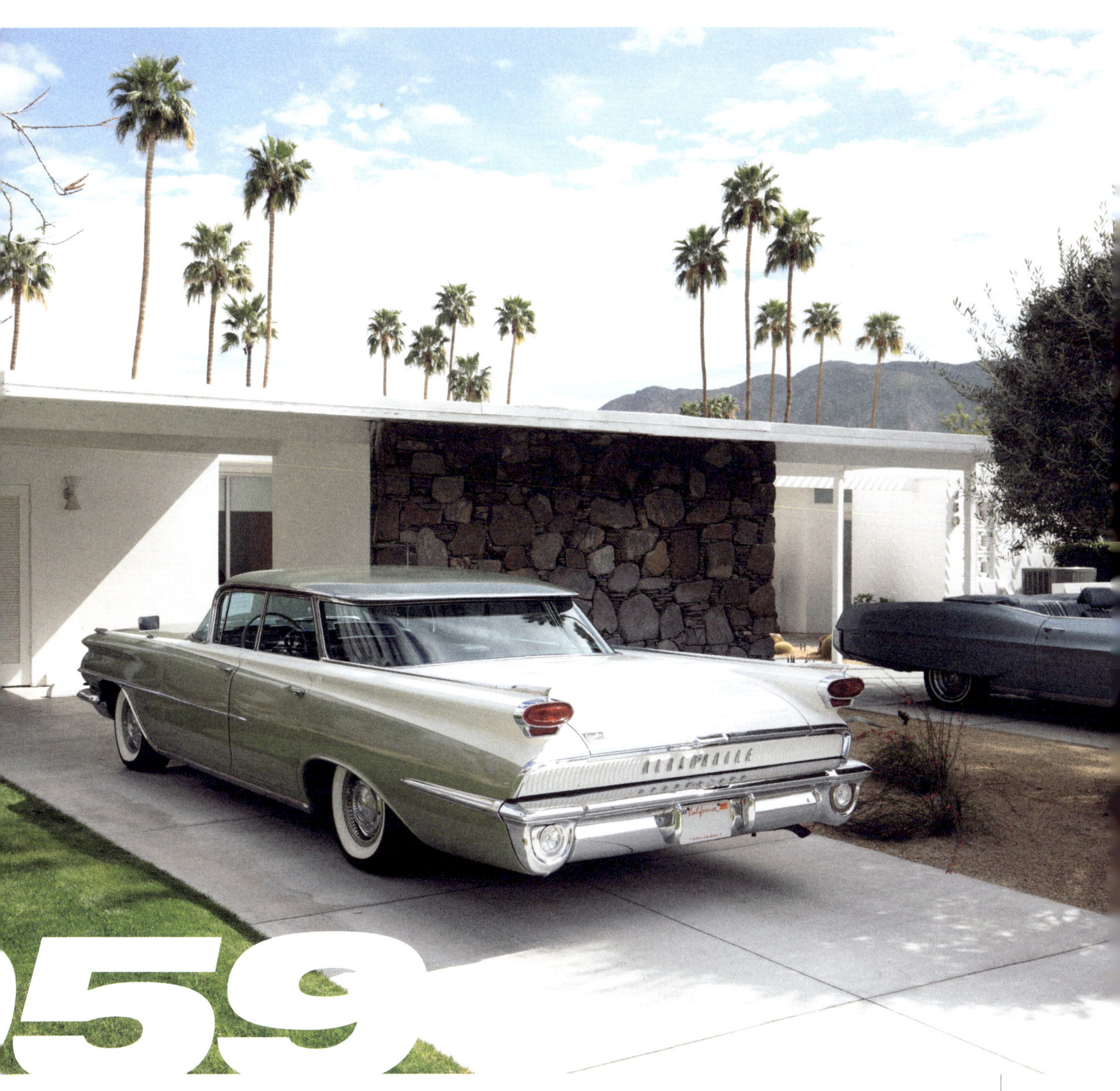
59

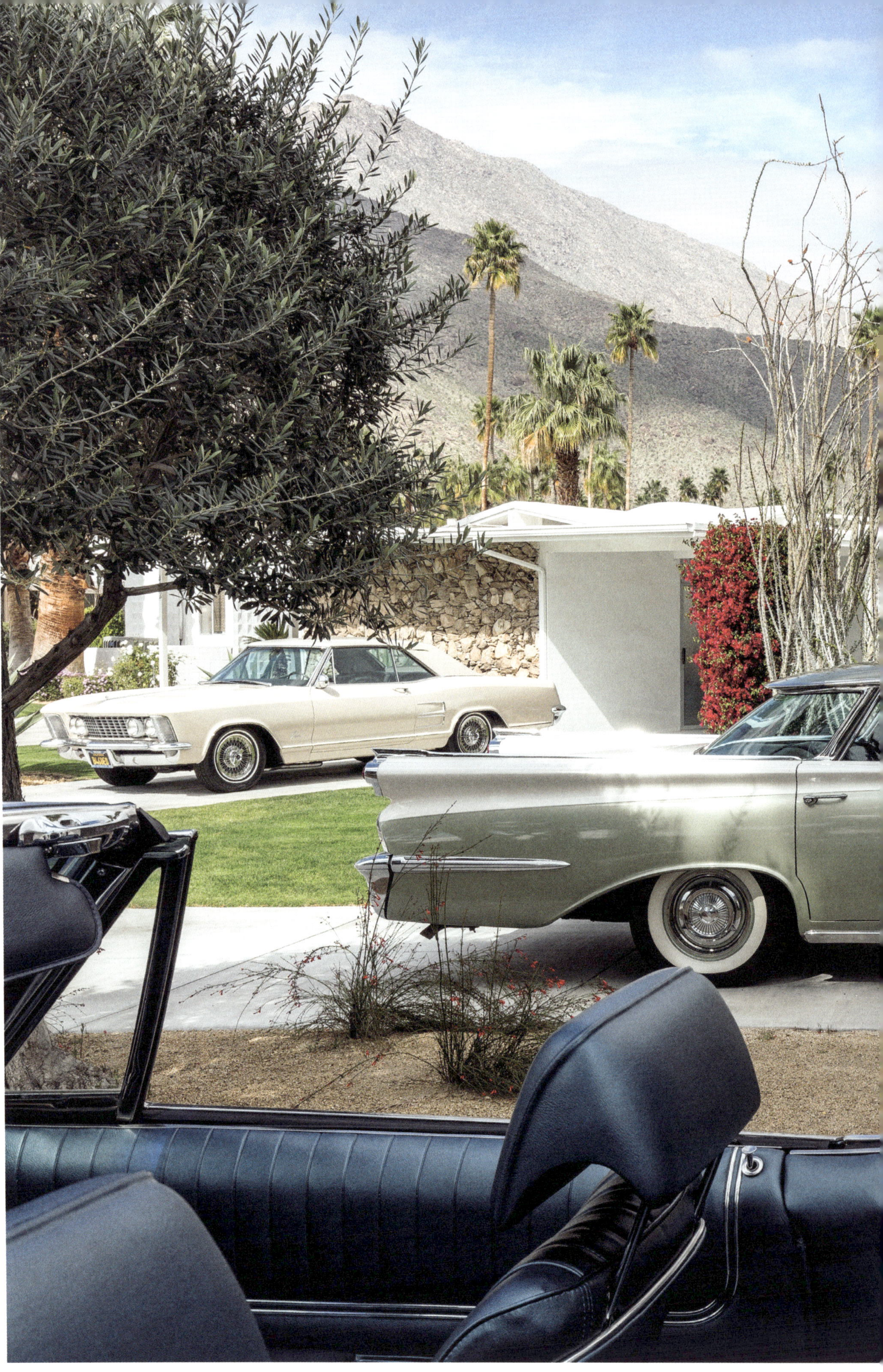

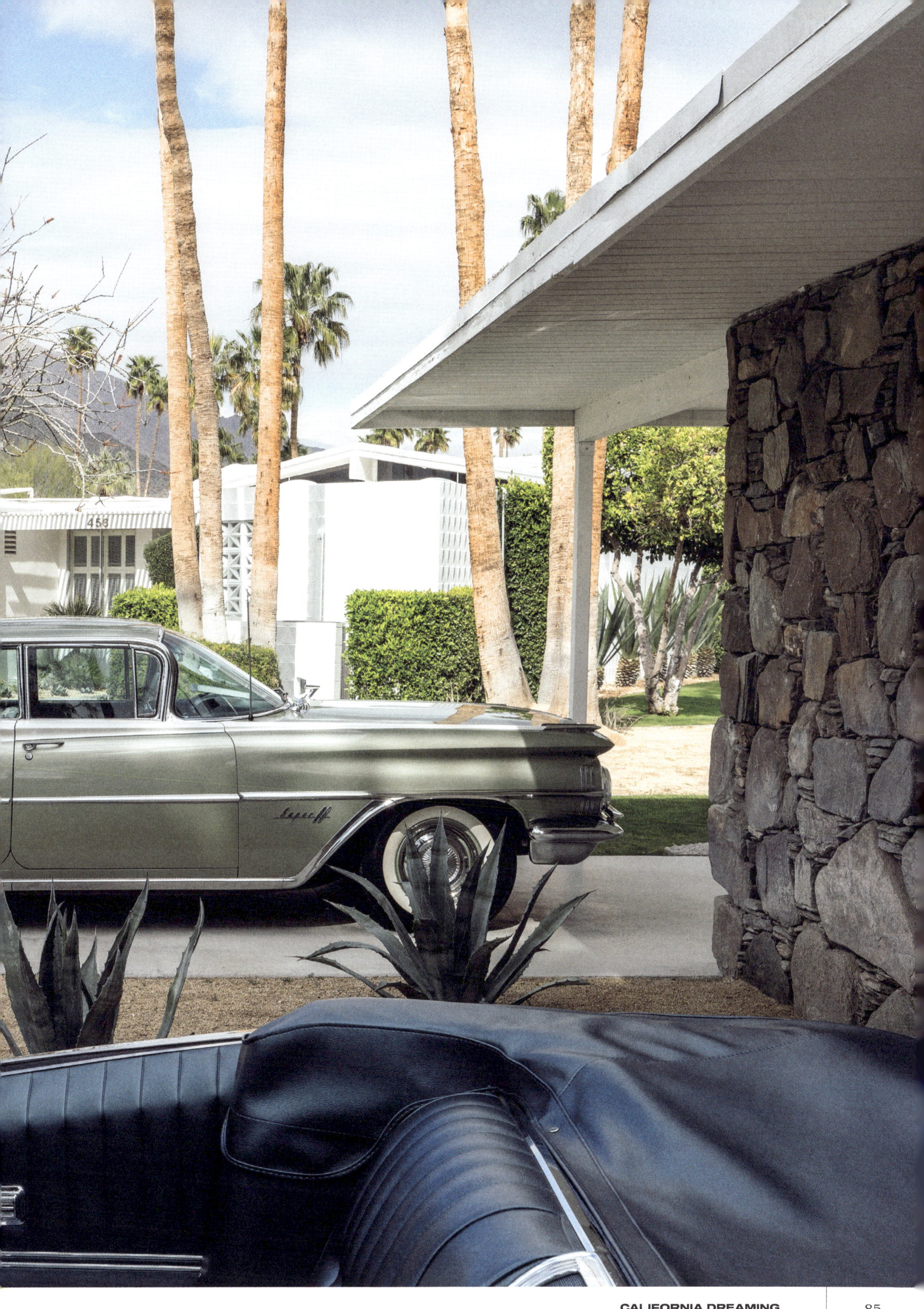
458

Mercury Montclair
2-door hardtop (Phaeton Coupé)

ARCHITECTURE 1070 E. Apache Road, Palms Springs is an address cherished by architectural enthusiasts. Constructed in 1957 by the Alexander Construction Company and designed by the eminent William Krisel, the renowned Alexander Home stands as a testament to mid-century modern design. Notably, the home's distinctive 'floating butterfly' roof—a feature only found in 12 Alexander houses in the Twin Palms area—captivates attention.

What sets this residence apart is the collaborative effort between architect William Krisel and owner Chris Menrad to restore both its interior and exterior in 2006. Not only were the original colors reinstated, but the front garden was also revitalized, echoing the vibrant spirit of 1957.

CAR In 1939, Edsel Ford founded the Mercury division with the aim of bridging the gap within the Ford Motor Company between the mainstream Ford brand and the luxury marque Lincoln. Additionally, he sought to position Mercury as a competitor to Buick and Oldsmobile in the mid-range automotive segment.

The Montclair was introduced in 1955 as Mercury's flagship model. The car showcased here belongs to the second generation, which served as the mid-range offering during the 1958 and 1959 model years, positioned below the Park Lane trim level.

In 1958 the Montclair-312 V8 engine was replaced by a 383 cubic-inch version, generating an impressive 330 hp. For those seeking even greater performance, the optional 430 cubic-inch 'Super Marauder' engine was available upon request. Remarkably, this engine marked a significant milestone as the first mass-produced American powerplant capable of delivering a staggering 400 hp.

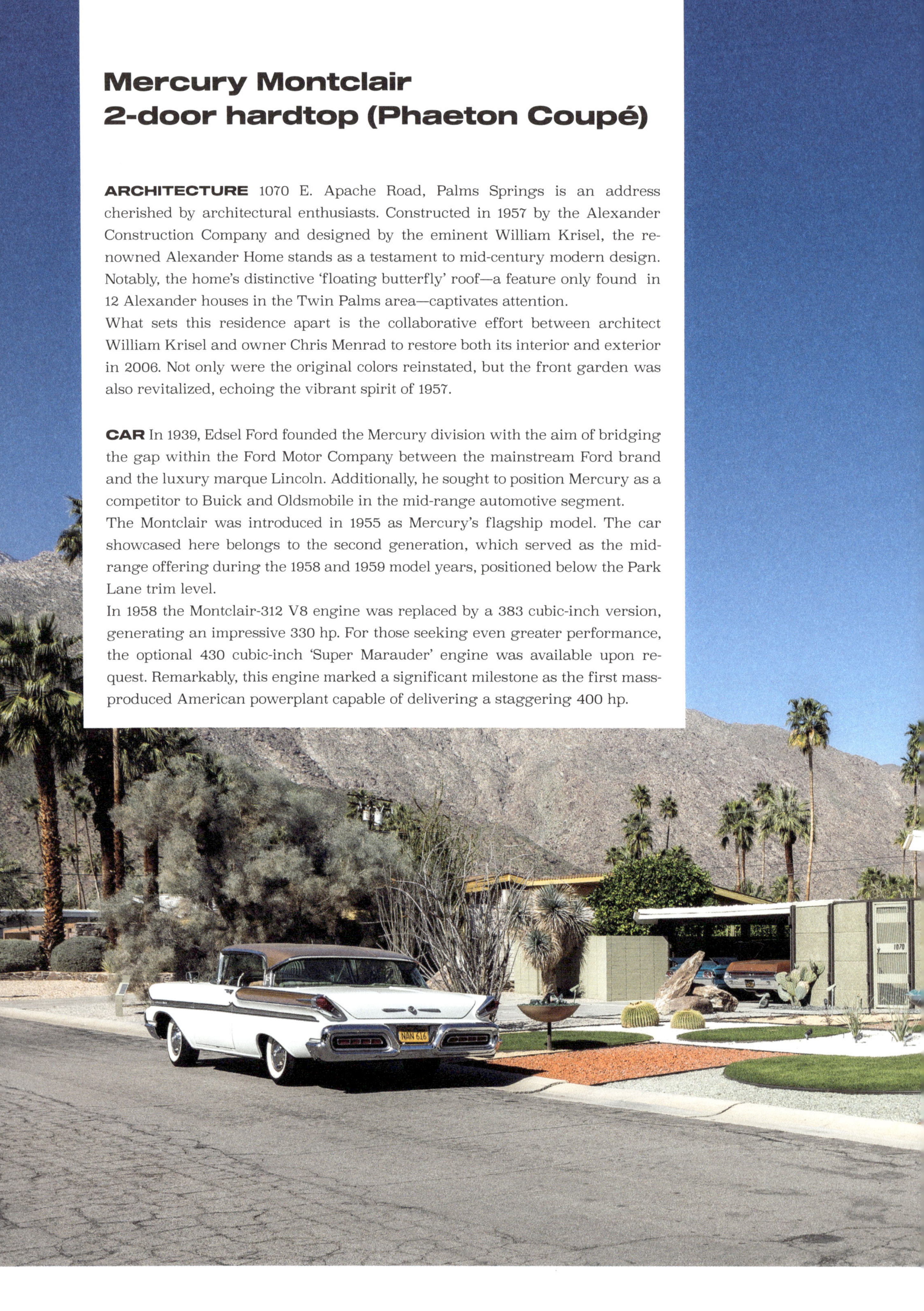

1958

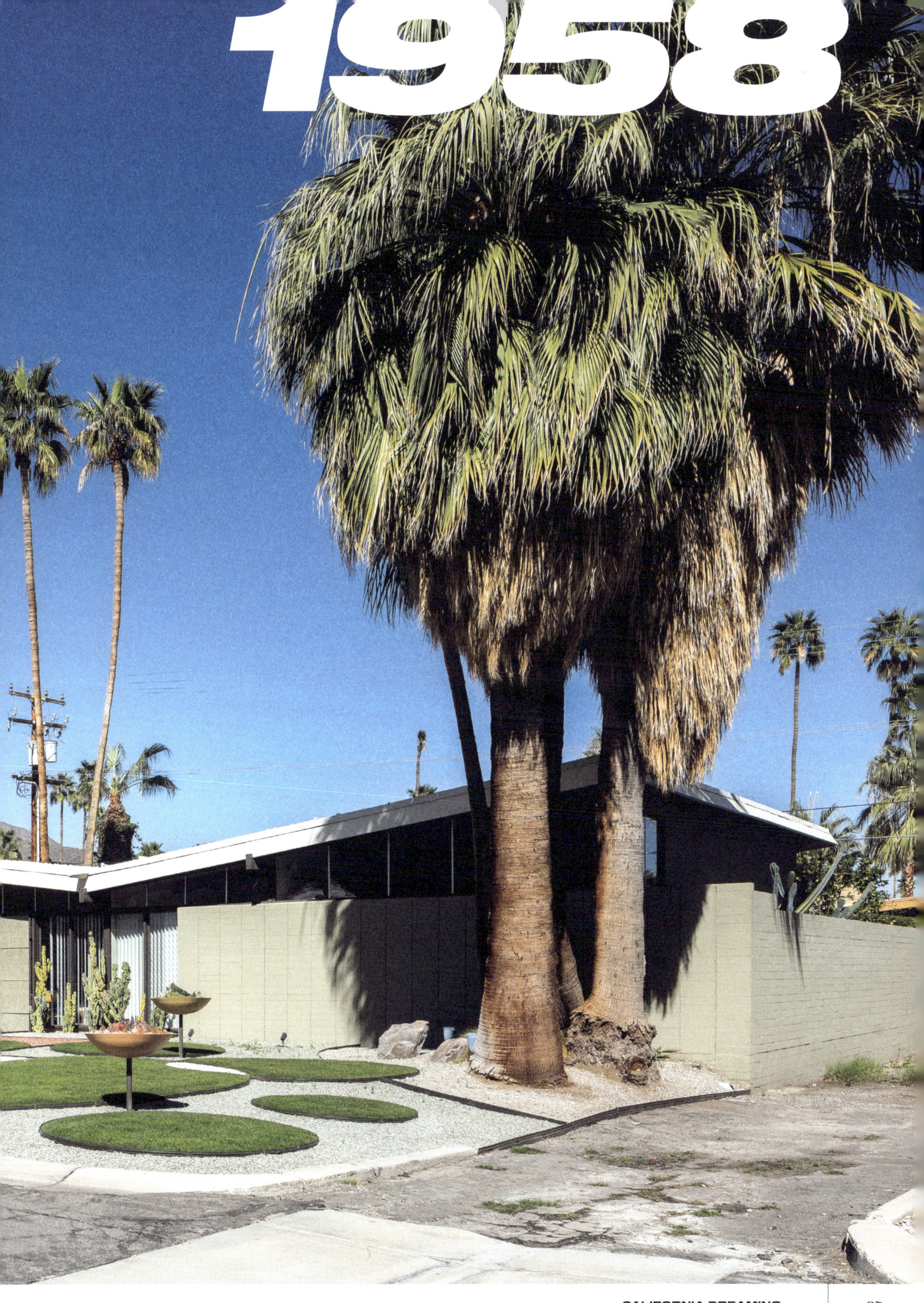

How to Accessorize a House with a Car

DOS AND DON'TS IN CARCHITECTURE

Ever wondered why luxury accessories sell so well? It's simple: no model-like measurements are required to effortlessly 'wear' them. A luxury brand handbag complements anyone's appearance, but the 'ideal' body for a skinny dress isn't everyone's reality. Much like a luxury handbag, an exclusive car functions as a chic vessel, a stylish conveyance. A mode of transportation, yes, but also a medium of expression, whose message is never neutral. In today's world, those who opt for an ordinary bag are labeled 'normcore.'

Just as an accessory completes a personal look, a car completes a home. It is the essence of carchitecture. Admittedly, for diehard car enthusiasts, a car often holds more significance than a house; sometimes it might even surpass a house in literal value. However, let's keep things in balance here.

An accessory conveys a statement, a declaration of individuality. Do you like to play it safe? Or do you prefer the allure of items that are recognizable as costly by their logos? Perhaps you like browsing vintage designer boutiques in search of a preloved accessory that no one else wears? Or are you post-ironic, with a penchant for accessories that embrace kitsch or low-end aesthetics with renewed coolness? In all these scenarios, paralels can be drawn with the automotive world. We once knew someone who loved the first-generation Fiat Panda because it reflected his fondness for marginality. Every choice says something about your sense of style, fashion sense and image—whether or not you acknowledge it.

PISTACHIO GREEN CHEVROLET

Tell me the connection between your car and your home, and I'll tell you who you are. Admittedly it's a quip, but when it comes to your carchitecture—the pairing of architecture and car—you could easily miss the mark. Fortunately, a few rules of thumb can steer you toward successful carchitecture. The simplest strategy: go for *ton sur ton* (matching tones). This is really for beginners, and it works particularly well in neighborhoods where houses stand out. Are you the proud owner of a mid-century bungalow with a pistachio green front door? If so, then go for a pistachio green Chevrolet Corvair.

Do you live in a Barbie-pink house in Daly City, California? Then make it a pink Corvette. A house with a Frida Kahlo blue façade? It'll stand out even more with a blue car in front of it, no matter the brand. Passers-by are guaranteed to stop and take a photo of the killer combination. If the striking effect is what you're after, have no doubt about matching tones. Now onto something a bit more daring: combining colors. This strategy hinges on the match of colors between architecture and car. Beware: carchitecture *à la* Wes Anderson is enticing, but requires greater color sensitivity than those who go for a *ton sur ton* look.

ART DECO CARS

Are you after something more sophisticated? Then try a *pairing* according to style period. What matches an intact ocean liner-style art deco house better than a car with streamlined shapes from the interwar period? Purists will say a Talbot-Lago T150-C SS Goutte d'Eau, the last word in that genre. However, a more understated option like a Pontiac Silver Streak or Lincoln-Zephyr will equally do the trick. Do you live in a decidedly post-modernist house from the 1980s? Then park an Alfa Romeo SZ in front of your glass entrance. It's not only a visual delight, but promises a great driving experience as well.

Stylistically, pure carchitecture exudes a sense of cohesion. However, it can be somewhat predictable, because in both fashion and interior design, a total look in a single style can lack vibrancy. Imagine a party where each guest adheres precisely to the dress code: it might make for nice photos, but those looks won't be memorable. And the same principle will likely apply to the party itself. Striving for stylistic purity is an easy, yet boring solution. Even in the most 'classical' milieux, it's a rarity. Consider King Louis XIV of France, who didn't restrict the embellishments of Versailles solely to French creations from his era. He preferred to mix and match them with precious curiosities from other periods and continents. Is anyone waiting for such a carchitecture-inspired time machine akin to that scenario? Unlikely. Compare it to a medieval castle around which a landscape architect must design a garden. Would they opt for a strictly medieval garden? Or would they, instead, favor a contemporary reinterpretation infused with elements reminiscent of medieval times? The latter option, in our opinion, holds greater allure.

SPOILER ALERT

Anyone who is not a fetishist of period styles can still easily discover formal paralels between house and car. Spoiler alert: a 1950s bungalow with butterfly roof cries out for a Cadillac Eldorado Biarritz with impressive tail fins, a pioneering feature introduced by Cadillac in 1948. Likewise, a robust brutalist concrete home from the 1960s or 1970s calls for a bold, angular car, preferably one painted a subdued color, accompanied by a firm suspension. Consider a gray Volvo 262C, for example: though opinions on its aesthetics differ, this 'beautiful brick' complements such a house, outshining even an elegant Jaguar XK-E.

In our opinion, carchitecture gets really interesting when the architecture—car fusion is bold and daring. Put bluntly, the fusion is a real success if it meets the three criteria of intelligence, taste and personality.

Admittedly, this is by far the most complex and sophisticated form of carchitecture. Matching a car with a house based on shape or color alone doesn't require a tremendous amount of skill. And while selecting a car from the right era does call for some historical insight into architectural and automotive design, it doesn't require a sense of style. Let's face it, how many of your former history teachers could be deemed style icons?

PRAIRIE CAR

Imagine you live in a Usonian or Prairie style house, archetypes of American residential architecture which Frank Lloyd Wright became famous for. Over the course of the 20th century, this style was endlessly copied and interpreted by other architects. So which car would you choose, assuming you have a generous budget? An intelligent choice would be a type that Frank Lloyd Wright—a car freak—once drove, such as a Cord L-29 Phaeton, a Bentley R-Type or a Lincoln Continental, the car for which he himself designed the Sedanca de Ville bodywork (open at the front, closed at the back). If you live in a highly contemporary, futuristic house, seek out a DeLorean DMC-12, the mythical car from the well-known movie *Back to the Future*.

Then there is a category of carchitecture specifically for Gen Z—the Zoomers who grew up on the internet and are adept at blurring the boundaries between high and low culture, taste and kitsch. Their taste (and sense of humour) is post-ironic where irony envelopes what they deem as cool and uncool to the extent that self-identity becomes an enigma. Yet this is of no consequence; in their meme-driven culture, humour has become so meta that it is mostly confusing. Now, you might ask, what does that have to do with carchitecture? The answer lies in the hands of Gen Z: under their influence, all conceivable forms of car pairing are possible. Even an unpretentious Honda Civic or Lada Niva can add luster to your home. Then again, perhaps Gen Z will be the first generation to totally renounce car ownership.

“Architecture and car design are both about creating functional spaces that inspire and enhance the human experience.”

Frank Gehry, architect

CLASSICAL GAZ

1971

Citroën DS

ARCHITECTURE Is this European car in front of San Francisco City Hall a carchitectural mismatch? Absolutely not. The rather pompous building is firmly rooted in European architectural tradition. The City Hall looks baroque, yet was only completed in 1916. The dome closely resembles that of St Peter's Basilica in Rome and the Hôtel des Invalides in Paris. It is noteworthy that America openly embraced European (neo) classical architectural styles, particularly for its institutional buildings, from its independence until the mid-20th century. It was only with the advent of Frank Lloyd Wright that America began its own architectural tradition. When leading European Bauhaus architects moved to America from the interwar period onwards, American architecture received an infusion of talent, shaping its trajectory to the present day.
Yet there have always been reactionary voices in the architectural debate. When President Donald Trump openly spoke out against modern architecture and advocated a return to classical styles through his 'Make Federal Buildings Beautiful Again' campaign. In his view, neoclassicism, Greek revival and Georgian styles were the architectural norm, and not what he called the 'monstrosities' produced by modernism. San Francisco City Hall is an anachronism anyway, as it replaced the previous neoclassical City Hall, which was badly damaged in the 1906 earthquake. That building had only been completed in 1899, after 27 years of construction.

CAR The Citroën DS—*déesse* means goddess—may well have been the most innovative car of the 20th century. When it was presented at the Paris Motor Show on October 6, 1955, fairgoers were blown away: as many as 12,000 DS's were ordered on the first day. Former aeronautical engineer and racing driver André Lefèbvre, who had previously designed the Traction Avant and the 2CV, led the technical development. The hydraulic system, with its hydropneumatic suspension that also operated the steering, brakes and even the transmission and clutch, was considered a miracle that had been previously thought impossible. It was the idea of the barely trained but brilliant Paul Magès. The level of comfort on uneven road surfaces was and remains unprecedented: you can simply ignore speed bumps. The bodywork is by Flaminio Bertoni, who was also a sculptor and architect. In his collection of essays *Mythologies*, French philosopher Roland Barthes compared the DS to the 'great Gothic cathedrals.' A panel of car designers put together by British magazine *Classic & Sports Car* proclaimed the DS the most beautiful car of all time. It was in production for 20 years.

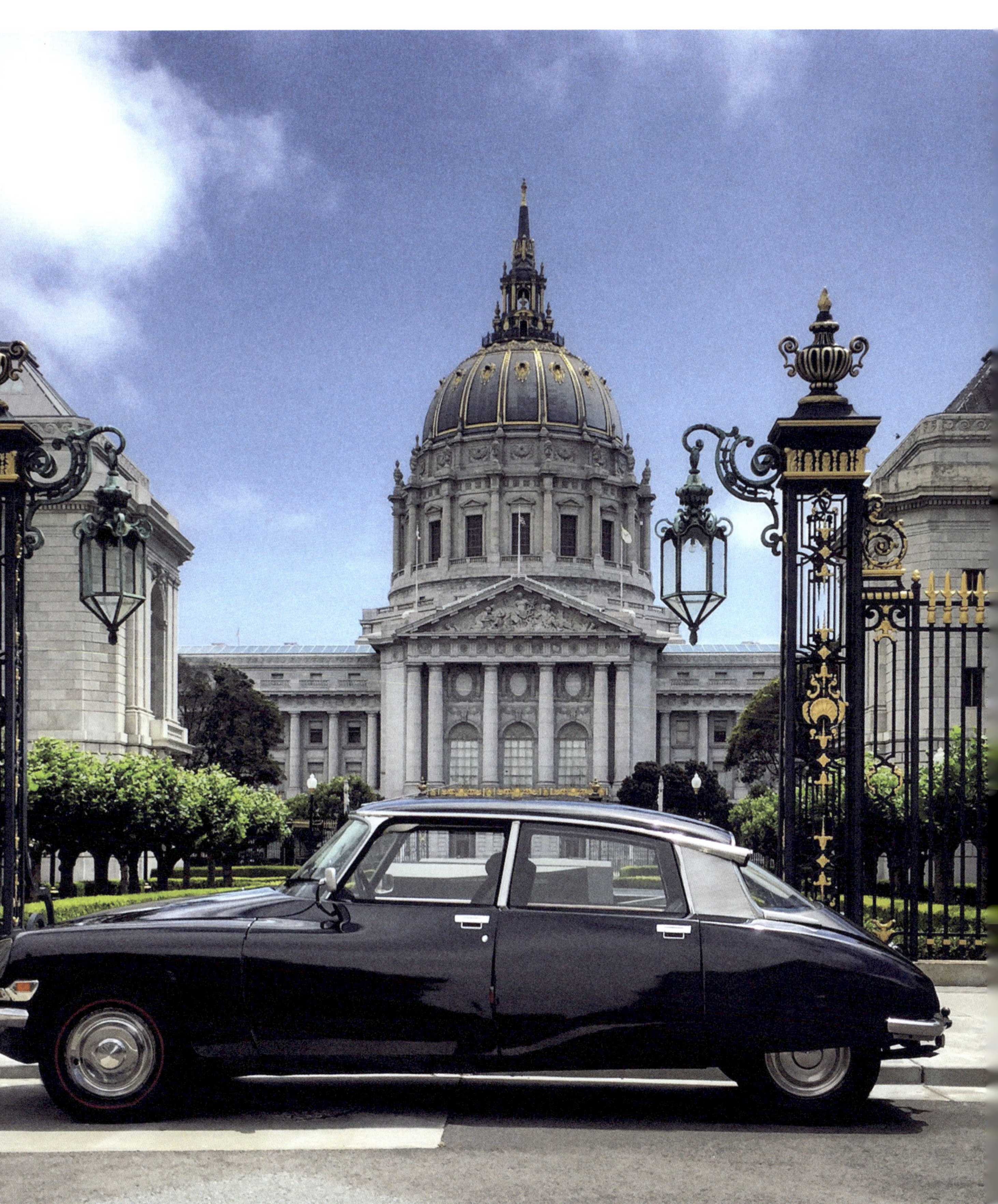

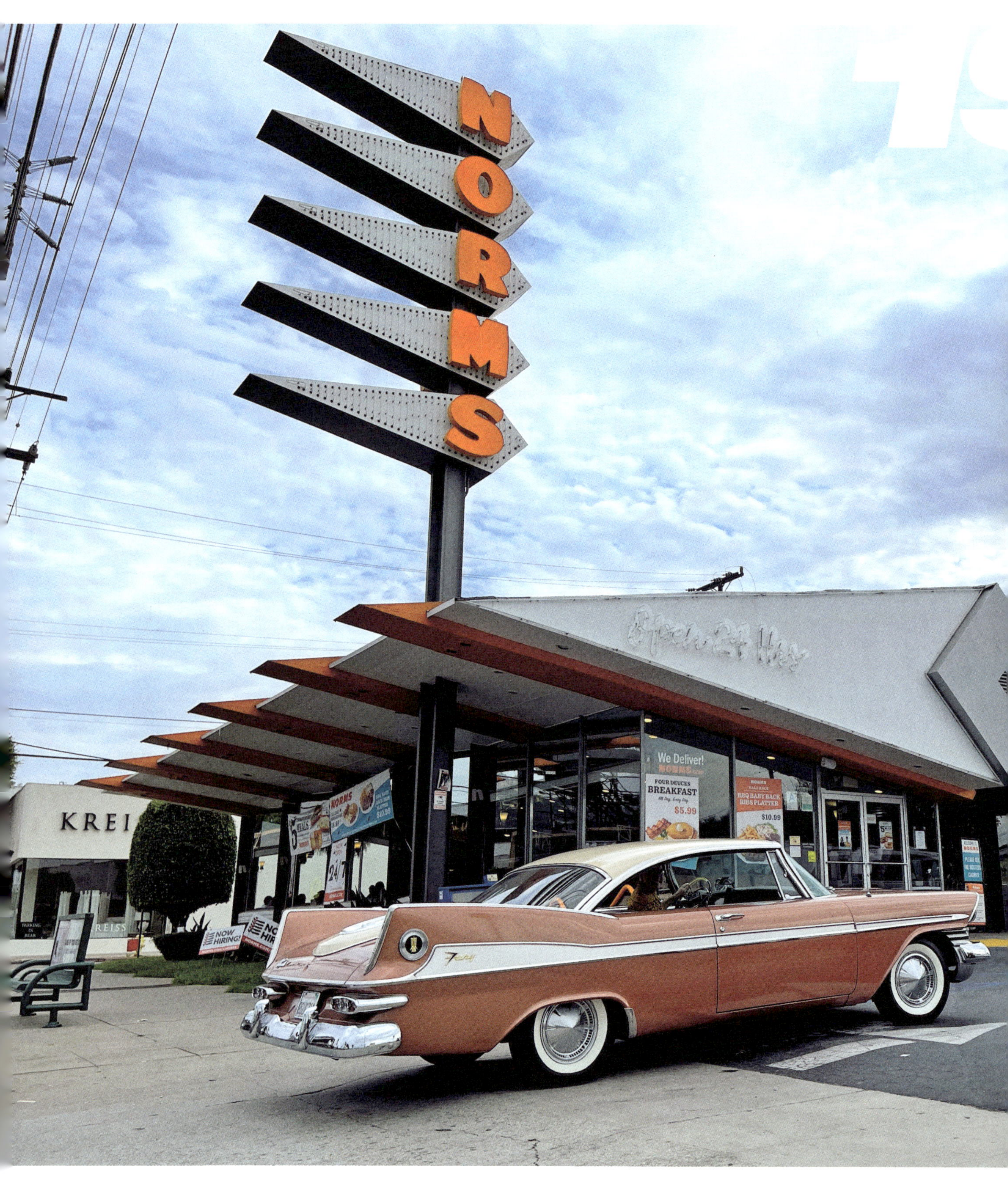
NORMS
Open 24 Hrs
We Deliver!
FOUR DEUCES
BREAKFAST
$5.99
BBQ BABY BACK
RIBS PLATTER
$10.99
NOW HIRING!
KREI

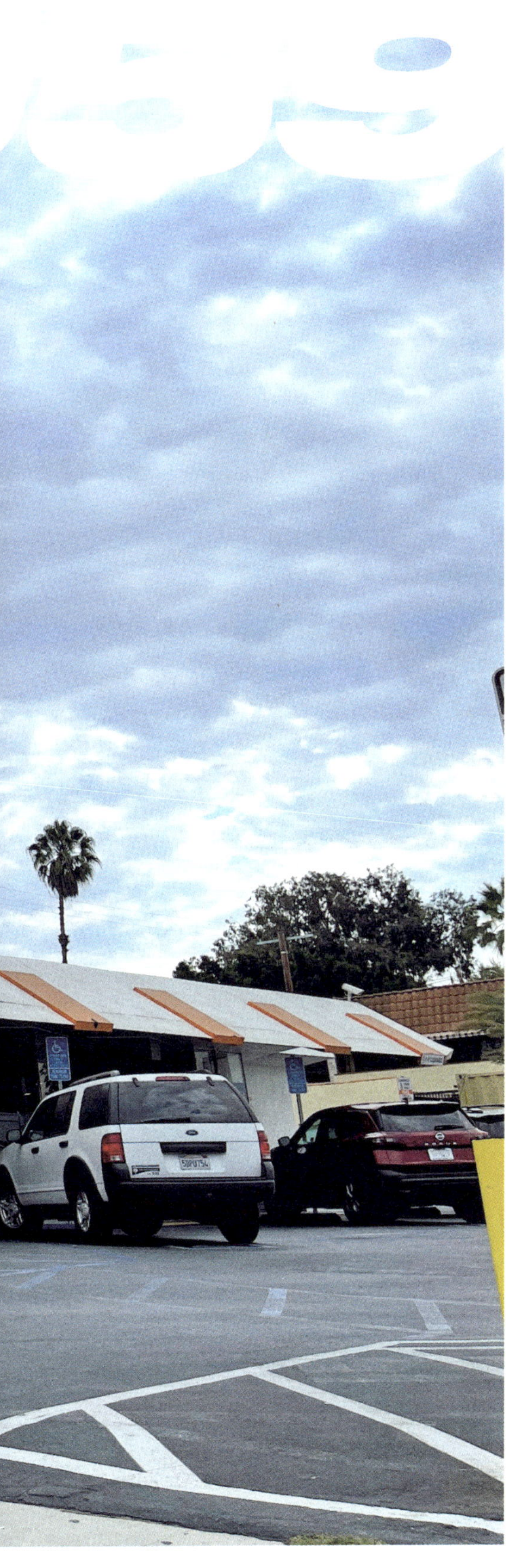

Plymouth Sport Fury

ARCHITECTURE Like the Plymouth Sport Fury in the foreground, Norms La Cienega in the background hardly requires an introduction. This iconic eatery has been a Los Angeles staple since 1957, thanks to the entrepreneurial spirit of Norm Roybark, who opened one of the first 24/7 diners in Hollywood back in 1949. With its welcoming atmosphere and good value for money, Norms has been drawing customers to its various locations for decades. The flagship establishment, Norms La Cienega in West Hollywood, is a prime example of mid-century modern design, crafted by architects Louis Armet and Eldon Davis, celebrated for their contributions to Googie architecture. The engineer, Richard Bradshaw, known for his work on the Theme Building at LAX (also an icon of Googie architecture mentioned in this book), lent his expertise to this project.
The architects drew inspiration from the futuristic aesthetic of cars and car garages, evident in the diner's asymmetrical sawtooth roof, protruding fins, and funky neon signage .
Not surprisingly, Norms has frequently served as a backdrop in film and television. In his popular series *Comedians in Cars Getting Coffee*, Jerry Seinfeld drove into a Norms diner in a Rolls-Royce Silver Cloud II. Norms La Cienega also holds a place in art history, with Ed Ruscha immortalizing it in his 1964 painting *Norms, La Cienega, on Fire*, which hangs in the collection of The Broad.

CAR The Plymouth Fury was introduced in 1955 (for the 1956 model year) as a subseries of the Belvedere. By 1959, it had evolved into a standalone model positioned above the Belvedere lineup, with the Sport Fury reigning as its top-tier model. It epitomised Chrysler Corporation's celebrated Forward Look design philosophy, spearheaded by the visionary Virgil Exner a few years before. Characterized by a long and low design, slender C pillars and an abundance of glass that bathed the cabin in natural light, the Fury embodied the essence of the Forward Look aesthetic. Notably, it featured the elegant tail fins that defined the era's automotive styling.

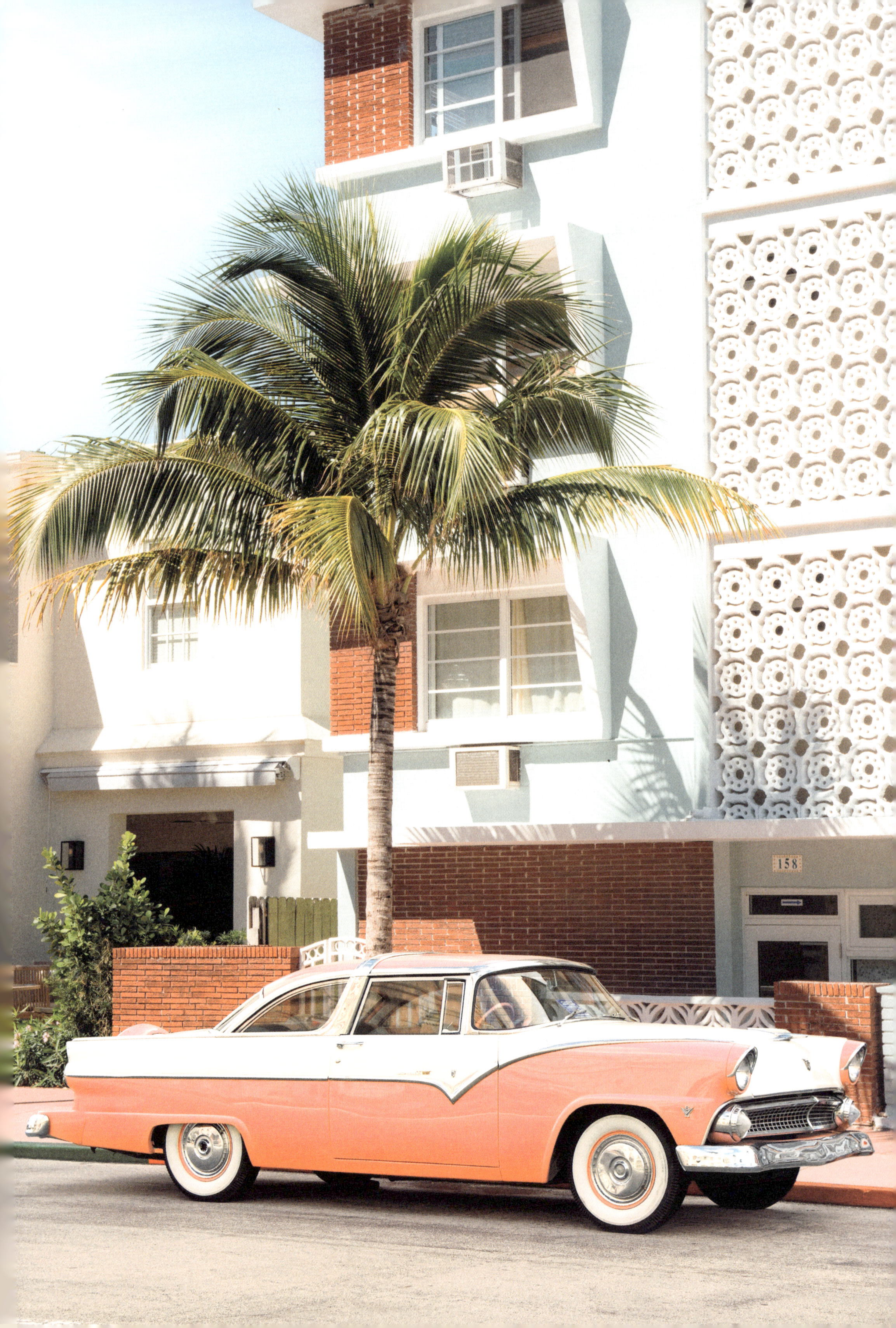
158

Ford Fairlane Crown Victoria

ARCHITECTURE 158 Ocean Drive in Miami Beach transports you to a holiday state of mind with just its address. Nestled within this retro block of flats, the allure is undeniable. Ocean Drive isn't just a destination for architecture fans, it's also steeped in cinematic history. Miami Beach's most famous street has served as the backdrop for box-office hits such as *Scarface*, *8MM* and *Charlie's Angels*. With its enchanting ocean views, swaying palm trees, glamorous hotels and art deco architecture, there is no reason not to cruise along Ocean Drive. However, if you're searching for the Sunray Apartments, the location of the famous chainsaw scene from *Scarface* at number 728, you'll be disappointed to learn that the building has since been demolished. What is still standing though is The Villa Casa Casuarina at 1116 Ocean Drive where Gianni Versace met his tragic fate in 1997, and which has been transformed into a boutique hotel, adorned in the decadent style synonymous with Versace.

CAR Named after Henry Ford's estate in Dearborn, Michigan, the Fairlane enjoyed a production run from 1955 to 1970, offering a diverse array of variants. These included sedans and hardtops available in both two-door and four-door configurations, station wagons and convertibles, some of which came with removable hardtops.

In this image, we see the first generation (1955–56), Ford's flagship at the time. Its noteworthy features include the charming 1950s-era color palettes, and the distinctive Fairlane Stripe, crafted from stainless steel that adorns the sides of all body styles.

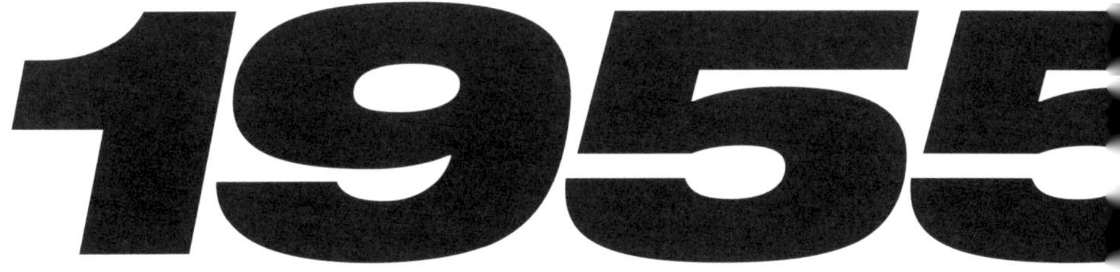

Cadillac Deville Convertible

ARCHITECTURE Some carchitecture purists may argue that the Lincoln Theatre in Miami Beach, which opened in 1936, should feature a Lincoln Zephyr from the same year at its entrance. However, this Cadillac Eldorado Convertible is equally fitting: it's the very car famously driven by Tony Montana (Al Pacino) in the 1983 crime drama *Scarface*, directed by Brian de Palma and set in Miami. While the Lincoln Theatre ceased to function as a cinema in the 1980s, it was restored in 2012 by Shulman + Associates, who converted the art deco building into an office complex with an H&M department store on its first floor. Remarkably, you can still feel the original vibe from 1936, both inside and outside the building. In its heyday, the Lincoln Theatre was a prestigious 'cinema palace,' designed by the era's most renowned cinema and theatre architect, Thomas W. Lamb (1871–1942). Lincoln Road in Miami Beach, adorned with art deco architecture, is a delightful treat for aficionados of this style. The Miami Beach Architectural District is home to about 800 art-deco-style buildings dating from 1923 to 1943. Cruising through this district in a vintage interwar car is an architectural adventure.

CAR The third-generation Cadillac Deville was in production from 1965 to 1970, adhering to the era's tradition of annual restyling. Initially, it featured the familiar 429 cu in (7.030 cc) V8 engine, delivering 340 hp. In 1968 that engine was replaced by a more potent 472 cu in (7.730 cc) variant producing 375 hp and a phenomenal torque of 525 Ft-Lbs, enabling the car to reach speeds of up to 110 mph.
While these cars exude timeless beauty and serve as remarkable time capsules, they are typically considered a budget-friendly option compared to many other collector cars available today. The price range can vary greatly depending on the condition or quality of the restoration, but for $20,000 you can pick up a fine car.

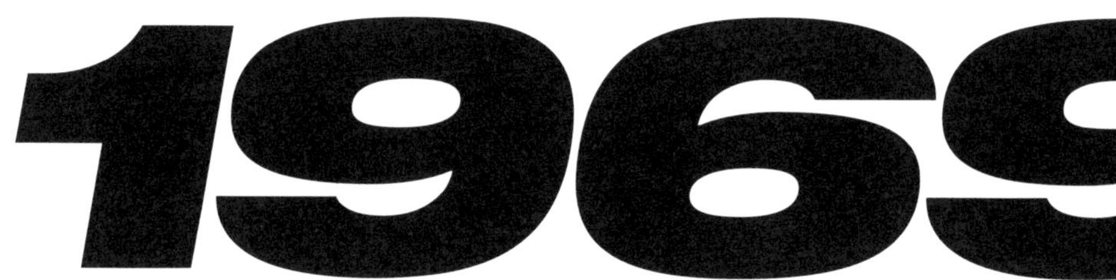

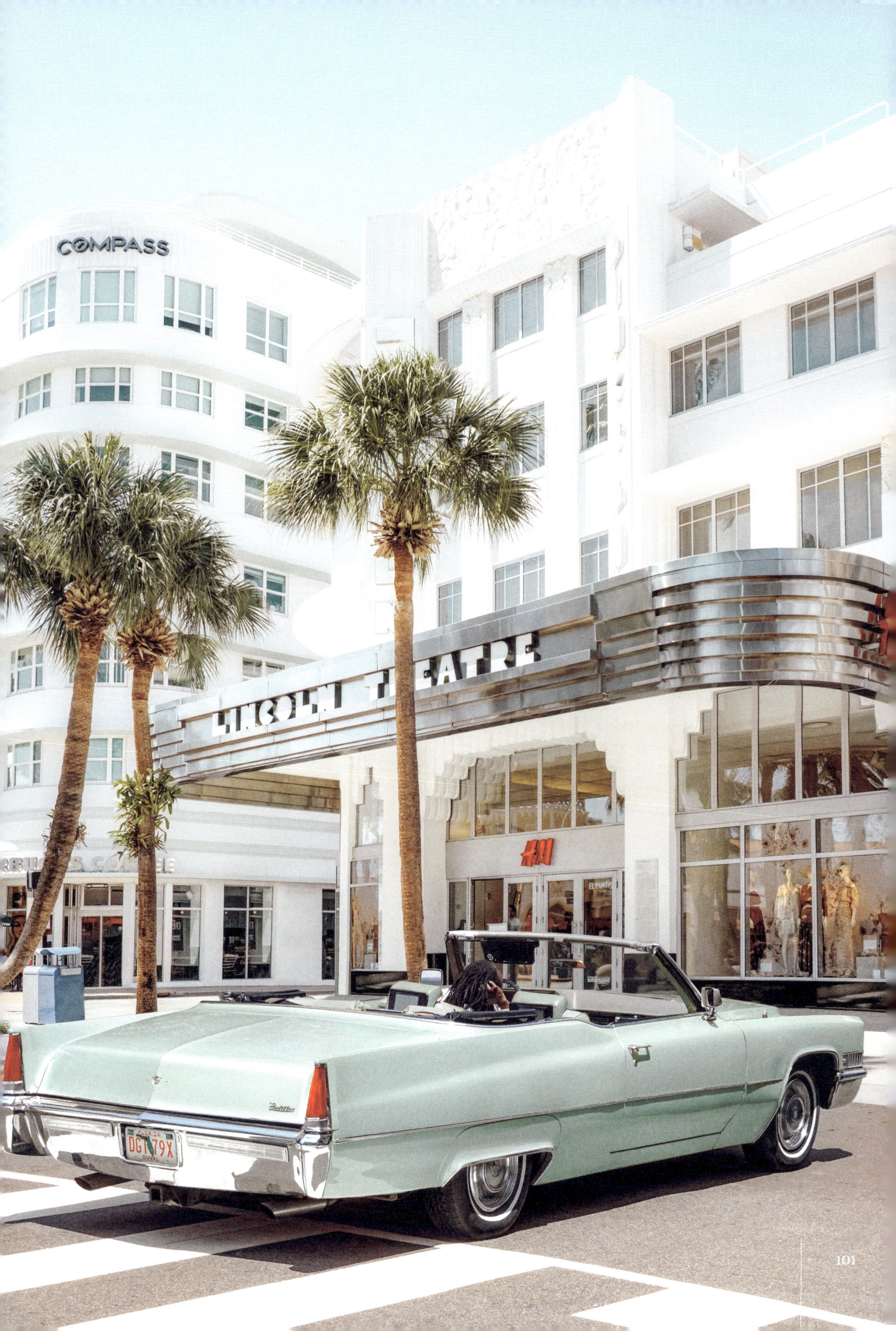
COMPASS
LINCOLN
H&M

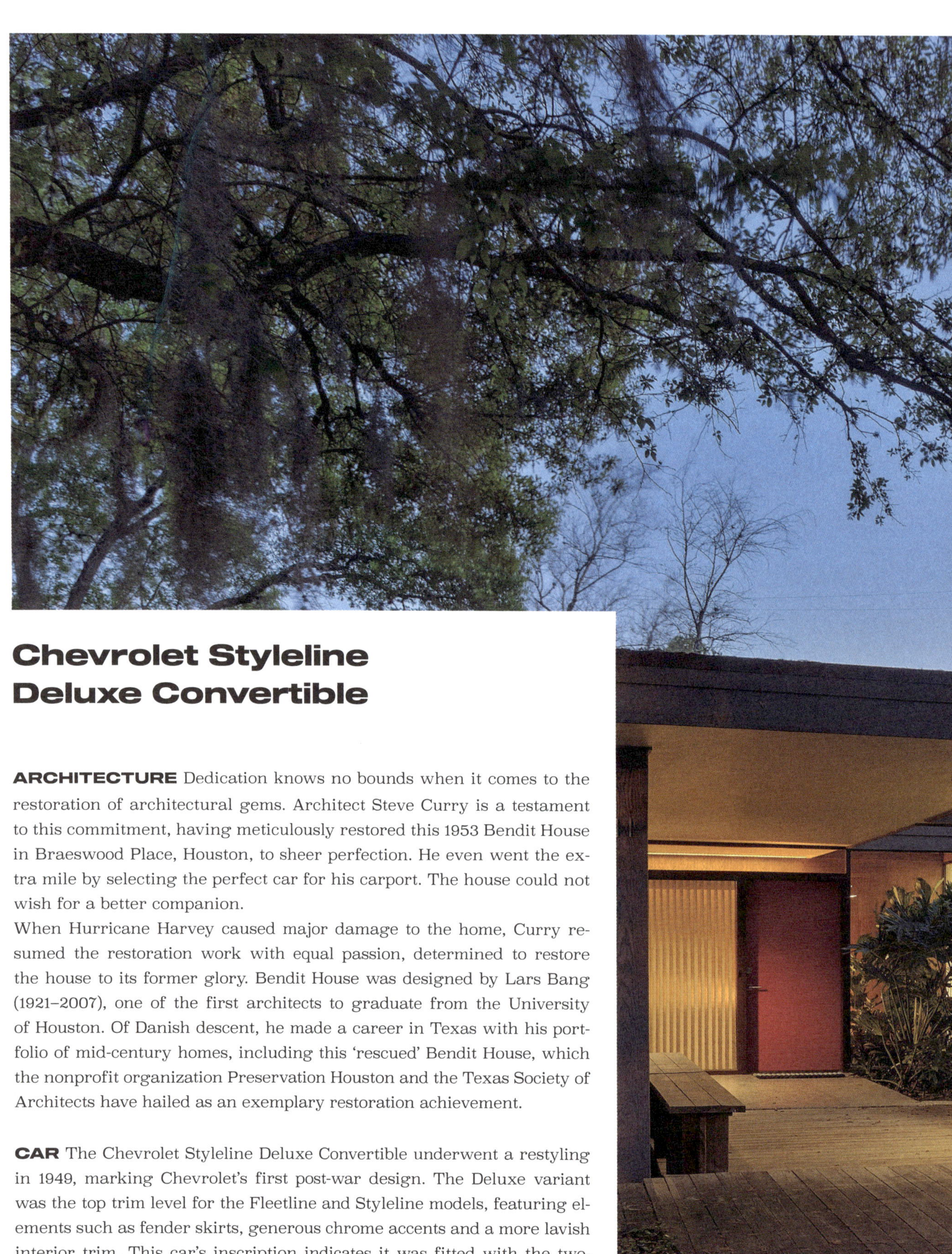

Chevrolet Styleline Deluxe Convertible

ARCHITECTURE Dedication knows no bounds when it comes to the restoration of architectural gems. Architect Steve Curry is a testament to this commitment, having meticulously restored this 1953 Bendit House in Braeswood Place, Houston, to sheer perfection. He even went the extra mile by selecting the perfect car for his carport. The house could not wish for a better companion.

When Hurricane Harvey caused major damage to the home, Curry resumed the restoration work with equal passion, determined to restore the house to its former glory. Bendit House was designed by Lars Bang (1921–2007), one of the first architects to graduate from the University of Houston. Of Danish descent, he made a career in Texas with his portfolio of mid-century homes, including this 'rescued' Bendit House, which the nonprofit organization Preservation Houston and the Texas Society of Architects have hailed as an exemplary restoration achievement.

CAR The Chevrolet Styleline Deluxe Convertible underwent a restyling in 1949, marking Chevrolet's first post-war design. The Deluxe variant was the top trim level for the Fleetline and Styleline models, featuring elements such as fender skirts, generous chrome accents and a more lavish interior trim. This car's inscription indicates it was fitted with the two-speed 'Powerglide' automatic transmission, a $159 option at the time. This transmission was paired with a larger 235-cubic-inch-6-cylinder engine producing an incredible 105 hp, which was particularly powerful for an affordable 1950s car.

1950

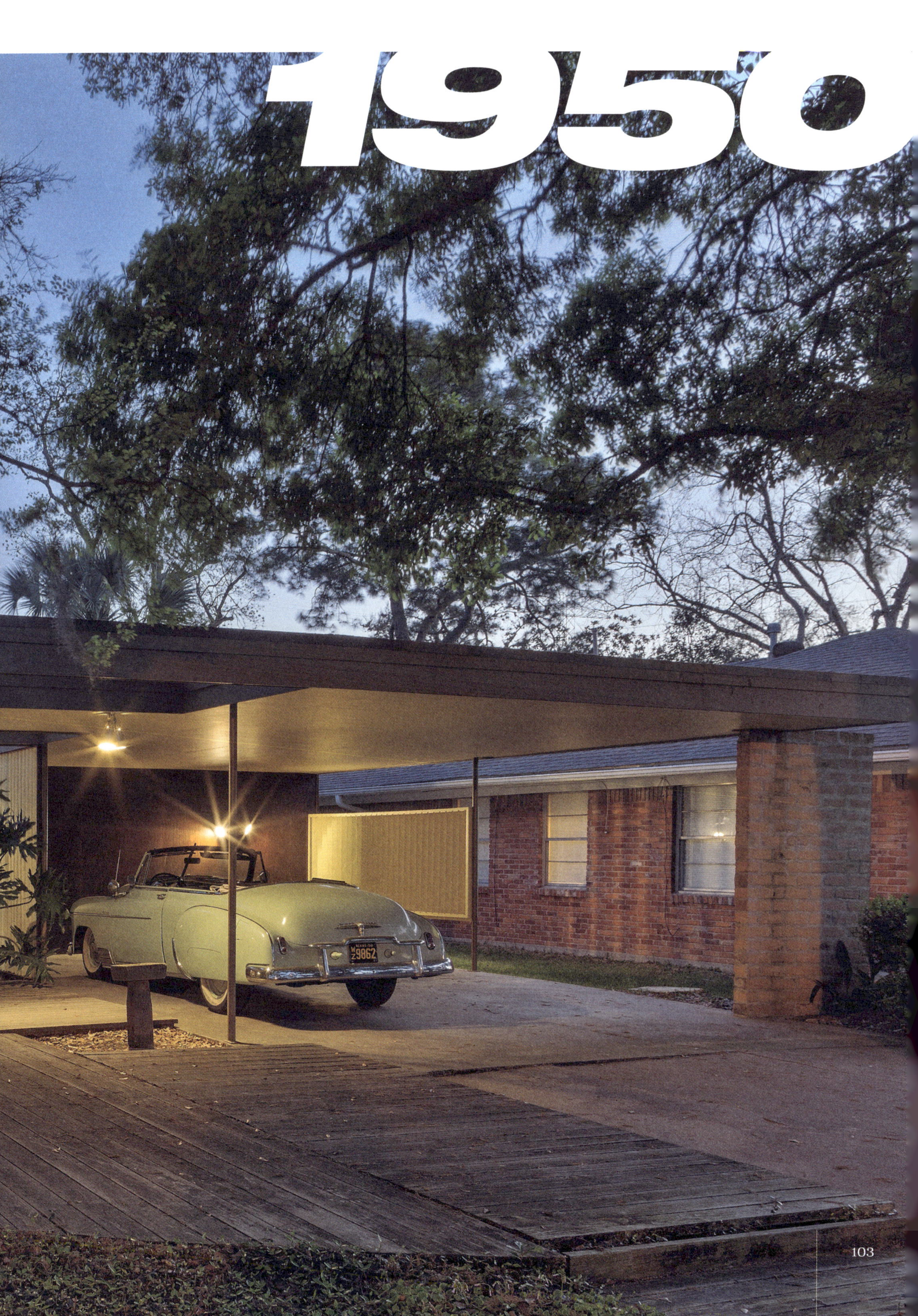

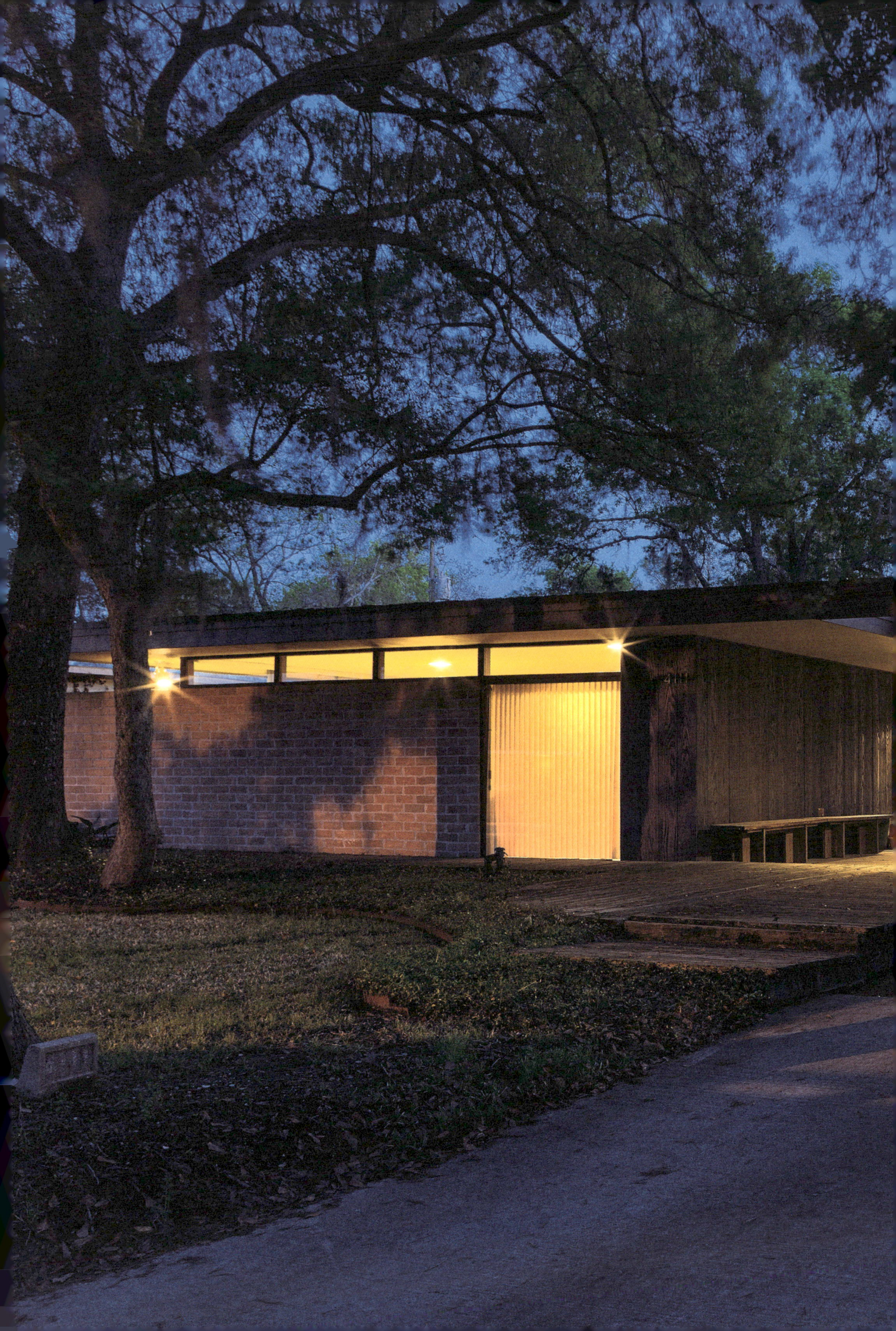

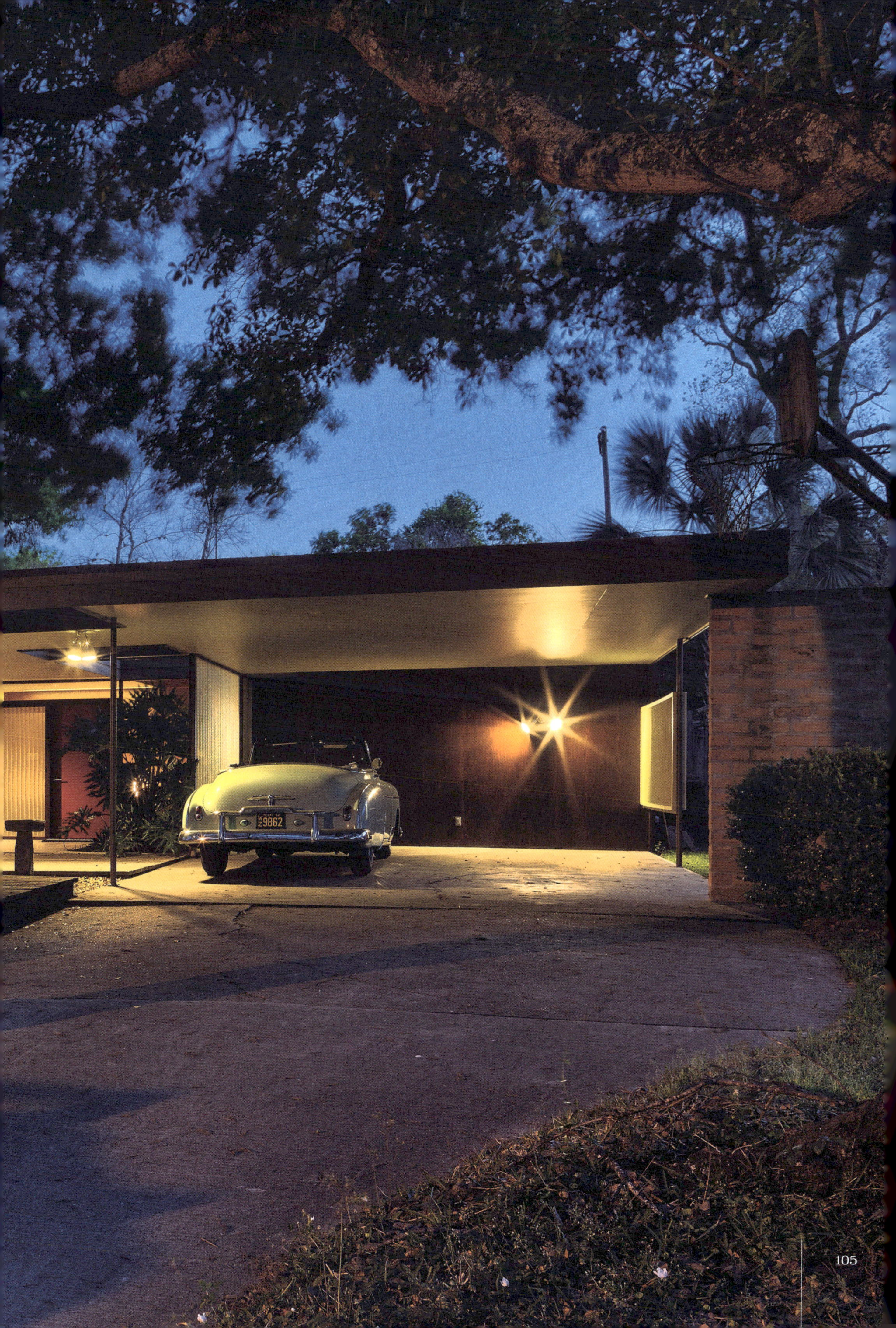
9862

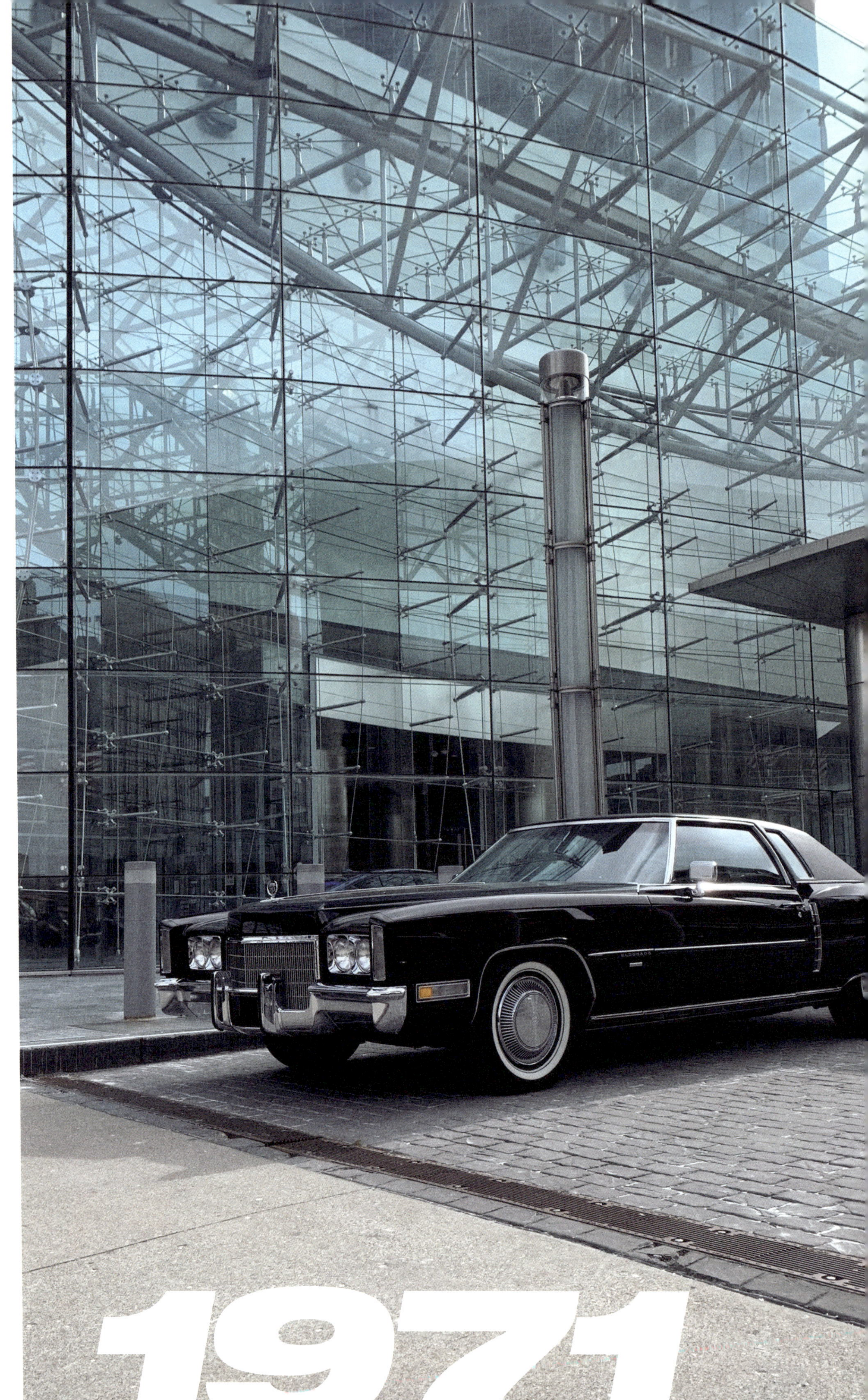
1971

Cadillac Eldorado Coupé

ARCHITECTURE The GM Renaissance Center, the global headquarters of General Motors in Detroit, stands as an emblematic example of carchitecture. With its seven interconnected skyscrapers, the gigantic building complex has dominated the skyline of the Motor City since the 1970s. John Portman, the original architect, ambitiously envisioned a 73-story hotel, a shopping center, numerous restaurants, and even banks within the complex. Since its comprehensive renovation in the early 2000s, the once isolated complex has become deeply entwined with the city and the Detroit River. Several architectural firms, including Skidmore, Owings & Merrill (SOM) and SmithGroup contributed to this development. The refurbishment efforts focused on softening the brutalist interior details, creating more openness and transparency, facilitated by the addition of a winter garden and a glass entrance pavilion.

CAR In the early 1970s, the Cadillac Eldorado Coupé boasted an enormous 500 cubic-inch V8 engine, making it the largest V8 ever used in a production car. In 1971, this engine produced 365 hp and a whopping 725 Nm of torque. Despite these impressive figures, the Eldorado's top speed only reached 117 mph, and it took 9.2 seconds to accelerate to 60 mph. The car's substantial weight, at 4,806 lb, and a fuel consumption of 10.6 mpg were characteristics that became less viable in response to the mounting oil crisis and environmental concerns, leading to the trend of smaller and more fuel-efficient cars.

Peugeot-Darl'mat 402 Spécial Sport

ARCHITECTURE When real-estate professional Lee Munder noticed a 'for sale' sign hanging at this beautiful art deco home in Palm Beach, he immediately went to explore further. Munder's daily commute had acquainted him well with this property in the El Cid Historic District, and he had long been fascinated by its late art deco charm, originally designed in 1937. The opulent residence, located in West Palm Beach, had been commissioned for engineer Ralph Wagner, who also served as the president of the Palm Beach Art League at the time.

Upon acquiring the property, Munder had Wagner's 'W' on the wrought-iron gate transformed into his own initial, 'M'. Munder also left his imprint inside the house, and had it thoroughly converted by the New York-based firm Pembrooke & Ives. The interior did not undergo a complete restoration: the firm artfully blended contemporary techniques and materials with the existing art deco volumes, resulting in a tasteful yet somewhat drastic departure from the original design.

The house dates from the early days of architect Belford Shoumate's own career. Active in Palm Beach from the late 1930s until his death in 1991, Shoumate completed hundreds of homes and public buildings in a variety of architectural styles ranging from colonial to art deco. This Wagner House also bears the hallmark of Shoumate's signature style—a fusion of nautical and floral elements. Early in his career, Shoumate recognized the importance of protecting and restoring Palm Beach's architectural heritage. To that end, he generously donated his personal archive to the Preservation Foundation of Palm Beach, an organization in which he himself was actively involved. It would be intriguing to know what Shoumate's thoughts would have been on this renovation of Villa Wagner.

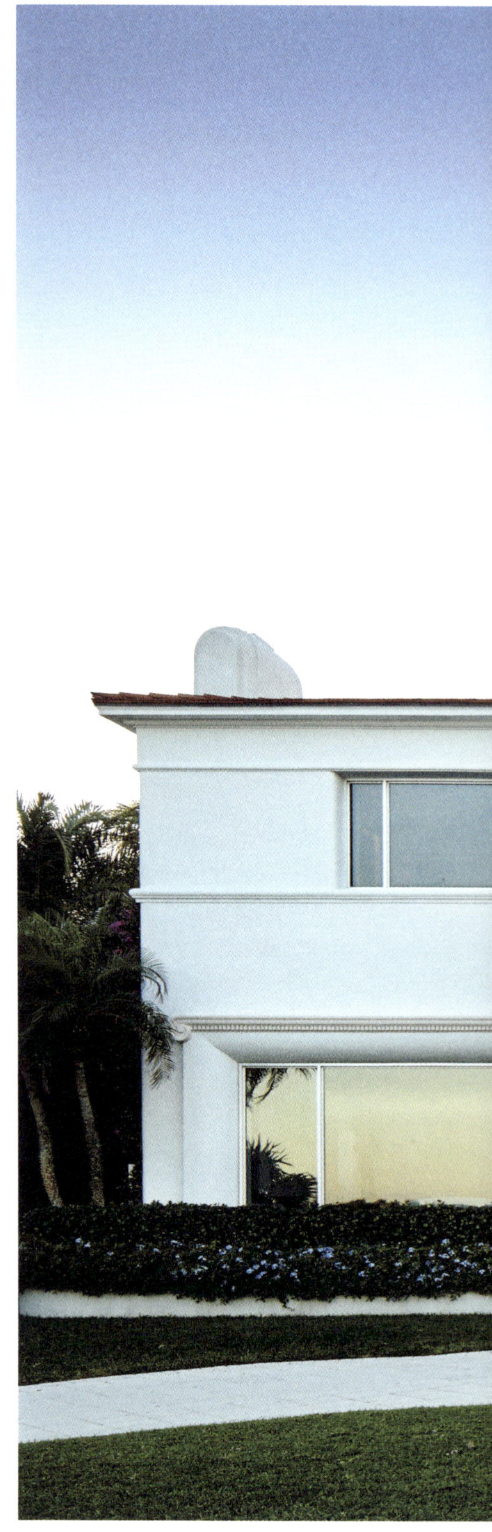

CAR Parisian mechanic, coachbuilder and Peugeot distributor Emile Darl'mat made a name for himself in the 1930s by personalizing existing Peugeots. He also produced his own bodyworks, initially in small volumes in his own workshop and later at Peugeot itself. The Peugeot-Darl'mat 302 from 1937 and the 402 from 1938 featured bodywork by Pourtout, designed by former dentist Georges Paulin. These cars, along with the aerodynamic trends of those years, boasted beautiful lines and art deco features such as the slanting grille and sculpted, non-integrated mudguards. The cars were fairly successful at the 24 Hours of Le Mans in 1938, winning in the up-to-2-liter category, and they also garnered significant admiration at Concours d'Élegances. It is estimated that 105 cars were built, including coupés, convertibles and roadsters, of which 22 are still known to exist. Even after World War II, Emile Darl'mat continued to build racing cars until 1956, when his son Roger returned to being a distributor, a role he held until 1980.

1938

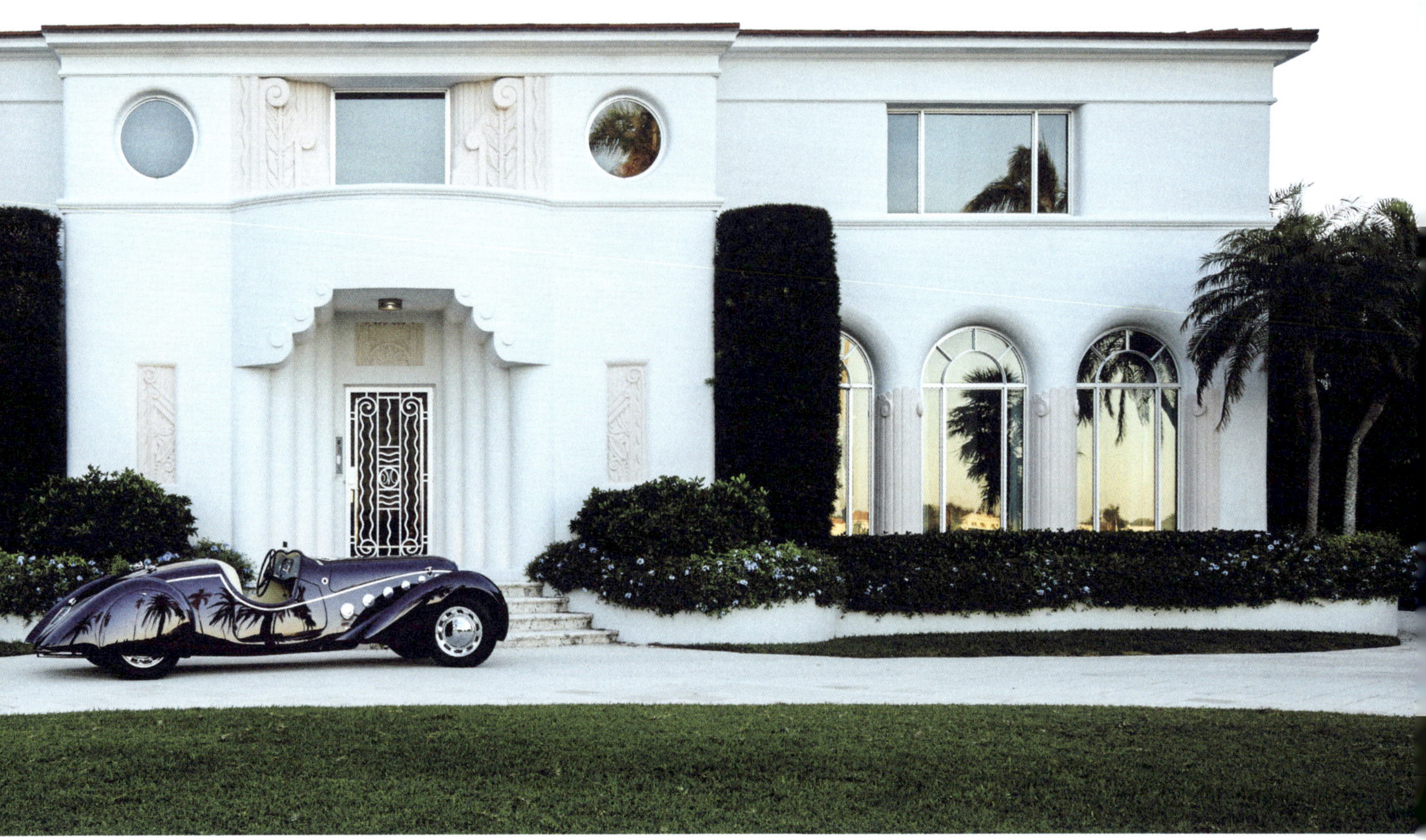

“Convertibles are for American playboys.”

Enzo Ferrari, automobile manufacturer

MATCH MY FAÇADE

1956

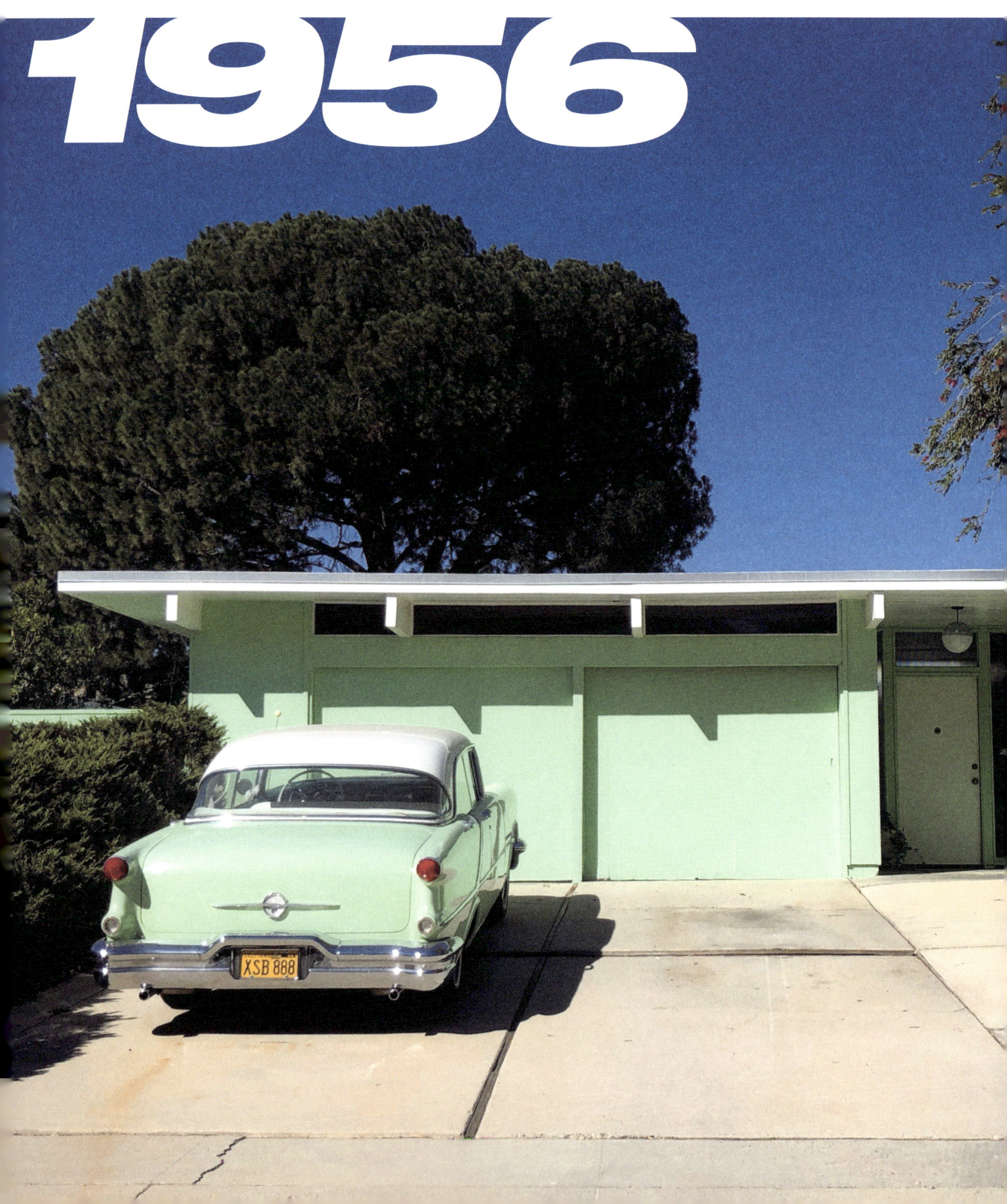

Oldsmobile 88 Holiday Hardtop Coupé

ARCHITECTURE Nestled in the San Fernando Valley in Granada Hills, Los Angeles, Balboa Highlands is the perfect destination for a carchitecture tour. Within the neighborhood lies an interesting cluster of mid-century houses, attributed to Californian developer Joseph Eichler, who, along with the Alexander and Meiselman families, played a pivotal role in Palm Springs. Most of his projects are in northern California, specifically in Palo Alto, San Jose, San Francisco, Sacramento, San Mateo and East Bay. Yet, Balboa Highlands, a community brought to life between 1962 and 1964, stands as a testament to his ventures in southern California.
After having himself lived in a Frank Lloyd Wright house, Eichler realized that good architecture could have a huge impact on quality of life. Driven by this insight, his construction company built affordable housing for the masses, exposing them to high-quality modern architecture—expansive spaces suffused with light. Eichler championed inclusivity within his architectural ethos, ensuring that people of diverse ethnic backgrounds were afforded the opportunity to own a home within his visionary projects. This commitment to social equity manifested explicitly when in 1958 he resigned from the National Association of Home Builders as a protest against racial discrimination in the housing market.
Balboa Highlands is home to three distinctive house designs, masterminded by architects such as A. Quincy Jones, Frederick Emmons and Claude Oakland. The latter duo conceived the pistachio green house with a double carport. Finding the right car was dead easy.

CAR The 1950s was a remarkable decade for General Motors, with each of its brands—Chevrolet, Buick, Oldsmobile, Pontiac and Cadillac—boasting a distinct identity and booming sales. The Oldsmobile 88 made its debut in 1949 and remained in production until 1999, spanning ten generations. Equipped with the Rocket V8 engine and featuring a relatively small and lightweight body, it can be considered one of the earliest muscle cars and quickly earned the title 'King of NASCAR'. The car we see here belonged to the second and largest generation, which was produced from 1954 to 1956, but also underwent annual modifications, as was common at the time. This specific car dates from 1956.

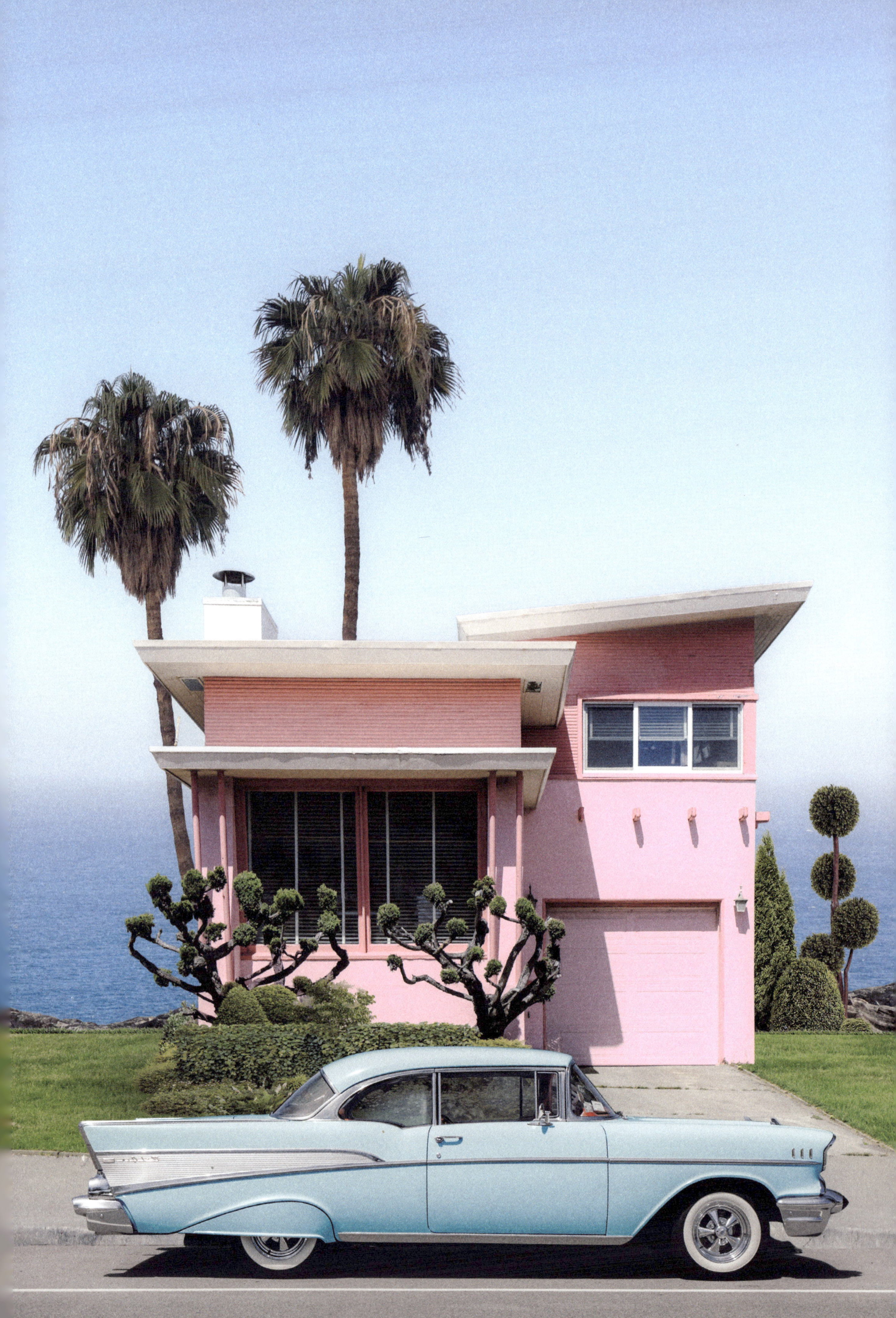

Chevrolet Bel Air

ARCHITECTURE Is this an exquisite set plucked from a Wes Anderson film or perhaps a page ripped from Barbie's dream world? It is in all respects the embodiment of a 'dream house'. American digital artist Jeffrey Czum creates visual compositions consisting of both real and fake elements. The surreal fusion of the vivid pink home in Daly City, the Pacific's serene expanse and the pastel-blue Chevrolet Bel Air, feels almost too good to be true. It undeniably serves as a picture-perfect textbook example of carchitecture. Czum, an artist of our era, elegantly dances across the boundary and reality and fiction, utilizing real-life photographs as a launchpad for his digital images. 'Ninety per cent of all my photos were taken from my car,' he says. 'I'll drive aimlessly around if I have to in order to find something interesting.'

CAR From 1953 onwards, Bel Air was synonymous with the biggest hits in the Chevrolet range. At the same time, it was an affordable but very elegant car for large families. Stylistic features such as the low roofline, the curved one-piece windscreen, the two-tone body and the rich use of chrome made the car look like a house. Models from the second generation from 1955, 1956 and mainly 1957—as in this picture—are among the most recognizable and sought-after American cars of all time, especially the 8-cylinder variants. In 1955 the grille was still inspired by that of Ferrari, but it was less popular and was replaced in 1956 by a more conventional variant. Here we see a 2-Door Hard Top, but the Bel Air came in numerous body types, including a sport sedan, convertible, station wagon and even panel van. The name would be retained until 1975, in Canada even until 1981. However, after seven generations, the Bel Air had been stripped considerably, including of almost all luxury.

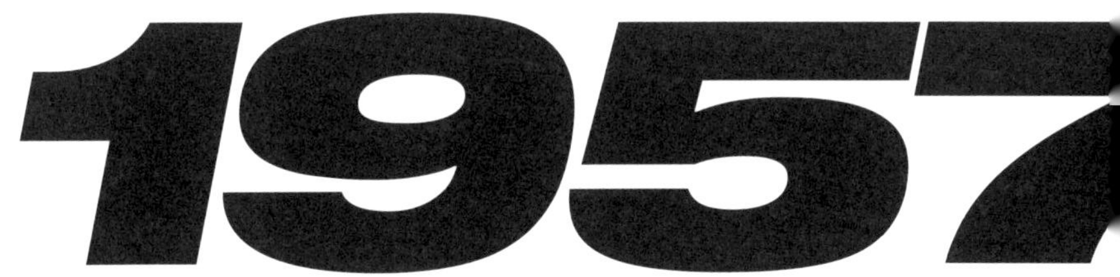

1972

VW Karmann Ghia Type 14

ARCHITECTURE *Parked Portraits* is a photography project launched by American graphic designer Vivienne Scholl. Roaming the streets of San Francisco, she looks for photogenic examples of carchitecture: cool cars parked next to matching buildings. The blue Victorian façade with colonial elements would easily be spotted in Bogota, Mexico City or Cape Town. But Scholl discovered it in San Francisco on Stanyan Street in the Cole Valley neighborhood. When she saw the bright blue Volkswagen Karmann Ghia, she immediately took the photo.

CAR In the post-war penchant for style, Volkswagen wanted to launch an elegant sports car in addition to economical and reliable vehicles. For this, it addressed itself to Karmann, a coachbuilding house from Osnabrück, Lower Saxony, which in turn commissioned the Turin-based Ghia design office. Ghia had previously created a design for Chrysler that had been shelved, so they adapted the project to fit a slightly widened Beetle chassis. The original air-cooled boxer engine with barely 30 hp from that Beetle was a bit light for a sports car, but courtesy of its looks, the Karmann Ghia exceeded all expectations, even in the US. There was also a convertible, an expensive four-seater (Type 34) and a touring coupé (TC). The car appeared over three generations, the last of which we see here. More than half a million units were built, in Osnabrück until mid-1974, and in the Brazilian city of São Bernardo do Campo until 1976.

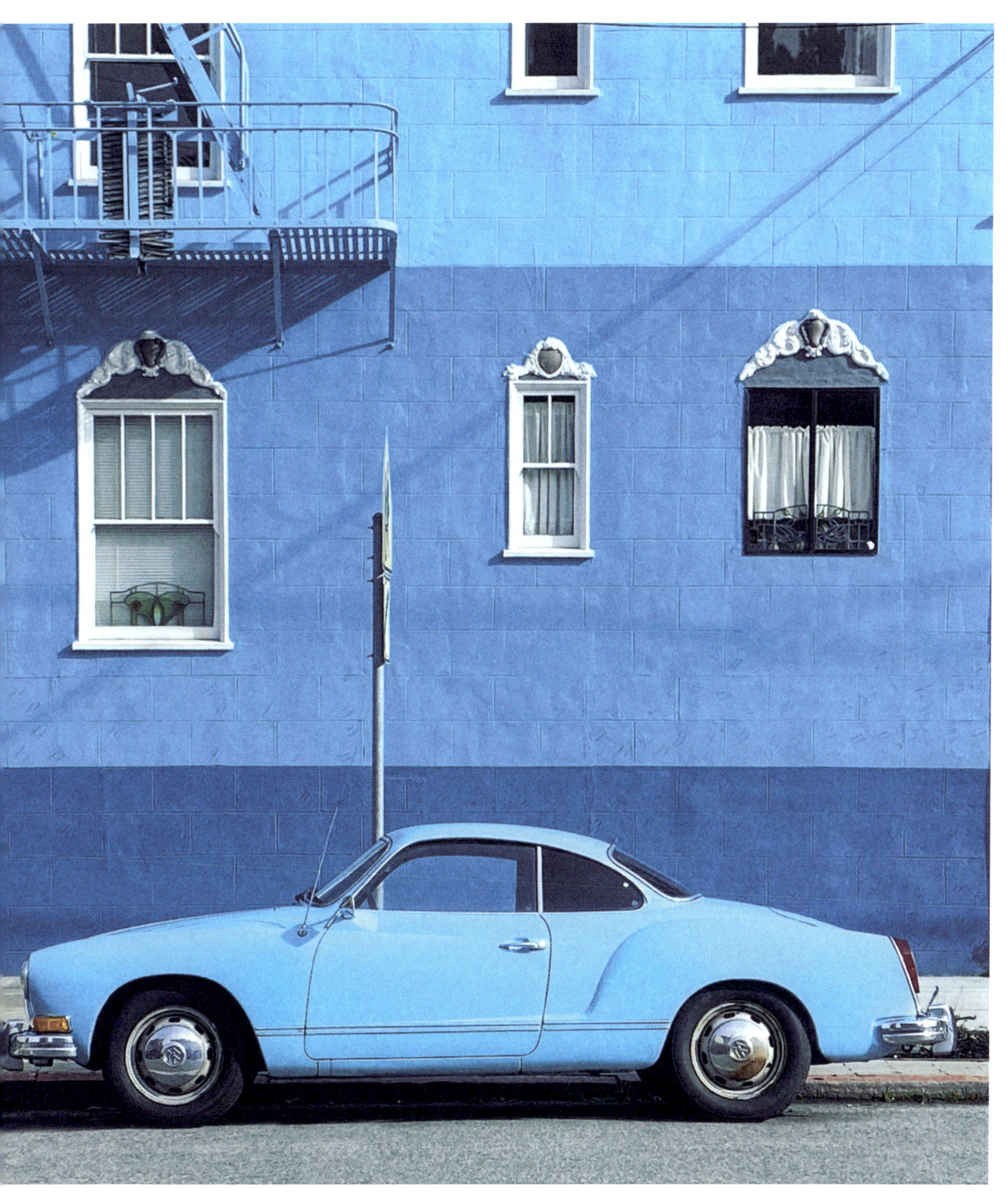

Mercedes-Benz 450 SEL

ARCHITECTURE In the bright midday sun, photo shoots in Palm Springs can sometimes 'burn out' with excessive brightness. Photographer Tom Blachford devised a solution by shooting the mid-century homes alongside complementary vintage cars illuminated solely by the soft glow of the full moon. His colleague, Ludwig Favre, adopts a slightly different approach. He shot this 450 SEL in the early hours of the day, when the morning light gently brightens the sky, perfectly harmonizing with the Mercedes' body color to create a captivating juxtaposition of carchitecture and nature.

CAR The W116 series made its debut in 1972 and marked the first time Mercedes-Benz officially designated its flagship model as the S-Class (which stands for *Sonderklasse* or special class). The man behind the design was Friedrich Geiger, a designer renowned for his work on pre-World War II classics, like the 540 K and the later 300 SL Gullwing. The styling represented a departure from the past, taking into account both passive safety and aerodynamics. As a result, Mercedes cars of this era were longer, wider and lower, boasting cleaner lines both externally and internally.

This 450 SEL, with an extended 10 cm wheelbase, was the top-tier model in the lineup. The base of the indestructible V8 engine had been in use since 1963 and now produced 225 hp. Later, Mercedes-Benz introduced the 6.9 variant, a hyperperformant car with a monstrous engine that produced 286 hp.

Traditionally, the S-Class has been the platform for Mercedes-Benz to introduce pioneering technical innovations. For instance, in 1978, the W116 model was among the first to offer ABS (Anti-lock Braking System) as an option, paving the way for developments that continued with the W126 in 1979.

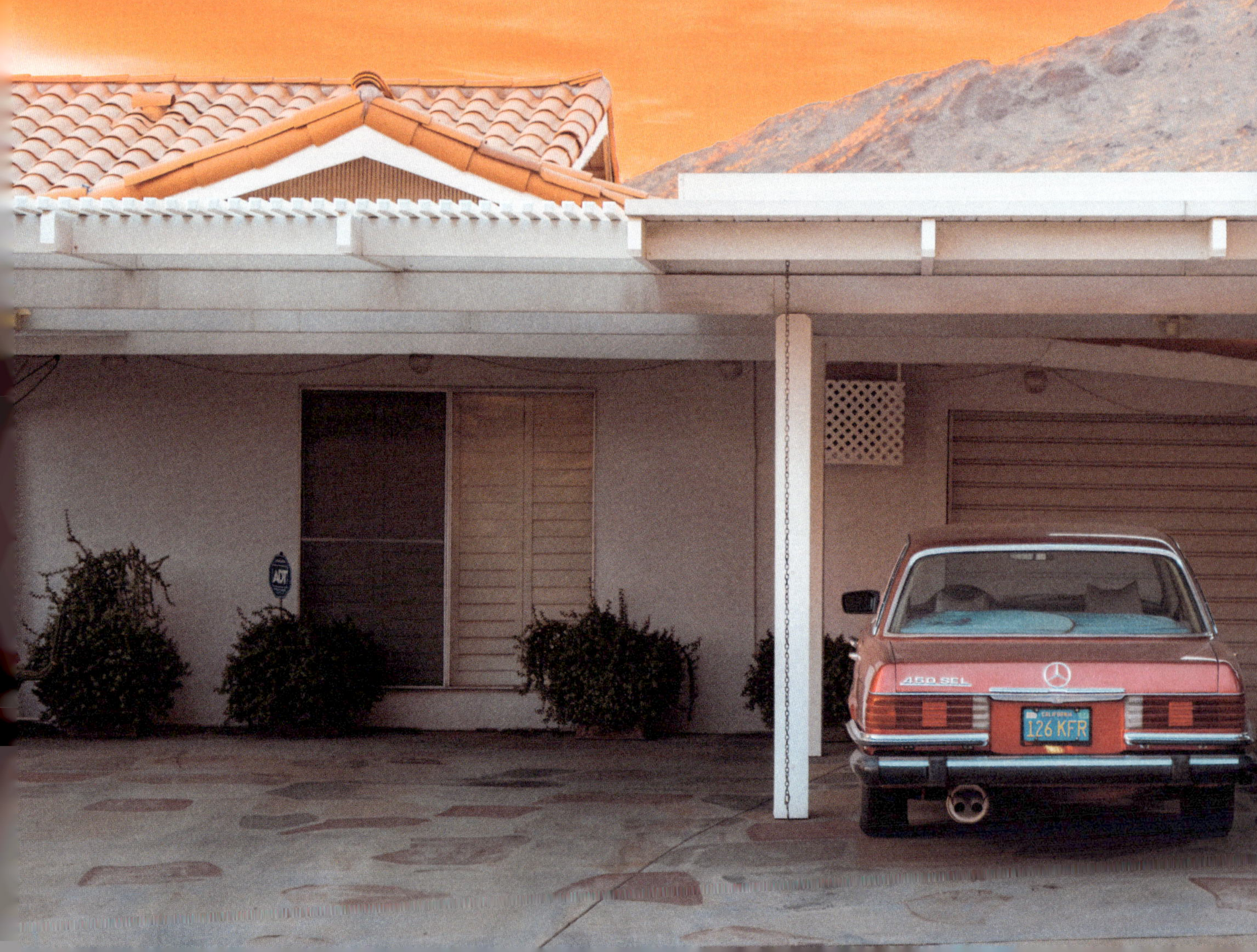

1973

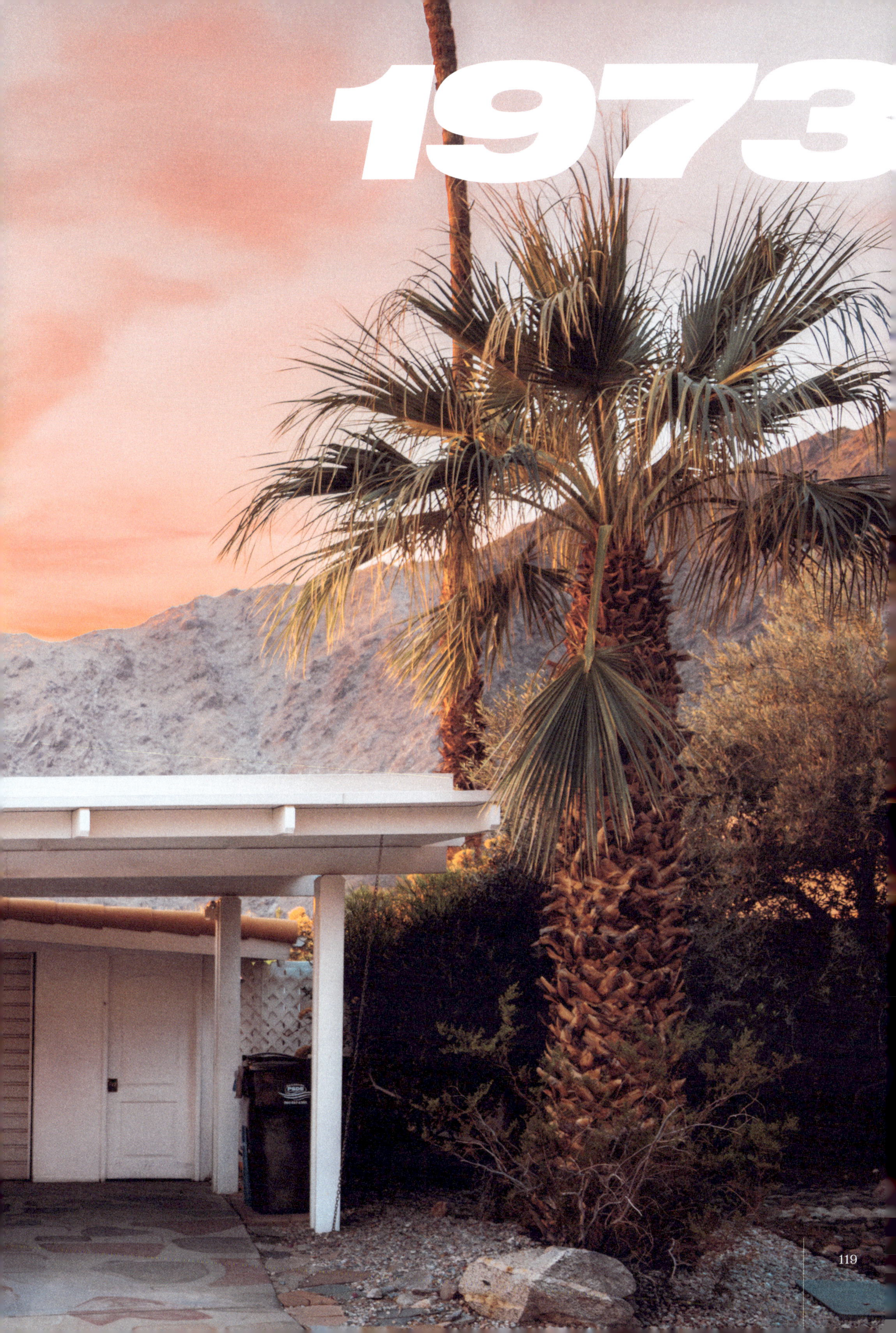

Porsche 914

ARCHITECTURE We couldn't, of course, overlook motels in a book on American carchitecture. Few things embody the essence of Americana more than these roadside hotels. They stand as iconic symbols of life on the American road. While similar roadside motels exist in Europe, Australia and Japan, it's the American motor lodges that are most closely associated with cinema.
The first motels sprang up in California in the 1920s, as the American road network expanded. They quickly became fashionable havens for motorists, bikers and truckers seeking rest or a quick bite while on their journey. However, it was the 1950s and 1960s that marked their true heyday, coinciding with the widespread ownership of automobiles across America.
Holiday Inn emerged as a chain of motels in 1952. However, motels began to decline in the 1990s as cheaper and larger roadside hotels sprang up along newly constructed highways. Nevertheless, in recent years, investors have rediscovered the charm of these nostalgic lodgings, leading to the restoration of many motor lodges into trendy boutique hotels. The revival has even garnered attention in popular culture, with Netflix series such as *Motel Make Over* and *Schitt's Creek* showcasing the allure of these revamped establishments. Welcome to Motel California!

CAR The Porsche 914, introduced in 1969, marked Porsche's entry-level model. Developed in collaboration with Volkswagen and Karmann, the car, sometimes referred to as the VW Porsche or the 'bastard Porsche,' was fitted with a mid-engine configuration, delivering superb handling. A fiberglass-reinforced targa roof added to the pleasure of open driving. Notable design features were an elongated wheelbase relative to the car's length, short overhangs, a wide roll bar, two trunks and pop-up headlights. When the Porsche 914 was launched, two boxer engines were available: a 1.7 liter-4-cylinder from Volkswagen and a 2-liter 6-cylinder from the 911T. For the US market, where the car sold well, a 1.8-liter engine was offered. Over 115,000 units of the 914/4 were produced, while the more expensive 914/6 saw a limited production of just over 3,300 units, making it the more sought-after version in the classic car market. The 914 was succeeded by the 924 in 1976.

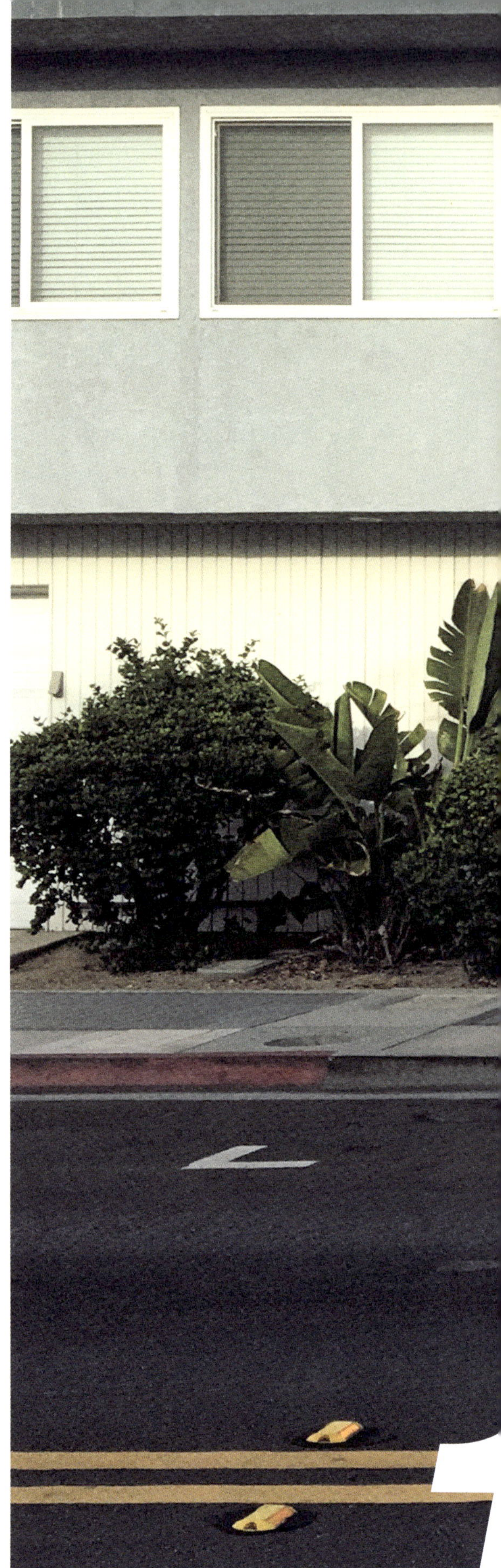

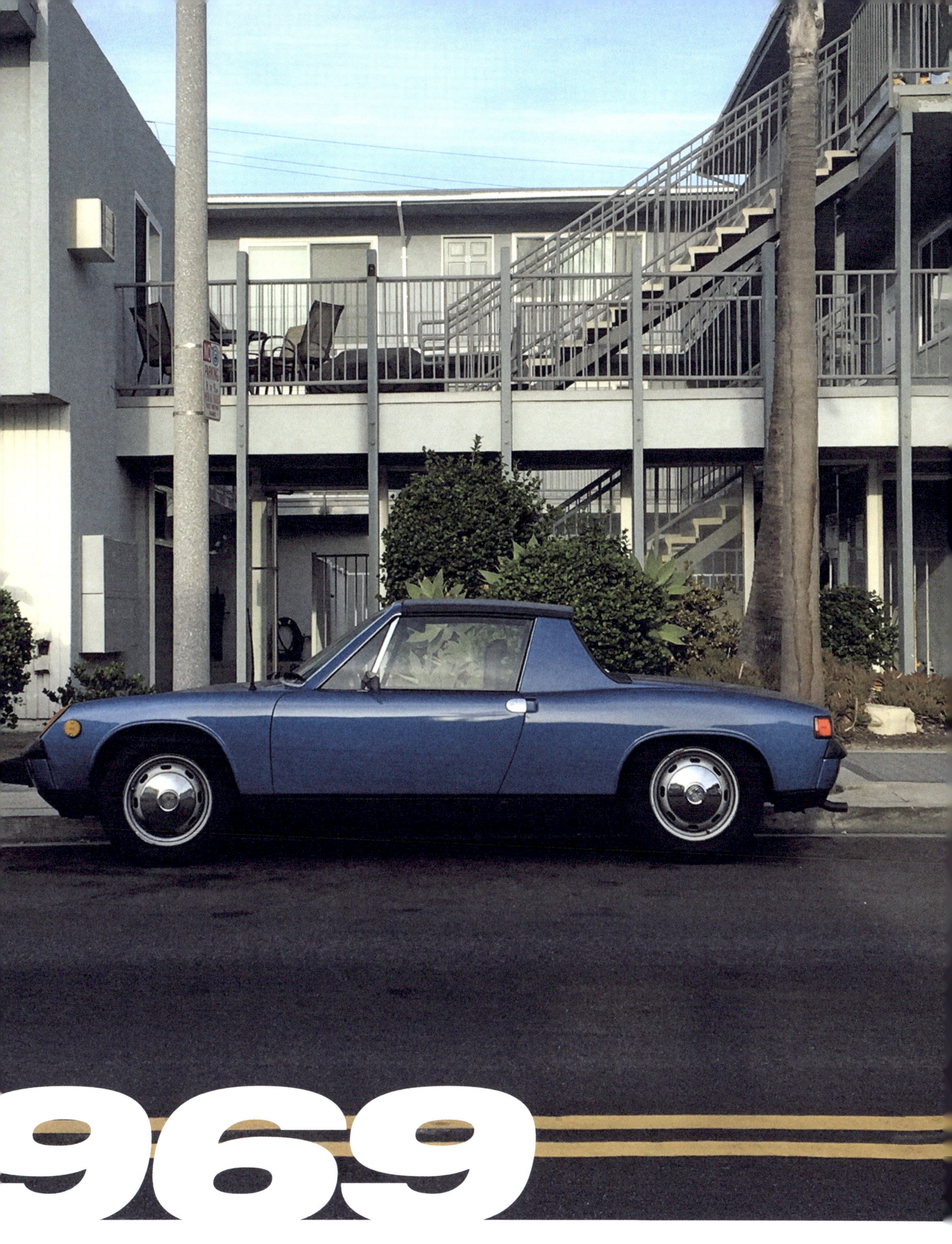
969

2007

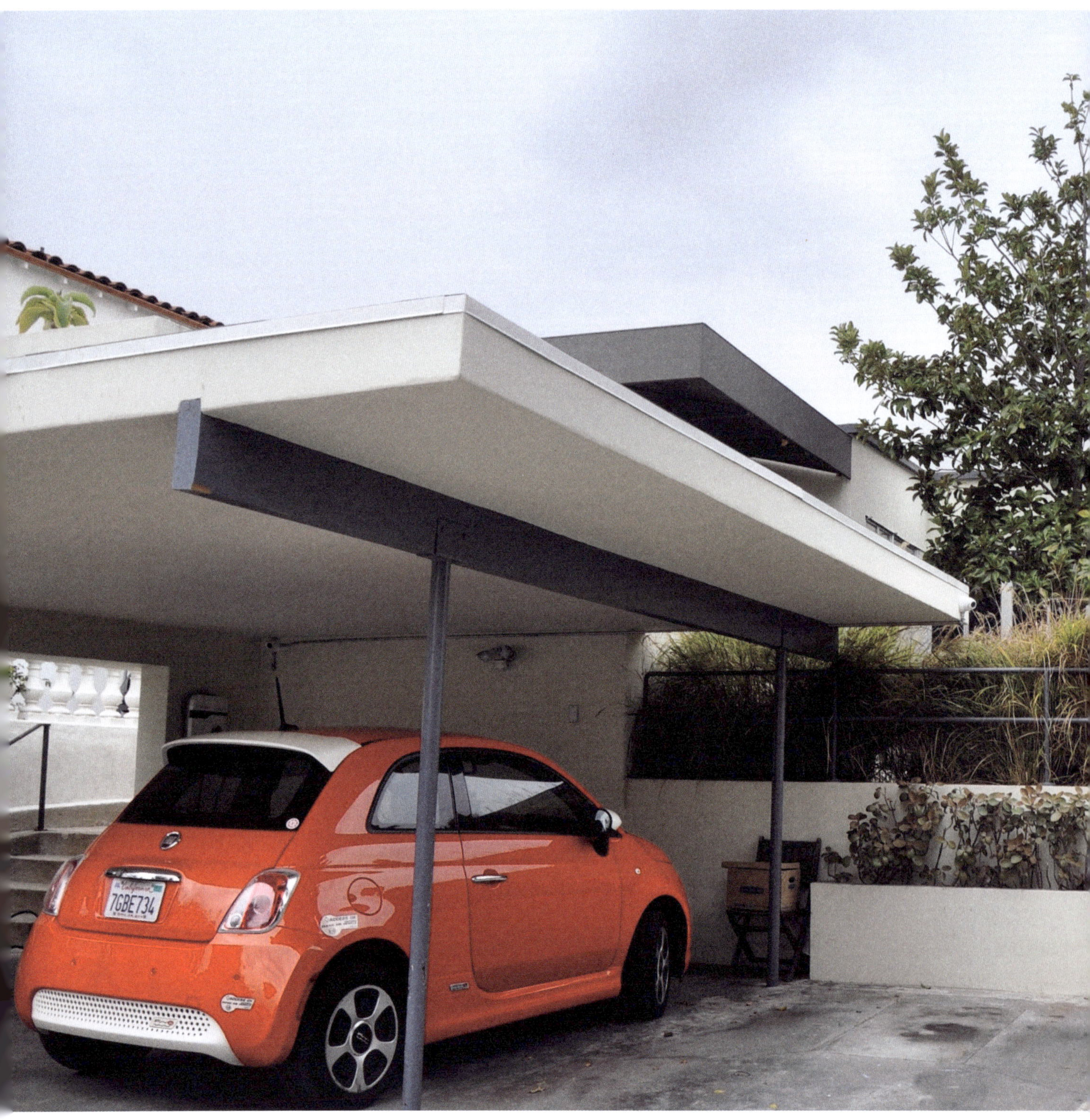

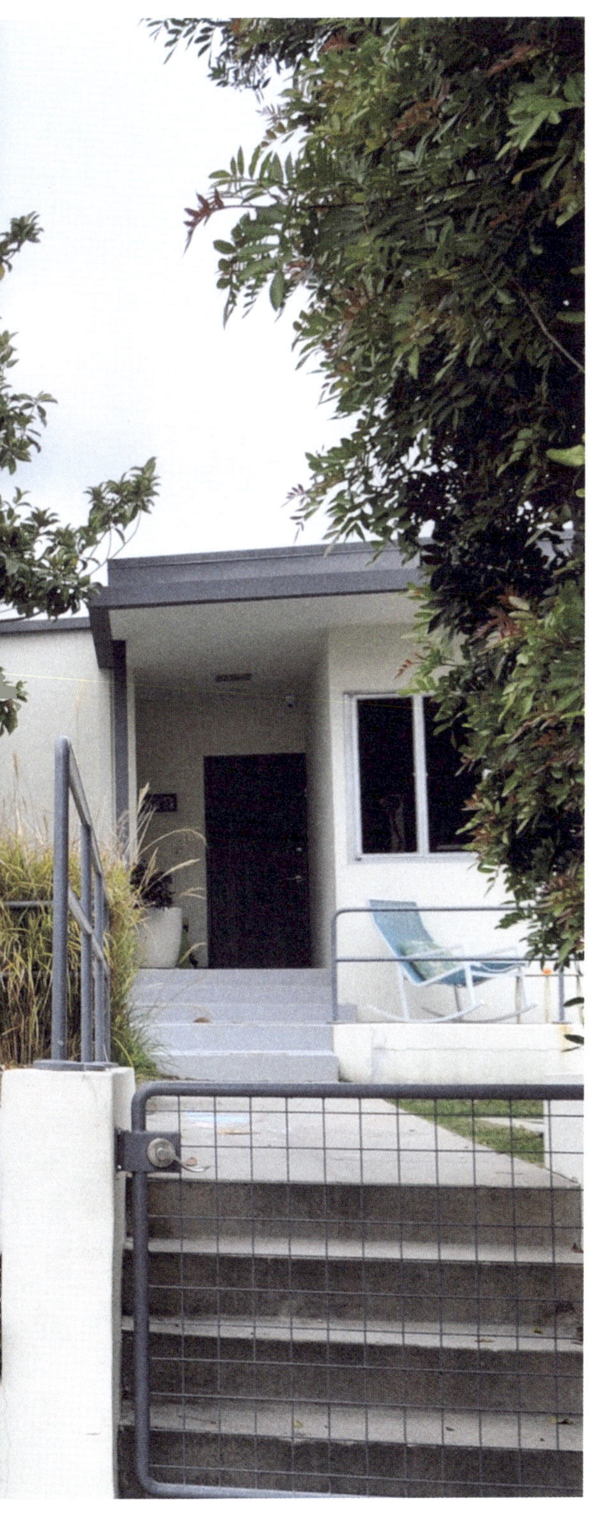

Fiat 500

ARCHITECTURE The growing popularity of the automobile in the early 20th century triggered the emergence of the carport, the ultimate carchitectural feature of a private home. Initially, cars were kept outdoors in barns or carriage houses. However, thanks to influential Prairie School architects, in particular Walter Burley Griffin and Frank Lloyd Wright, the carport became a much sought-after addition to private homes. The semi-open carport evolved to become an integral part of the architectural blueprint of homes, signifying the domestication of the private car in America. With the advent of electric vehicles flooding the market, carports now serve as essential charging stations, reflecting the evolving dynamics between individuals and their automobiles.

CAR Inspired by the original Fiat 500, designed by the brilliant engineer Dante Giacosa and launched 70 years earlier, the contemporary Fiat 500 has grown into a modern style icon since its introduction in 2007. The car derived from the Fiat Trepiùno, the striking 2004 concept car created by Roberto Giolito of Centro Stile Fiat, who was awarded the Compasso d'Oro for industrial design. Frank Stephenson, who previously designed the modern Mini, oversaw the transformation of this concept into a production model. The Fiat 500 encompasses various series, including the America edition, featuring American flag details. Incidentally, the US market version received a different rear axle for enhanced comfort. In recent years, the Fiat 500 has embraced the era of electric mobility.

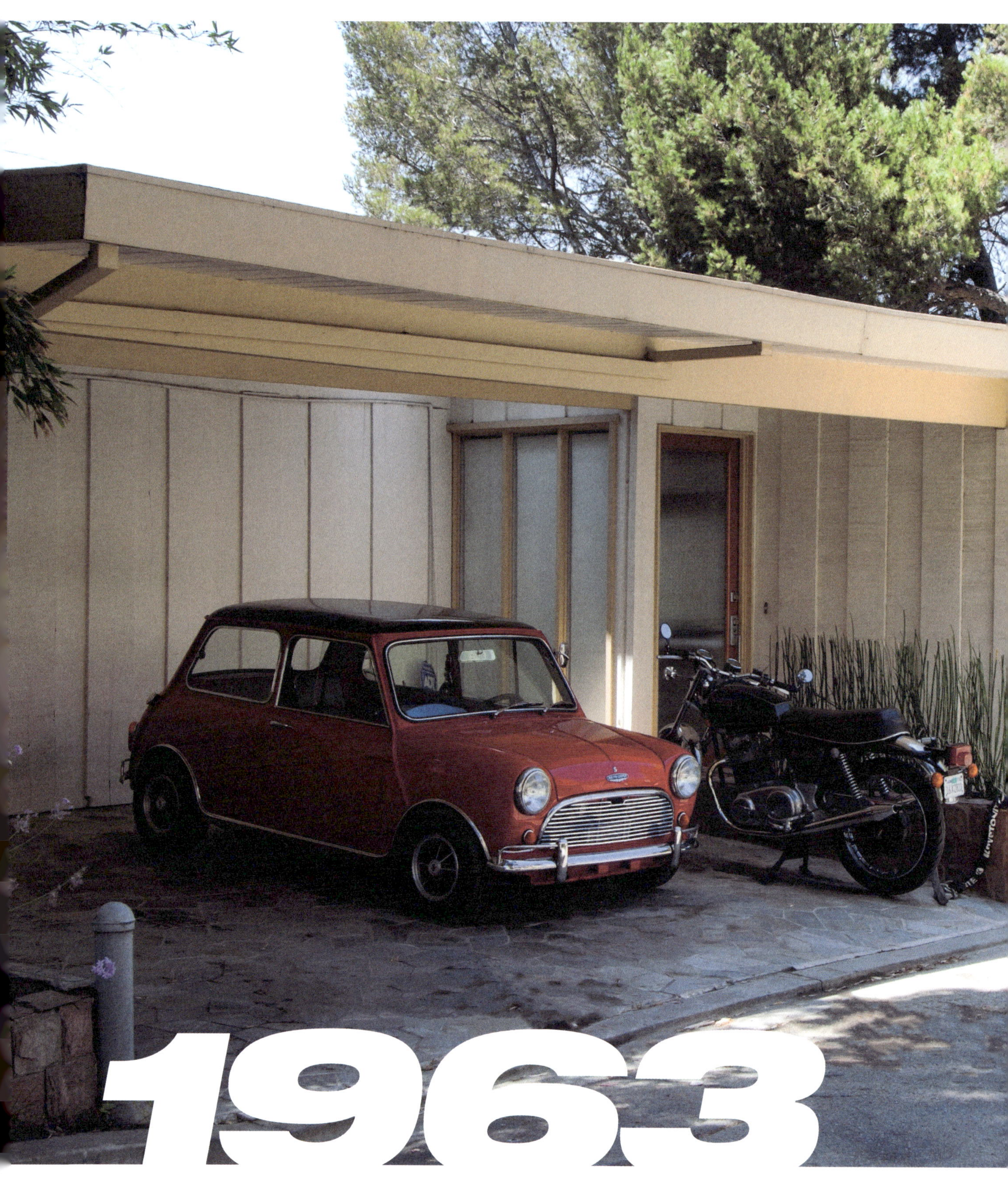
1963

Austin Mini Cooper S

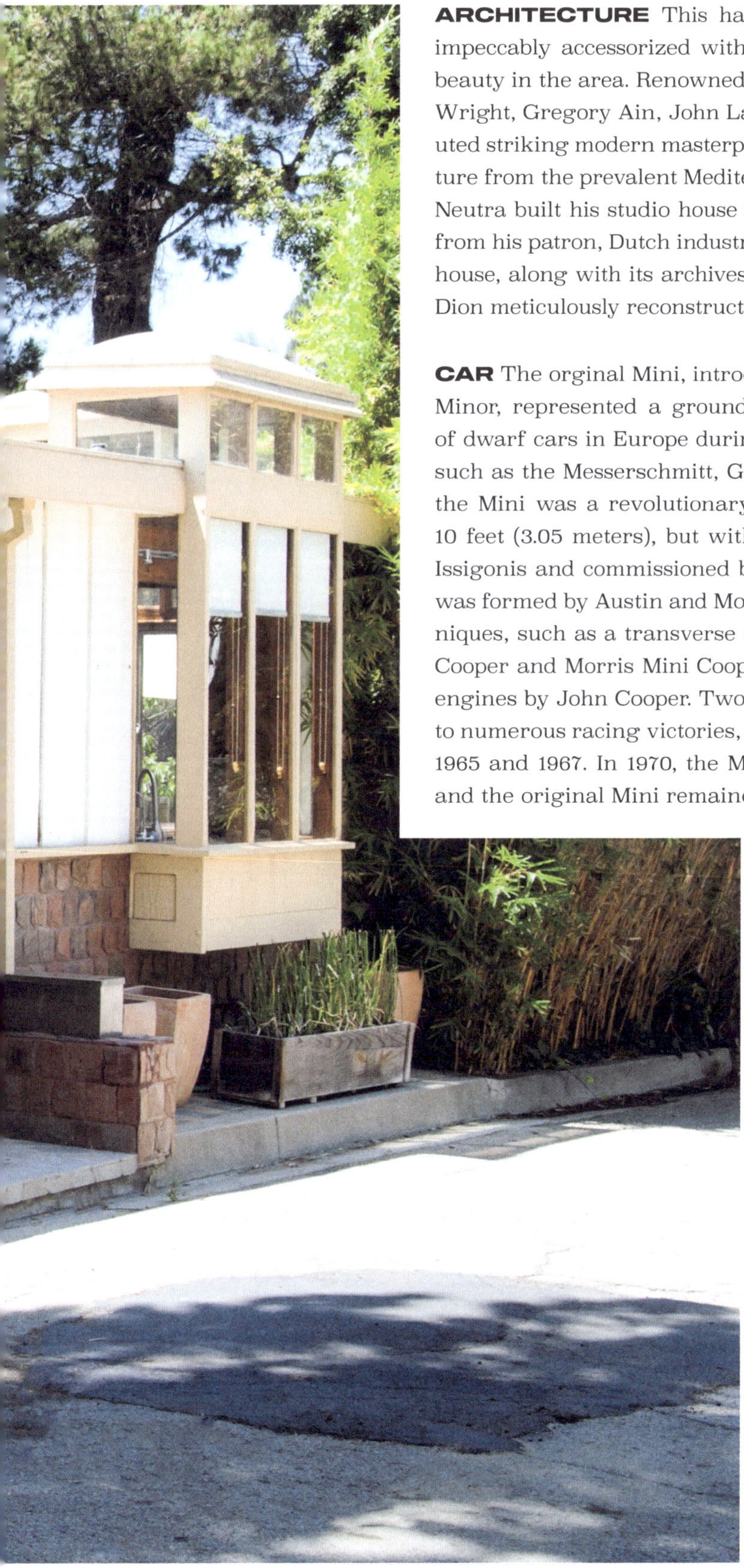

ARCHITECTURE This handsome home in Silver Lake, Los Angeles, is impeccably accessorized with motorized beauties. However, it's not the only beauty in the area. Renowned architects such as Richard Neutra, Frank Lloyd Wright, Gregory Ain, John Lautner and Rudolph Schindler have also contributed striking modern masterpieces in Silver Lake, offering a refreshing departure from the prevalent Mediterranean-inspired architecture. Notably, Richard Neutra built his studio house near this property in 1932, supported by a loan from his patron, Dutch industrialist Cees H. Van der Leeuw. While the original house, along with its archives, went up in flames in 1963, Neutra and his son Dion meticulously reconstructed it, almost identically to its former glory.

CAR The orginal Mini, introduced in 1959 as Austin Seven and Morris Mini-Minor, represented a groundbreaking response to the growing popularity of dwarf cars in Europe during the 1950s. Unlike its diminutive competitors, such as the Messerschmitt, Glas Goggomobil, Iso Isetta and the BMW Isetta, the Mini was a revolutionary and characterful little car measuring barely 10 feet (3.05 meters), but with room for four passengers. Designed by Alec Issigonis and commissioned by the British Motor Corporation (BMC), which was formed by Austin and Morris, the Mini employed space-maximizing techniques, such as a transverse engine and front-wheel drive. The Austin Mini Cooper and Morris Mini Cooper arrived in 1961 with performance-enhanced engines by John Cooper. Two years later, the Cooper S followed suit, leading to numerous racing victories, including three Monte Carlo Rally wins in 1964, 1965 and 1967. In 1970, the Mini brand was introduced as a separate entity, and the original Mini remained in production until 2000.

Volkswagen T2

ARCHITECTURE The T2 Volkswagen epitomizes 'carchitecture on wheels,' serving as both home and transportation for many surfers and hippies. This iconic model appears to be designed for road trips or surfing adventures. The resurgence of van life—living out of a van—in recent years is evident in the skyrocketing prices of vintage camper vans. However, while this nomadic lifestyle may be liberating, it has its downsides. Living on the road in such a compact space requires much discipline and a willingness to sacrifice comfort and luxury. Additionally, vintage vans present maintenance issues, adding another layer of complexity to this lifestyle.

CAR The Volkswagen T2, particularly its second generation, earned a reputation as a hippie van. Icons such as Bob Dylan and The Beach Boys featured the van on their album covers. However, the van also served various practical purposes, including use by police forces in many countries. Although around five million units of the T1 and T2 were produced, these simple vans have evolved into valuable collector's items, often surpassing the prices of many sports cars.

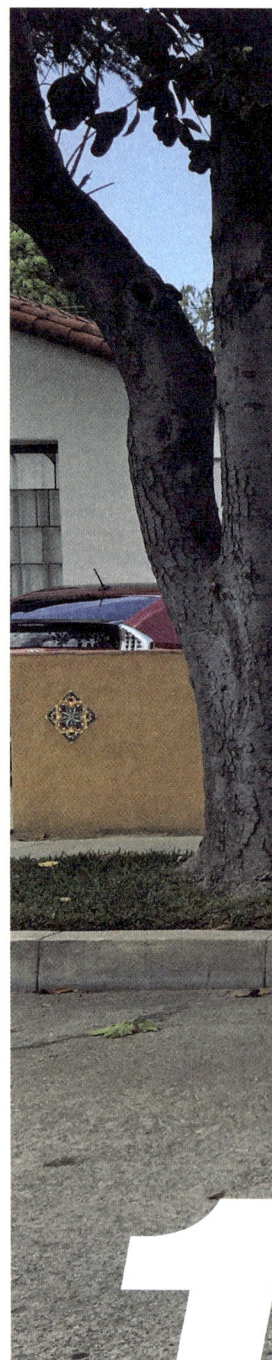

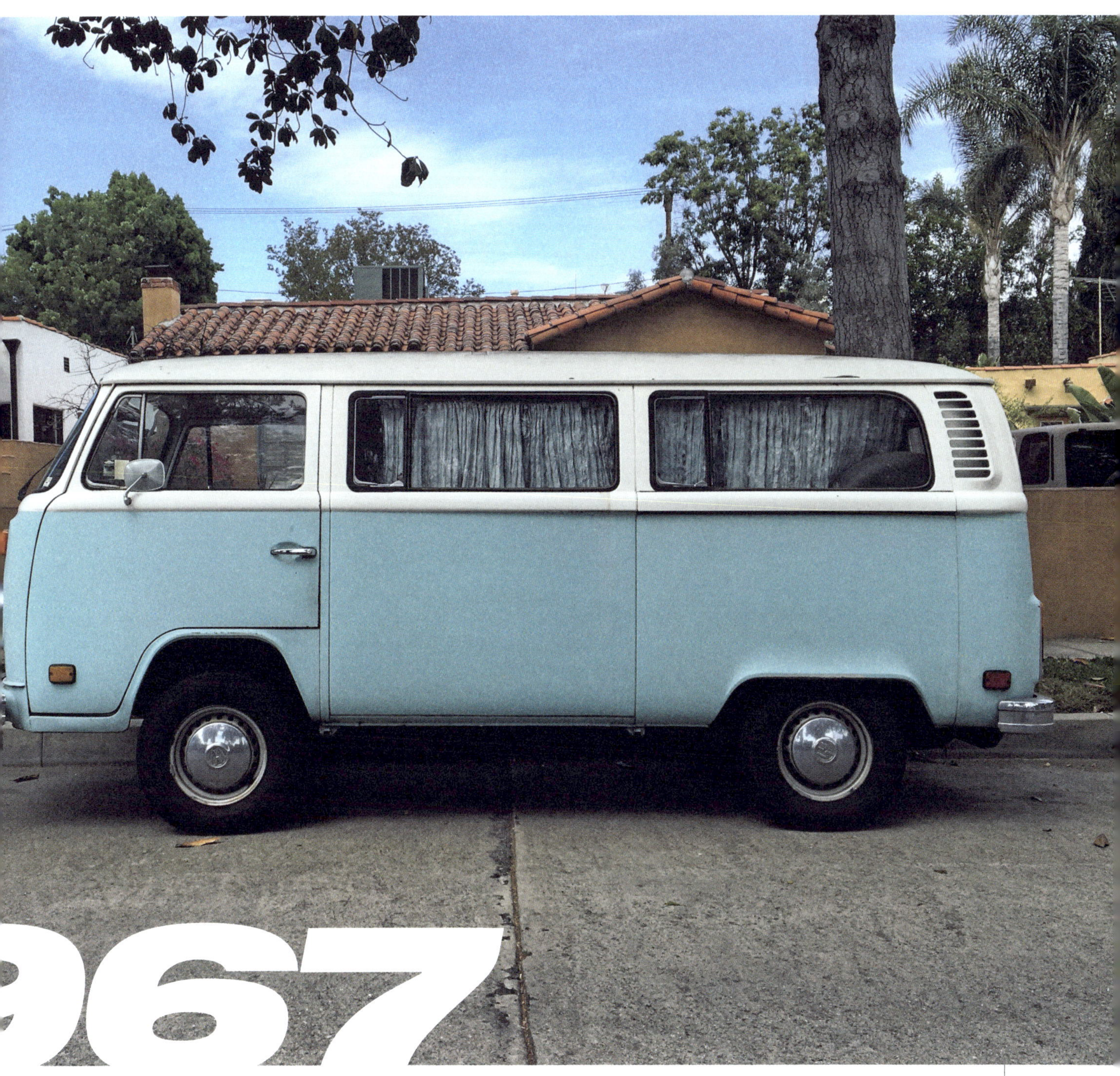
967

1965

AMC Rambler Marlin

ARCHITECTURE Exploring the northern districts of San Francisco unveils a treasure trove of architectural wonders. From Alamo Square to Pacific Heights and Haight-Ashbury, visitors are greeted with a myriad picture-perfect rowhouses showcasing various European neo-styles. It's no wonder these 19th-century streetscapes serve as backdrops for numerous series and films, attracting car enthusiasts seeking perfect examples of carchitecture. Like this AMC Rambler Marlin in the Castro neighborhood.

CAR American Motorcars Corporation (AMC) was formed in 1954 after a merger between the Hudson Motor Car Company and the Nash-Kelvinator Corporation. In 1965 it introduced the distinctively styled Rambler Marlin, which surfed along on the trend for large luxury cars. The next year it was called AMC Marlin and in 1967 simply Marlin. In that latter production year, the second generation was launched. The car had grown substantially; it became wider and got a longer hood, which improved the overall proportions. Under that stretched hood, 4.8 or 5.6-liter V8 engines could replace the 6-cylinder. Successfully so: the latter was barely ever ordered. Marlins are collectible anyway but with only about 2,500 built, the second generation is even more so.

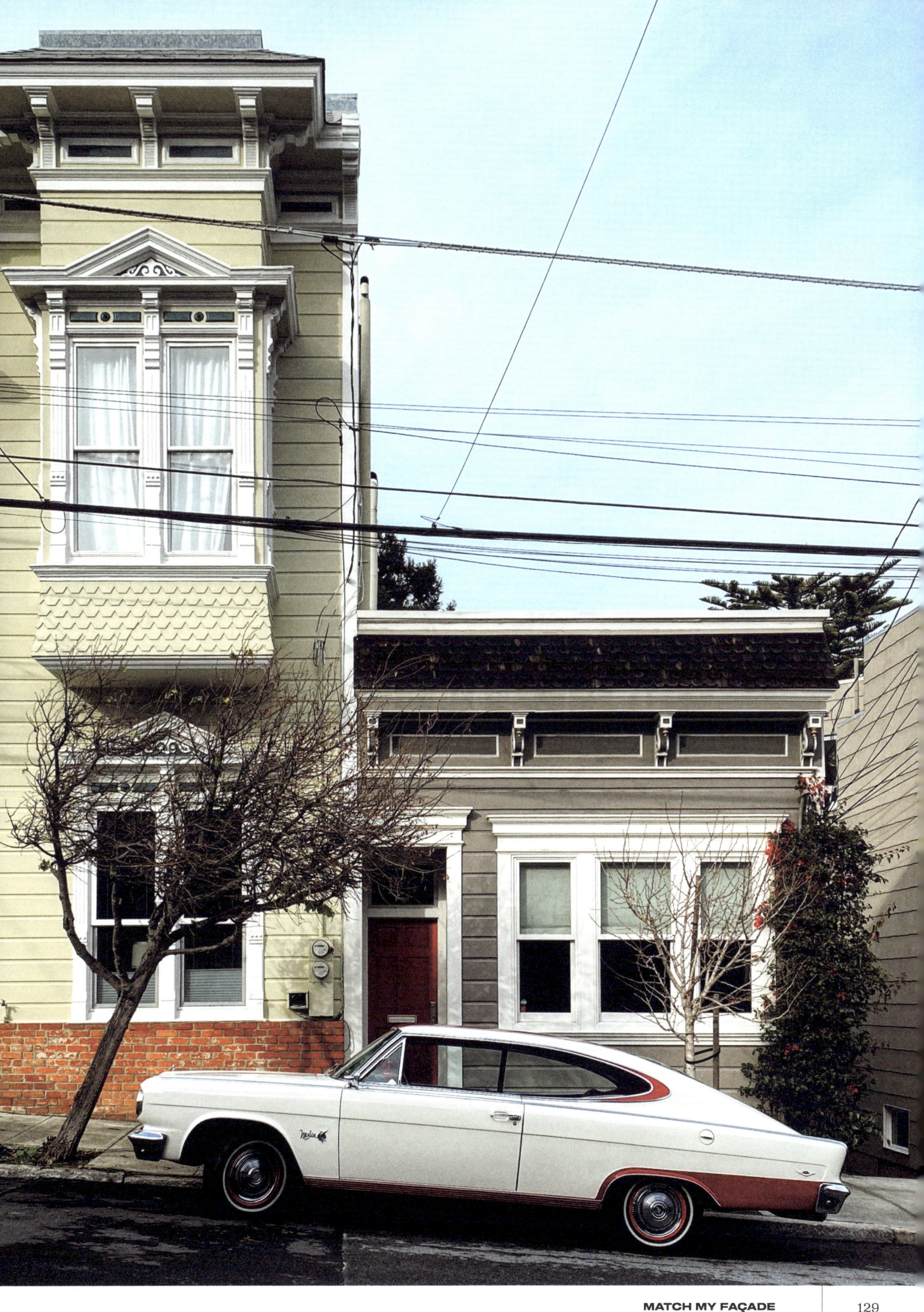

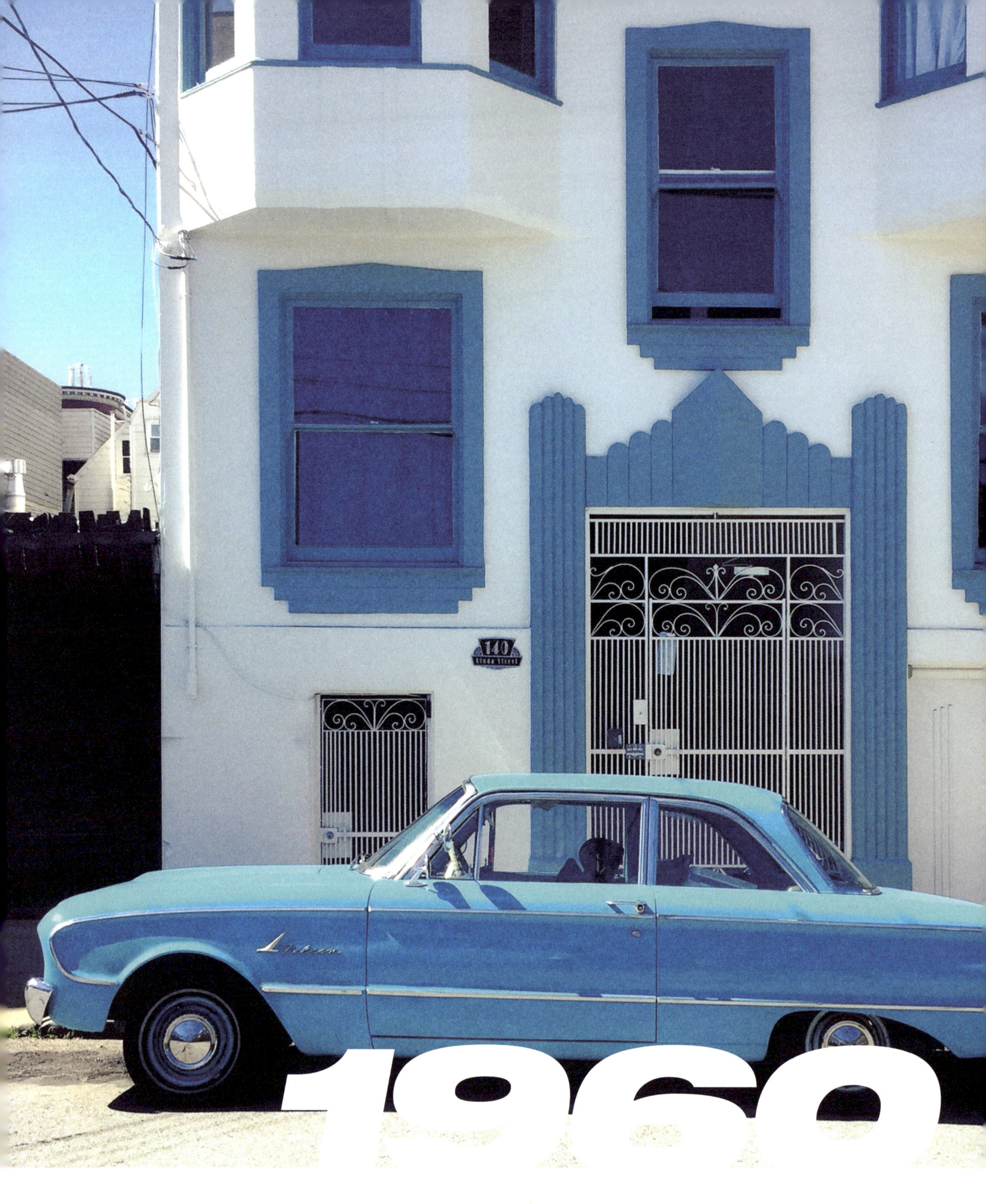

1960

Ford Falcon

ARCHITECTURE San Francisco was one of the first cities in the US to adopt British and French 19th-century architectural styles. Most of these houses were built between 1850 and 1915, when the city was booming, thanks to the Gold Rush. Although many of the city's estimated 40,000 Victorian houses were destroyed by the 1906 earthquake and the ensuing fire, they remain photogenic on account of their striking colors and lavish ornamentation, often complemented by vintage cars parked outside. Like this Blue Ford Falcon on Linda Street, right in the trendy Mission District.

CAR In 1960 the Ford Falcon ushered in a new car category to the United States, one that Europe was already familiar with: the compact midsize. Initially, it was powered by a small, relatively economical lightweight 2.4-liter 6-cylinder engine producing 90 hp. Later, it featured more powerful engines, including the V8, which would also power the Mustang. Within just two years, the Falcon achieved remarkable success, with over a million units sold. However, its triumph was soon met with competition from the Chevrolet Corvair and Plymouth Valiant. Here, we see the two-door coach, one of the numerous coachwork variants within the first generation. Two more would follow during the 1960s.

Chevrolet Corvette C2 Sting Ray Cabriolet

ARCHITECTURE This mid-century house in Richardson, Texas, while no longer completely original, has undergone extensive remodeling by architect Charles Bobo and interior designer Tavis Westbrook. Yet, amidst the changes, the essence of its 1963 vibe remains refreshingly intact, evident in the rough bricks and exposed beam structure. To complement its vintage charm, nothing suits better than an iconic car from the 1960s, such as a Corvette C2 Sting Ray Cabriolet.

CAR Two years after the appearance of the Jaguar XKR or E-type in 1961, Chevrolet astonished the automotive world with the Corvette Sting Ray. Unlike its predecessor, the C2 Corvette was an instant and resounding success, representing a significant leap forward in terms of both design and performance.

Constructed with fiberglass bodywork, the Sting Ray drew inspiration from the sleek lines of the 1952 Alfa Romeo Disco Volante, among other influences. Designed by Larry Shinoda, with an initial sketch by Peter Brock, the man behind the Shelby Cobra Daytona Coupé, the Sting Ray exuded a captivating blend of elegance and style.

Notably, the design team at GM meticulously crafted a radically symmetrical interior to complement the striking exterior. Initially, sales of coupés and convertibles were evenly split, but within two years, demand for convertibles surged, eventually accounting for two-thirds of overall sales.

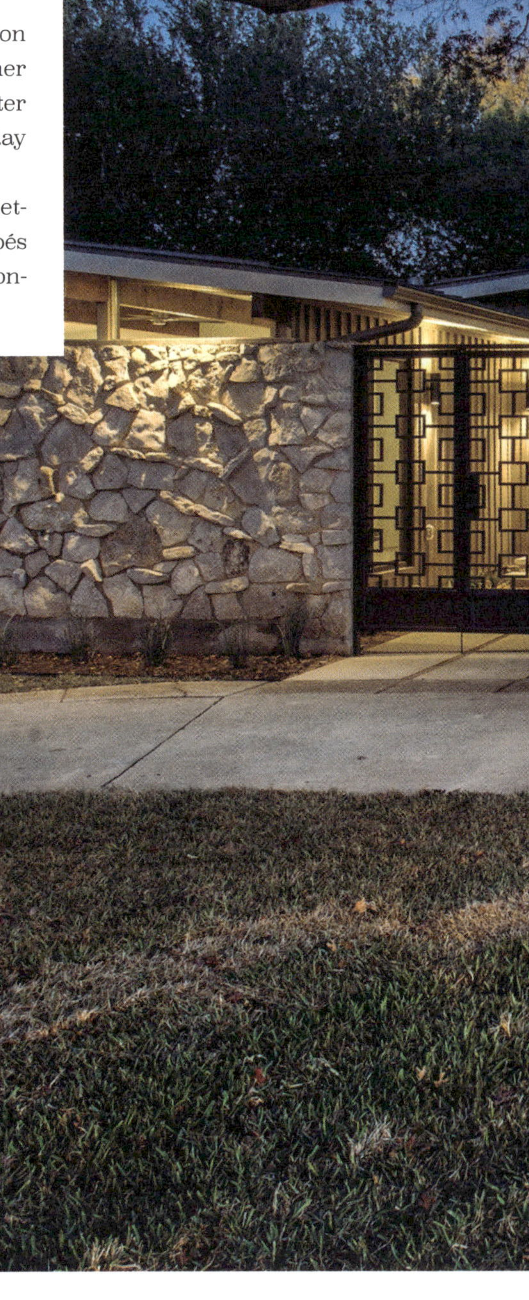

1965

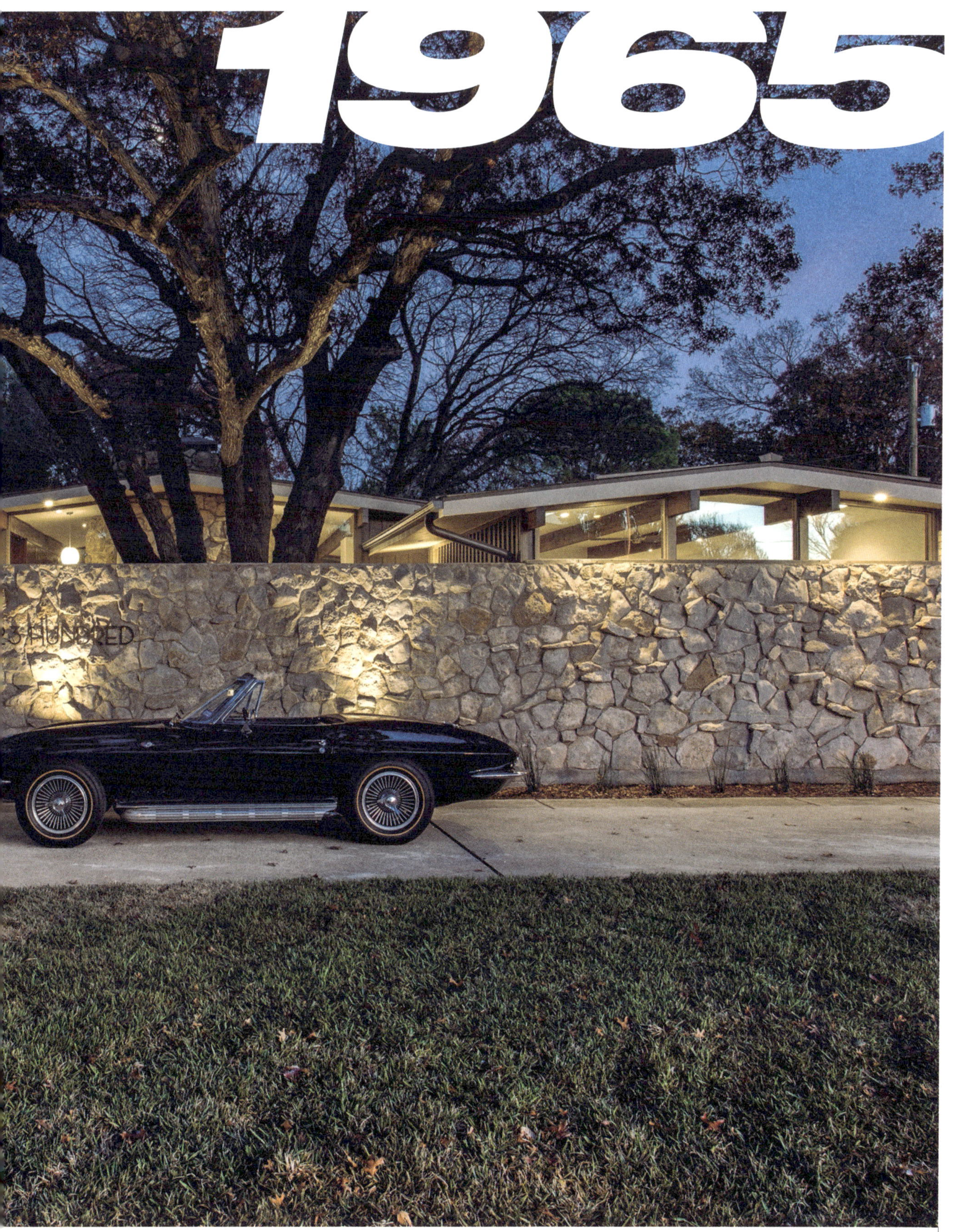

Cars to Live in: RV Culture in the US

Millions of Americans hold a deep affection for Recreational Vehicles (RVs). The term 'RV' encompasses a wide range of vehicles, from compact, minimalist caravans to luxurious motorized palaces on wheels. The styles evolved over time from the early landau carriages to the motorhomes of the 1930s and 1940s, inspired by art deco and aero-tech designs. The 1950s and 1960s witnessed the rise of space-age trailers, while the 1970s and 1980s embraced angular vehicles in earthy tones. Today, fully connected high-tech motorhomes cater to the needs of digital nomads, symbolizing the contemporary adaptation of RV culture. The RV has become an American institution, reflecting the spirit of adventure and freedom. In this article, we delve into the origins and evolution of this beloved phenomenon.

Savouring the serenity of a lakeside sunset with a small picnic table and a bottle of wine can feel like a slice of paradise on earth. And then, with the dawn of a new day, embarking on another adventure. This is the essence of RV life. Synonymous with freedom and flexibility, RVs offer the opportunity to traverse landscapes and cultures at your own pace, crafting your personalized journey. From solo travelers to large families, the allure of RVs is universal. Whether it's in a modest, weathered vehicle or an awe-inspiring mansion on wheels, the appeal remains undeniable.

RVs come in various forms, including caravans, motorhomes and fifth wheels: larger trailers towed by a pick-up or van with an open cargo area. Many are custom-built marvels, boasting two stories and expandable living areas, known as 'slide-outs.' Some embark on RV adventure in their youth, while others take the step after retirement, and still, there are those who postpone until it's too late to seize the moment.

INNOVATIVE TOURISM

Even before the invention of the automobile in the 1880s, camping and communing with nature were cherished pastimes for Americans. Horse-drawn carts facilitated these adventures, as depicted in publications such as *Popular Resorts and How to Reach Them* from the 1870s, which celebrated the wonders of California's Yosemite National Park. From the same period, *Adventures in the Wilderness; Or, Camp-Life in the Adirondacks* by clergyman William H.H. Murray inspired many to embrace outdoor escapades under the celestial canopy.

However, with the advent of automobiles, camping tourism underwent a transformative evolution. The 1910

Pierce-Arrow Touring Landau is often heralded as the first Recreational Vehicle, with 'Landau' harking back to a type of carriage, previously used for comfortable long-distance travel—a precursor to what we now know as a 'convertible.' Its debut at the tenth edition of the annual Madison Square Garden car show, a glamorous event spanning 7,000 square feet, and reminiscent of a Roman amphitheatre, marked a significant turning point. Initially reserved for the affluent, this early motorhome boasted amenities that included a folding bed, a collapsible sink and a toilet.

This era witnessed coastal towns such as Asbury Park in New Jersey embracing a new ethos of leisure, prompting a wave of innovation in recreational vehicles. Entrepreneurs such as Roland and Mary Conklin epitomized this spirit, converting a bus into a two-story motorhome for their cross-country journey from Huntington, New York, to San Francisco, California. Complete with a fully equipped kitchen, cosy sofas, sleeping berths and an onboard generator, their pioneering vehicle inspired DIY enthusiasts, thus setting in motion a new trend.

Another trailblazing model, the 1913 Earl emerged as one of the early modern travel trailers. It is named after its creator, a Cal State professor, for whom the vehicle was customized from a brand-new Ford Model T to facilitate dining and sleeping during trips. Not mass-produced by Ford, this bespoke RV was crafted by a coachbuilder in Los Angeles. Today, it is on display at the RV/MH Hall of Fame in Elkhart County, Indiana, the epicenter of RV culture and heritage.

TIN CAN TOURISTS

The concept of national parks was relatively new, having emerged less than half a century earlier. Destinations such as Yosemite, Yellowstone and Sequoia were rapidly gaining popularity, thanks in part to significant investments from railway companies. These companies not only laid down extensive railway lines but also erected glamorous lodges. However, during the 1920s boom of the US auto industry, these canvases became an appealing alternative to the luxurious lodges. Among the noteworthy mass-produced trailers of this era was the Curtiss Aerocar, often dubbed a 'motor bungalow' due to its inclusion of running water. Another notable model was the Auto-Kamp from Michigan, essentially a trailer with a fold-out tent featuring two mattresses, a dining table, a cooler, kitchen equipment, a two-burner gas stove and even electric lights. Some adventurers hitched it to a Ford Model T and traveled in it across the continent.

In 1919, the Tin Can Tourists club was established, the first RV camper club in the US. The name paid homage to the shiny silver caravans at the time, a style that endures to this day in the immortal and immensely popular Airstream trailers. The club fostered a sense of community among enthusiasts, encouraging gatherings at beautiful camping sites, although wild camping remained the preferred choice for many.

During the Great Depression, the rapid growth of RVs slowed down, but the number of cars and RVs continued to steadily grow. And as more people opted for holiday travel in trailers or motorhomes, the demand for reserved camping sites also rose. During World War II, production almost halted, but the post-war economic boom, coupled with affordable fuel prices, led to increasingly comfortable and well-equipped RVs with stylish lighting and cosy sofas. Self-built RVs remained popular during this time.

Airstream, established in 1931, rose to iconic status as a brand known for both trailers and motorhomes. In 1963, President Kennedy utilized one as a mobile office during weapon testing at a military base in the New Mexico desert. The Holiday Rambler, founded in 1953, also earned a solid reputation within the industry. And in 1958, Winnebago entered the scene, initially offering trailers, before expanding into well-insulated, mass-produced motorhomes that became more affordable than ever, thereby boosting RV culture. For further insights, James Twitchell's book *Winnebago Nation* (2014) offers a comprehensive account of the RV's origins and evolution over the 20th century.

The Wolverine Camper Co introduced RV variants with comfortable beds and compact yet fully equipped kitchens. RVs continued to grow in size, culminating in 'palaces on wheels' on the roads by the mid-1970s, complete with roof terraces. Subsequent models even featured built-in garages for a second vehicle.

The compact Volkswagen van, known as Type 2 and revered by enthusiasts, became an icon of RV culture, due in part to its streamlined design and practical camping equipment. Throughout the 1960s and 1970s, it symbolized love, peace and freedom, even gracing the cover of Bob Dylan's album *The Freewheelin' Bob Dylan*. To this day, it remains a sought-after and expensive classic, having evolved into its seventh generation under the name 'California.'

HOTELS ON WHEELS

The 1960s heralded the advent of more expansive highways, reflecting a burgeoning fascination among motorized Americans. Jack Kerouac's novel *On the Road* (1957) deeply resonated with this demographic. In 1960, the acclaimed writer John Steinbeck embarked on a quest to uncover the essence of the 'real' America, traversing the nation in a camper truck he affectionately named Rocinante, after Don Quixote's loyal horse. He chronicled his escapades in *Travels with Charley: In Search of America* (1962), thus contributing to the growing allure of motorhomes, which were steadily becoming ingrained into the fabric of popular culture.

This trend found early expression in movies such as *The Long, Long Trailer* (1953), featuring Desi Arnaz and Lucille Ball, who honeymoon in a 36-foot trailer. Subsequently, the RV gained prominence in productions such as the original *Blues Brothers* (1980), *Lost in America* (1985), *The Incredibles* (2004) and *Little Miss Sunshine* (2006). More recently, Brad Pitt's character in *Once upon a Time in Hollywood* (2019) epitomized the RV lifestyle, symbolizing quintessential American values of freedom, individuality, adventure and self-reliance, the RV became an iconic institution.

In their personal lives as well, celebrities were not immune to the allure, with luminaries such as Will Smith investing in 'The Heat,' a 30-tonne motorhome boasting a living area of 1,200 square feet and a price tag of $2.5 million. The manufacturer, Anderson Mobile Estates, also provided Mariah Carey and numerous others with custom-made double-deckers. Today, icons such as Justin Bieber, Gwen Stefani and Leonardo DiCaprio embrace the RV lifestyle as a refreshing alternative to hotels, with DiCaprio's RV resembling a luxurious cruise ship. Meanwhile, stalwarts such as Tom Hanks and Matthew McConaughey have demonstrated a longstanding affinity for the classic Airstream trailer, epitomizing elegance and comfort for almost two decades.

DIGITAL NOMADS

The digital age dawned in the 1990s, yet despite the allure of affordable air travel, the romance of the open road endured. Following 9/11, RVs experienced a resurgence in popularity, a trend that continued well into the 2010s. In 2016 the RV Industry Association reported the highest spike in 40 years, driven largely by adventurous millennials. This surge in enthusiasm harked back to before the ore–oil crisis era of the 1970s.

The appeal of RVs transcends mere transportation, encompassing a diverse array of activities from extreme sports to leisurely pursuits such as hiking and fishing, and fostering a deep connection with nature. Regardless of age, gender or social status, RV owners are united by a strong sense of community and camaraderie. Gathering at campsites, seminars, RV shows and national park rallies, they forge lasting friendships and exchange tales of their adventures, which are an integral part of camper culture.

A cornerstone of the RV lifestyle is the hands-on approach to customerization and maintenance. From restoring vintage RVs to personalizing modern ones with creative flair, DIY ethos permeates the community, embodying the American spirit of self-sufficiency.

The advent of rapid internet in the 2010s gave rise to digital nomads, enabling a significant portion of the population to work remotely while traversing the country. In 2018, an estimated one million Americans lived full-time in an RV or motorhome. Despite the switch to a minimalist and nomadic lifestyle, RV life is nevertheless associated with a high degree of comfort. This lifestyle shift offers an escape from the pressures, responsibilities and tediousness of modern life, inviting exploration and self-discovery off the beaten path.

Technological advancements have transformed the RV experience, integrating features such as solar power, constant connectivity and smart home amenities, enhancing both comfort and convenience. All this has changed the overall experience as well as RV culture. During the coronavirus pandemic, RV culture experienced a significant upsurge. Isolated travel in personal bubbles proved ideal for social distancing. As a result, the demand reached unprecedented levels, straining the supply chain. At the same time, the transition of RVs into the electric age has become a fact. And so it seems that the convergence of electric vehicle (EV) technology with RVs represents a progressive and eco-friendly concept for the future.

“Le Corbusier believed that architects should study machines such as automobiles in order to find standards on which to base modern architectural principles.”

Ivan Margolius, architect and author

WHEELS OF FORTUNE

Ferrari 410 Superamerica Series III

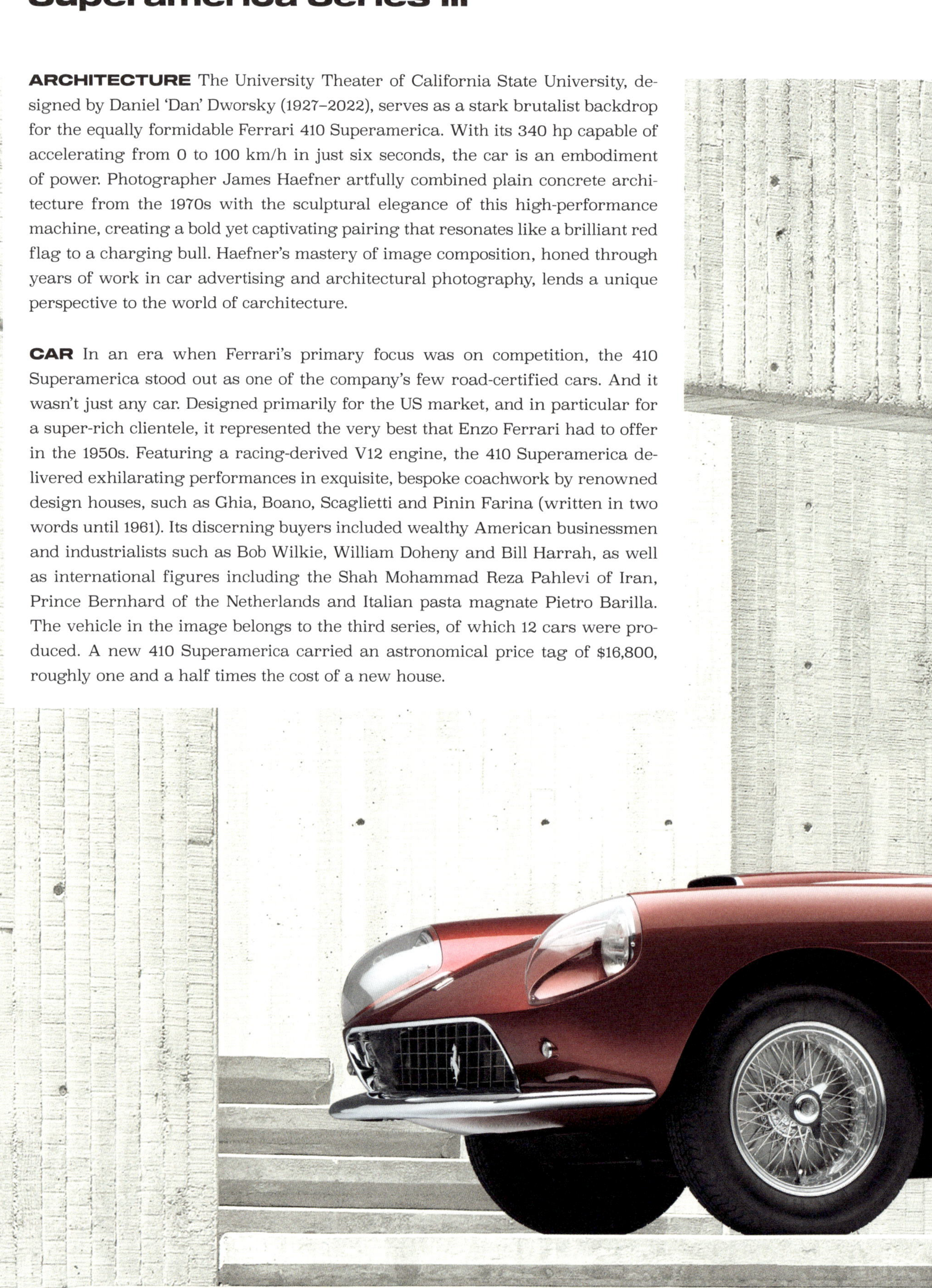

ARCHITECTURE The University Theater of California State University, designed by Daniel 'Dan' Dworsky (1927–2022), serves as a stark brutalist backdrop for the equally formidable Ferrari 410 Superamerica. With its 340 hp capable of accelerating from 0 to 100 km/h in just six seconds, the car is an embodiment of power. Photographer James Haefner artfully combined plain concrete architecture from the 1970s with the sculptural elegance of this high-performance machine, creating a bold yet captivating pairing that resonates like a brilliant red flag to a charging bull. Haefner's mastery of image composition, honed through years of work in car advertising and architectural photography, lends a unique perspective to the world of carchitecture.

CAR In an era when Ferrari's primary focus was on competition, the 410 Superamerica stood out as one of the company's few road-certified cars. And it wasn't just any car. Designed primarily for the US market, and in particular for a super-rich clientele, it represented the very best that Enzo Ferrari had to offer in the 1950s. Featuring a racing-derived V12 engine, the 410 Superamerica delivered exhilarating performances in exquisite, bespoke coachwork by renowned design houses, such as Ghia, Boano, Scaglietti and Pinin Farina (written in two words until 1961). Its discerning buyers included wealthy American businessmen and industrialists such as Bob Wilkie, William Doheny and Bill Harrah, as well as international figures including the Shah Mohammad Reza Pahlevi of Iran, Prince Bernhard of the Netherlands and Italian pasta magnate Pietro Barilla. The vehicle in the image belongs to the third series, of which 12 cars were produced. A new 410 Superamerica carried an astronomical price tag of $16,800, roughly one and a half times the cost of a new house.

1958

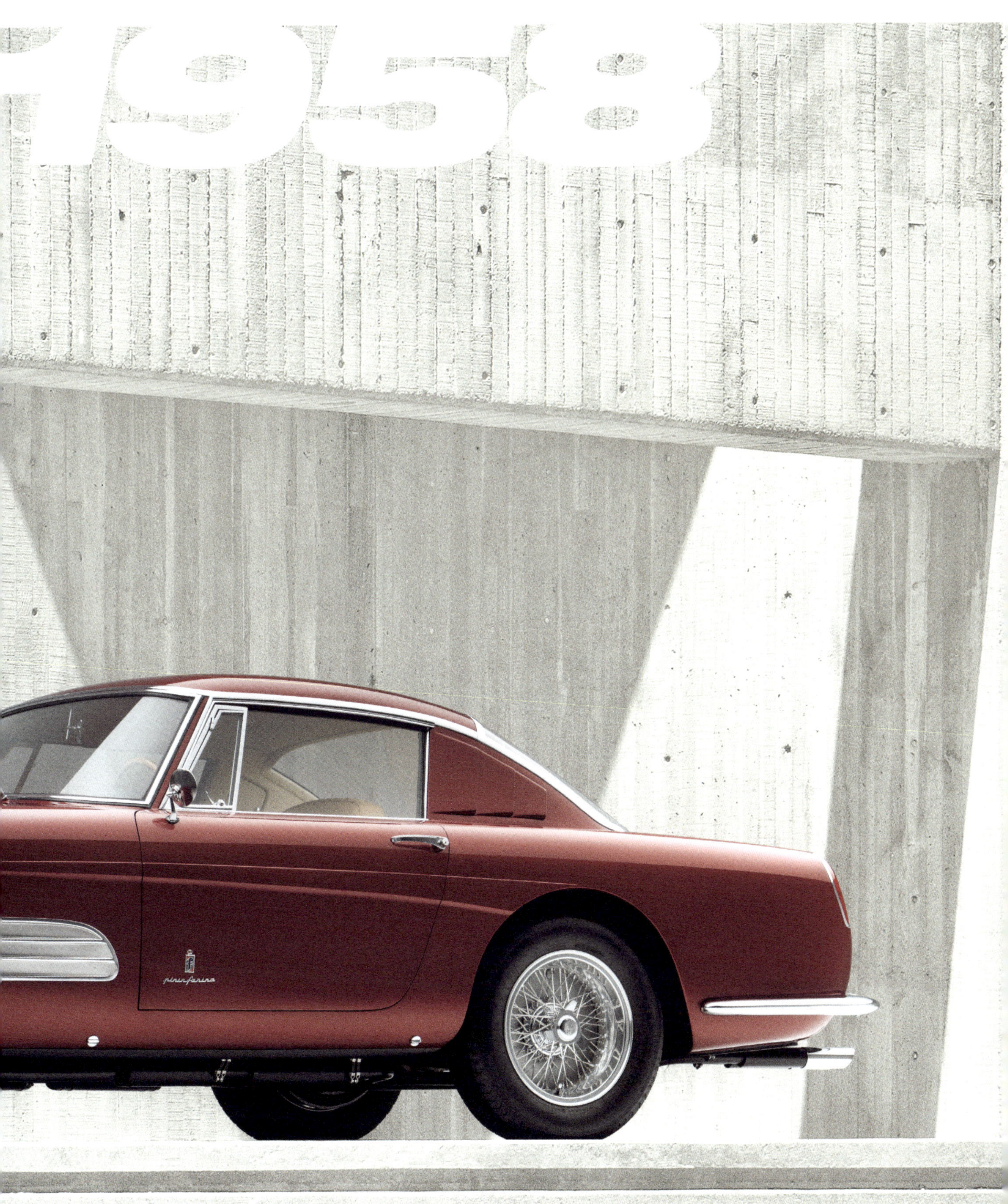

1953

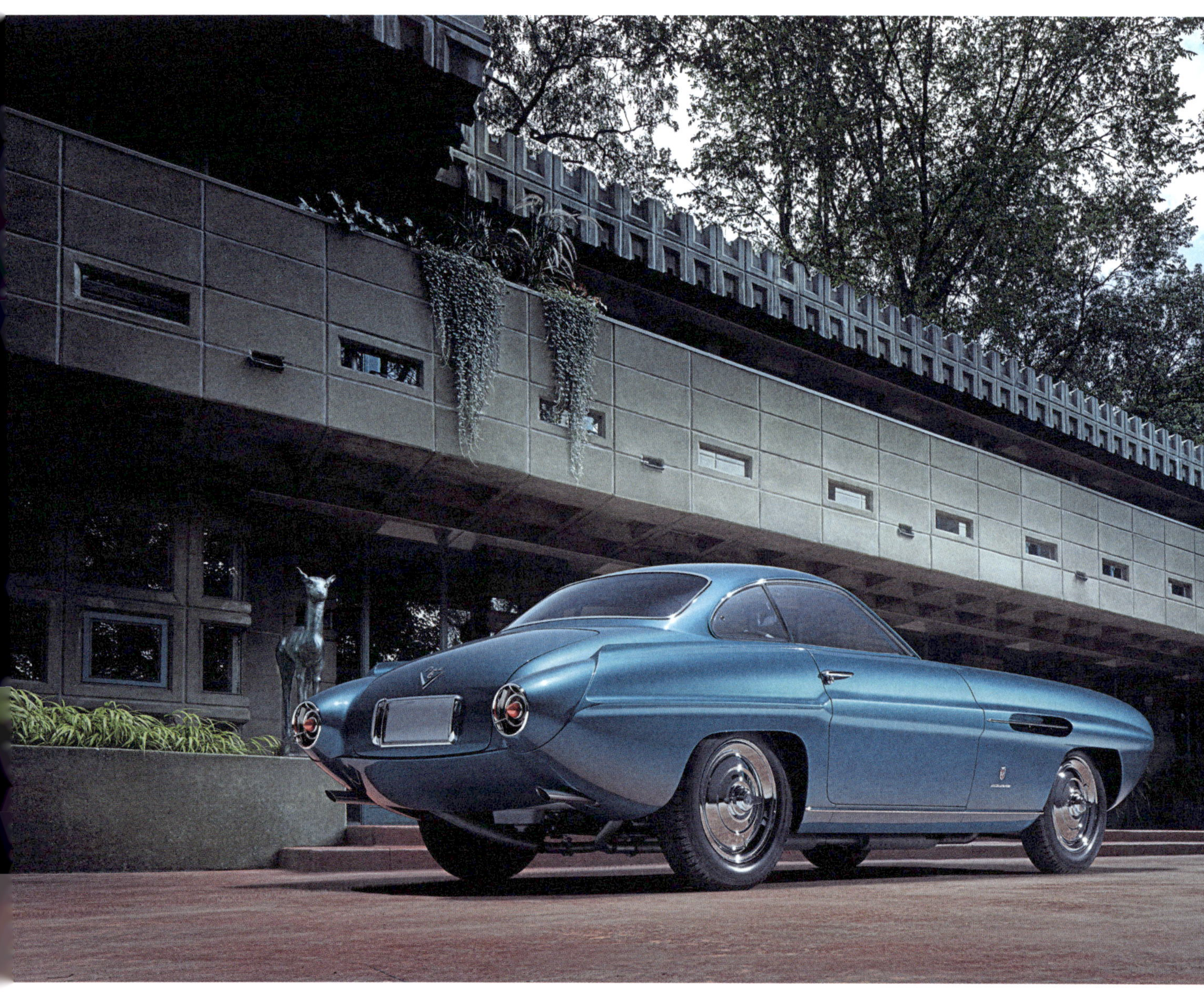

Fiat 8V Supersonic

ARCHITECTURE In 1952 *Road & Track* magazine described this Fiat 8V as 'the biggest surprise of the year.' Norm Silk and Dale Morgan experienced their own unexpected revelation in 2006 when they acquired a dilapidated property in Detroit, only to find out that it was the creation of Frank Lloyd Wright (1867–1959). Given Wright's affinity for automobiles, it's not surprising that his architectural footprints graced Detroit, the Motor City. However, Turkel House is his sole architectural venture in the city itself.
Erected in 1955–56 for Dorothy Turkel, Turkel House was in an advanced state of decay when Silk and Morgan bought it. Virtually every aspect of the house had to be renovated, replaced or restored. But thanks to the dedication of this couple, the remarkable house is once again the luminous Usonian gem that Wright once conceived. A striking feature is the grid that recurs throughout, integrated into windows, ceilings and crafted woodwork. However, the real showstopper is the way in which Frank Lloyd Wright draws nature and daylight into the living space: the dynamic interplay between organic forms and geometric precision is typically Wright.

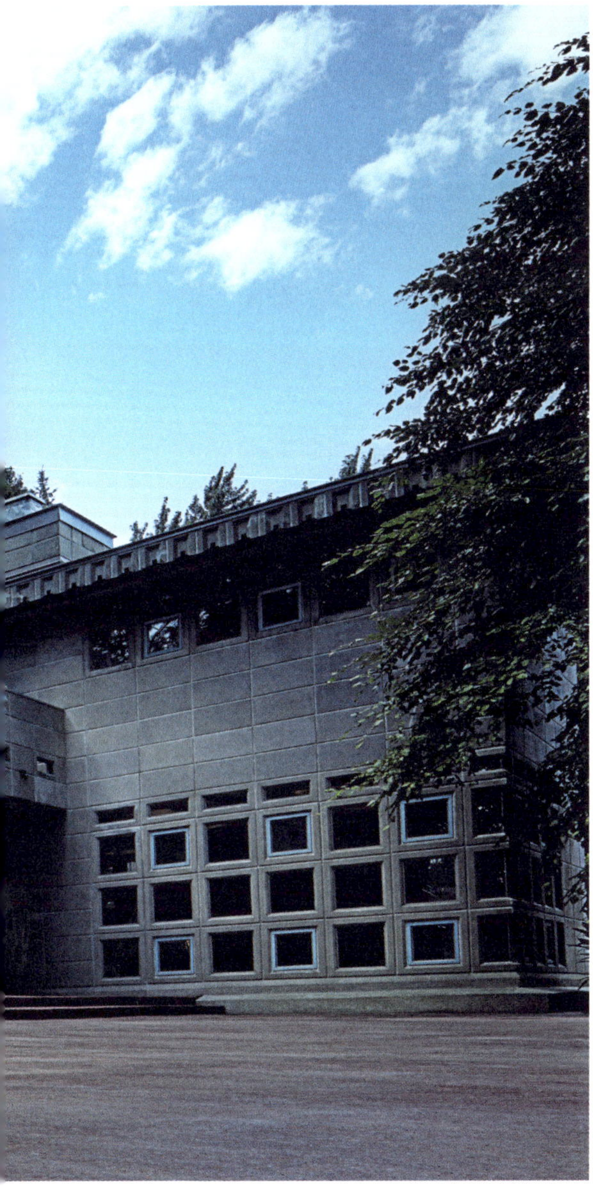

CAR Produced from 1952 to 1954, the Fiat 8V (Otto Vu) earned its name due to the fact that Fiat believed Ford had a copyright on the V8 designation. This car was a departure from Fiat's post World War II reputation for producing mass-market vehicles accessible to the average consumer. While the 8V performed admirably in racing, it fell short of commercial success, with only 114 units of this particularly ingenious 2-liter engine being manufactured.
The original bodywork design is credited to Luigi Rapi, the design director at Fiat's Dipartimento Carrozzerie Derivate e Speciali. or Special Bodies Department, with some 40 bodies constructed inhouse. Other engines were sold along with the chassis to external coachbuilders, such as Carrozzeria Zagato, Vignale and Ghia. It was the latter that built 15 Supersonic cars, primarily for the US market. Designed by Giovanni Savonuzzi, this avant-garde 'Jet Age' styling aimed to offer a glimpse into the future of automotive design. It has become the most beautiful of all 8Vs, and to this day exudes a modern appeal. It is also the most sought-after variant and a head-turner at concours d'elegance car shows around the world. Its current market value hovers around $2,000,000.

1965

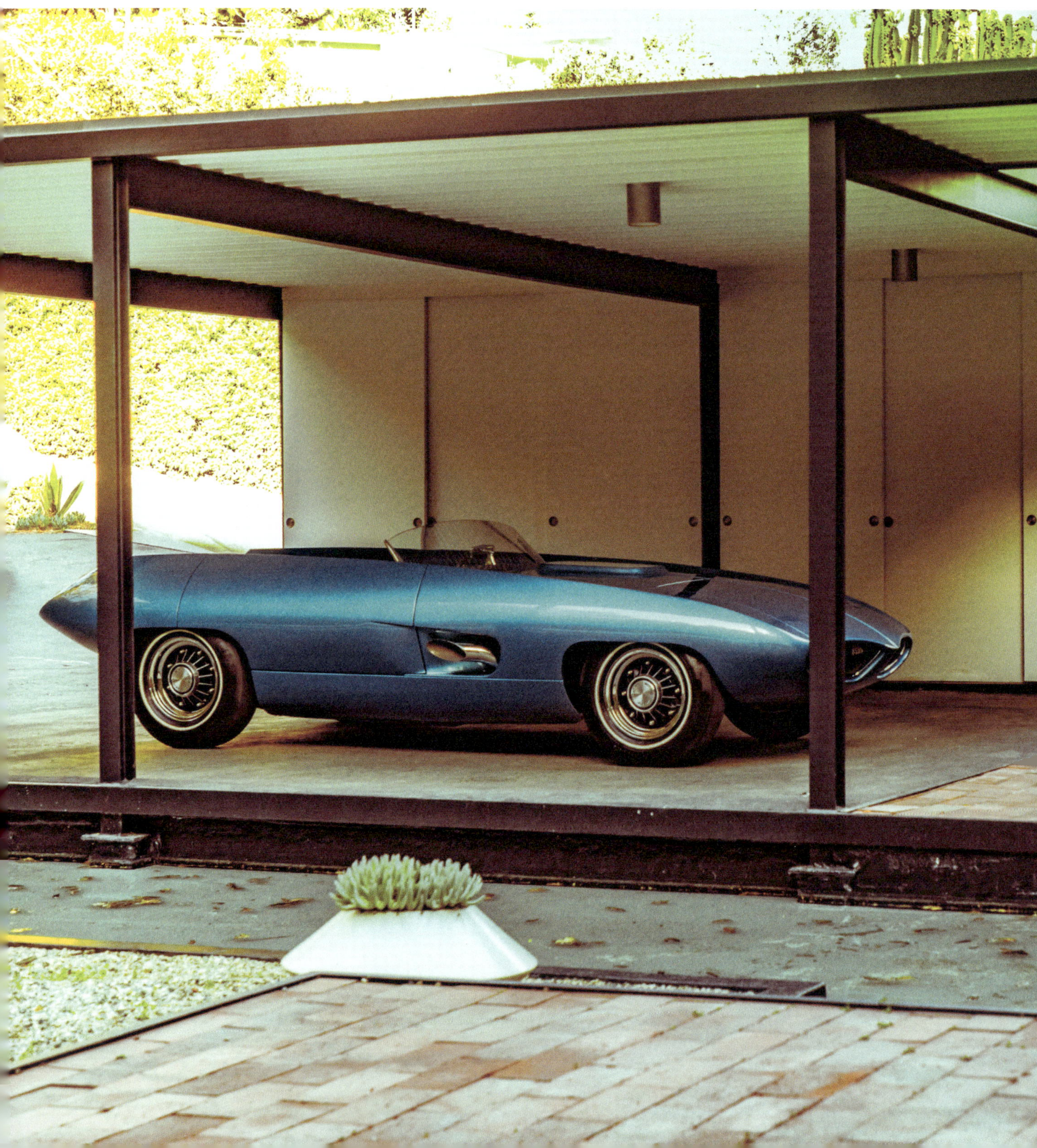

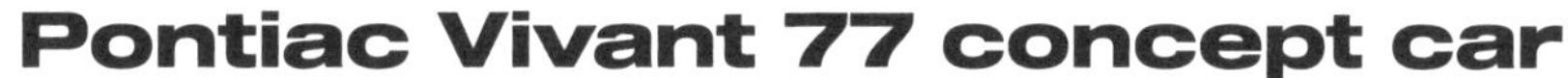

Pontiac Vivant 77 concept car

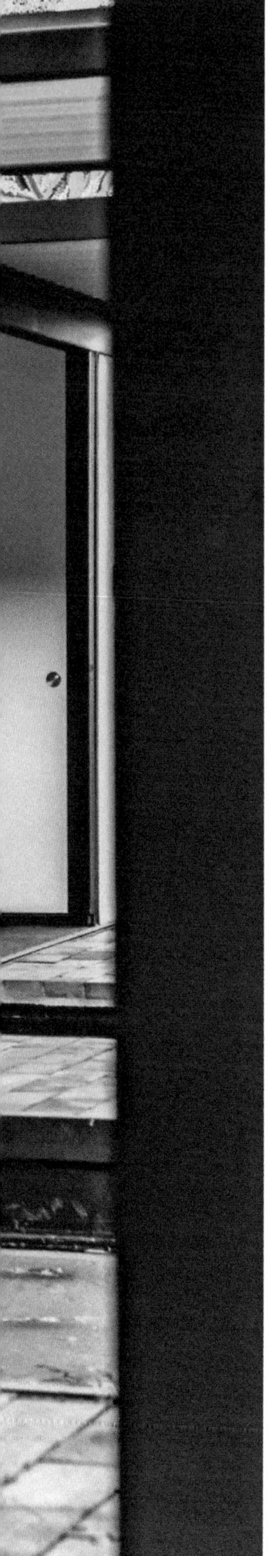

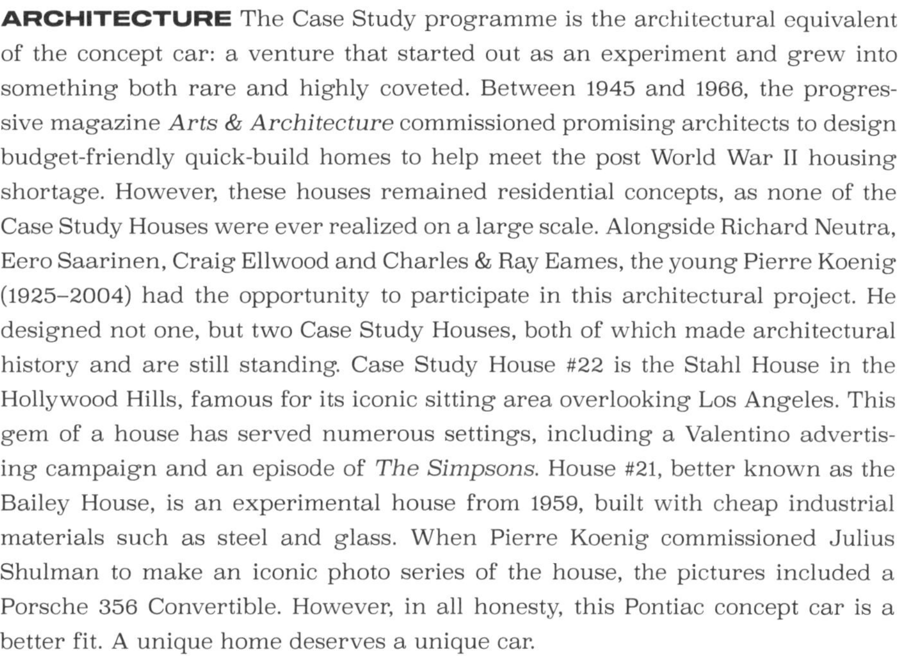

ARCHITECTURE The Case Study programme is the architectural equivalent of the concept car: a venture that started out as an experiment and grew into something both rare and highly coveted. Between 1945 and 1966, the progressive magazine *Arts & Architecture* commissioned promising architects to design budget-friendly quick-build homes to help meet the post World War II housing shortage. However, these houses remained residential concepts, as none of the Case Study Houses were ever realized on a large scale. Alongside Richard Neutra, Eero Saarinen, Craig Ellwood and Charles & Ray Eames, the young Pierre Koenig (1925–2004) had the opportunity to participate in this architectural project. He designed not one, but two Case Study Houses, both of which made architectural history and are still standing. Case Study House #22 is the Stahl House in the Hollywood Hills, famous for its iconic sitting area overlooking Los Angeles. This gem of a house has served numerous settings, including a Valentino advertising campaign and an episode of *The Simpsons*. House #21, better known as the Bailey House, is an experimental house from 1959, built with cheap industrial materials such as steel and glass. When Pierre Koenig commissioned Julius Shulman to make an iconic photo series of the house, the pictures included a Porsche 356 Convertible. However, in all honesty, this Pontiac concept car is a better fit. A unique home deserves a unique car.

CAR This remarkable automobile is the embodiment of a deeply personal automotive vision, brought to life by the ingenuity of Herb Adams. With a storied career engineering several muscle cars at the now-defunct Pontiac (formerly a division of General Motors), headed by the infamous John DeLorean, Adams self-financed the development of his personal dream car and dedicated considerable hands-on effort to its creation. To realize the car's aesthetic vision, he enlisted the expertise of the so-called Beatles of Troy, a trio of former Rolls-Royce coachbuilders. The result is a vehicle characterized by its clean, sharp lines and a distinctive wedge-shaped profile. The tail fins were inspired by the three Alfa Romeo BAT (Berlina Aerodinamica Tecnica) concept cars designed by Franco Scaglione at the Italian design house Bertone in the early 1950s.

At the 1966 Detroit Autorama, the Vivant 77's striking design left the crowd awestruck. As befitted a concept car or a one-off prototype, it had no roof, no bumpers, no wing mirrors and no door handles. However, in Michigan, where automotive freedom was greater than in other states, the car remained fully operational, and Adams continued to drive it regularly for over a decade. Under the hood, the Vivant 77 concealed a NASCAR-derived 370 cubic-inch V8, pumping out 405 hp. Adams ultimately sold the car to finance his racing pursuits. It subsequently changed hands several times before disappearing from public view for 35 years. Following an 8,000-hour restoration effort, this extraordinary car reemerged when it was displayed at Pebble Beach in 2017 and the Concorso d'Eleganza Villa d'Este in Italy in 2019.

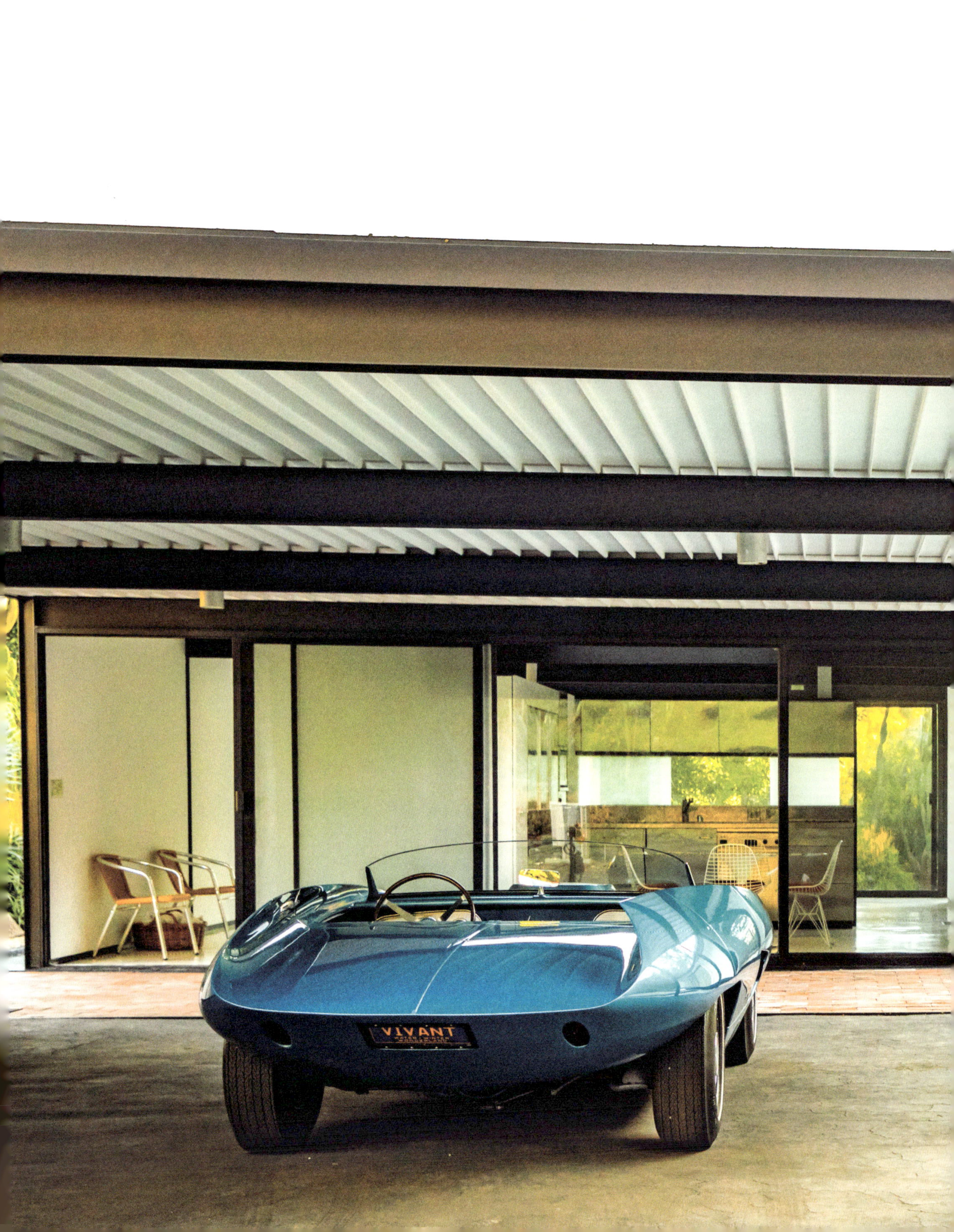
VIVANT

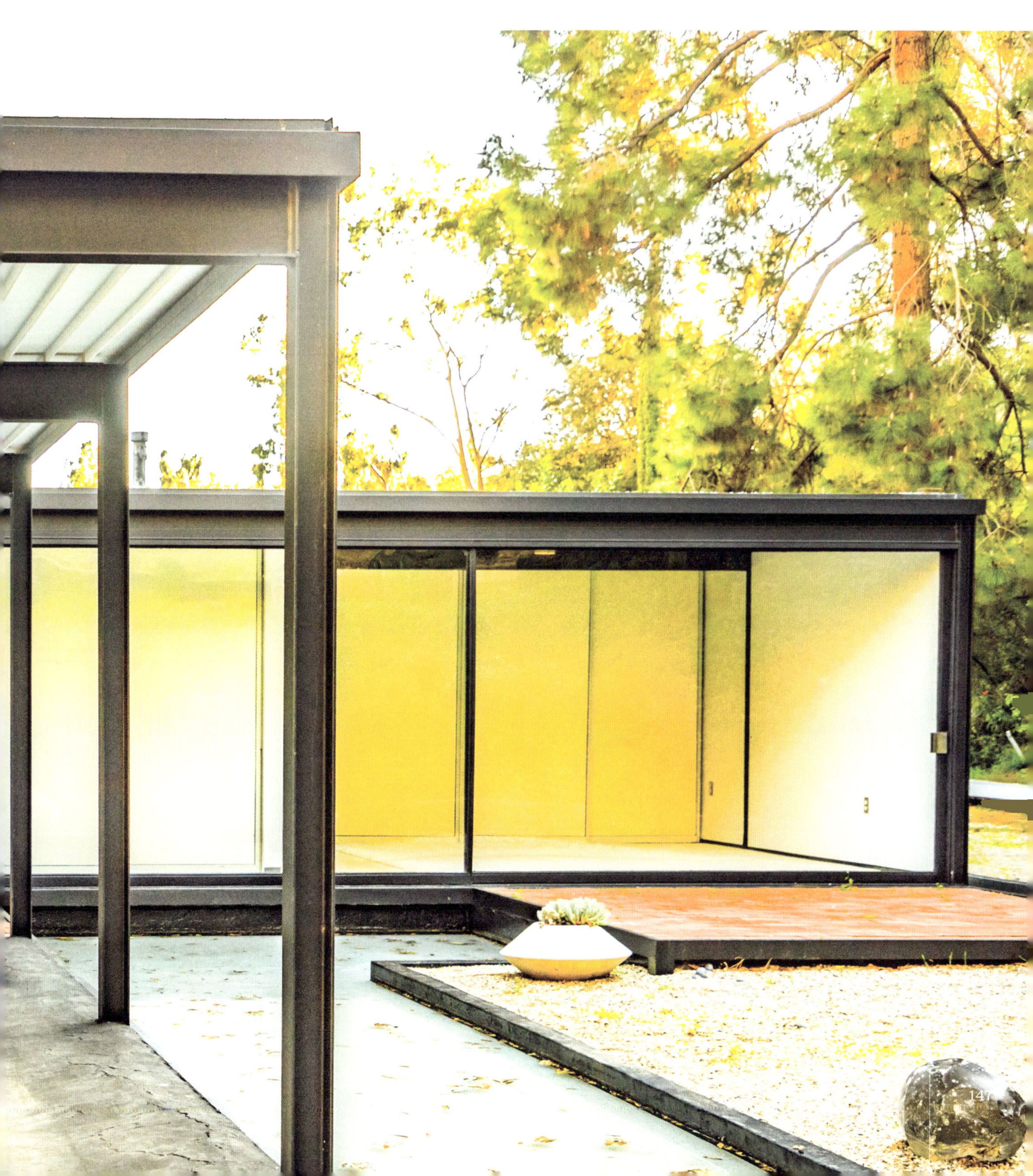

1963

Aston Martin DB5

ARCHITECTURE In the James Bond novels, 007 drives a Bentley, yet on the silver screen he swears by an Aston Martin DB5, a car that achieved movie stardom in its own right. Interestingly, Ian Fleming, the creator of the character, had a different preference altogether, favouring the Studebaker Avanti, which he called "an infinitely higher class of machine". Even without the iconic gray Aston Martin, this stunning 1960 William Krisel villa at 1164 North Rose Avenue in Vista Las Palmas exudes its own movie-star allure.

Vista Las Palmas used to be called the 'Beverly Hills of Palm Springs' owing to its popularity among Hollywood luminaries who either lived in or visited the neighborhood. Marilyn Monroe, for instance, regularly rented a house on Rose Avenue. Dean Martin, Frank Sinatra and Sammy Davis Jr. frequented the pool of fellow Rat Pack member, actor Peter Lawford, who lived with Patricia Kennedy, President Kennedy's sister, in a villa on North Via Monte Vista. More recently, Leonardo di Caprio acquired one of these famous movie-star homes in Palm Springs: the residence of Dinah Shore at 432 Hermosa, one of architect Donald Wexler's masterpieces. Palm Springs, with its cinematic heritage, continues to etch its name into the annals of film history.

CAR In 1964 the Aston Martin DB5 made its iconic debut in the movie *Goldfinger*, after which it would appear in a number of subsequent Bond films and become the quintessential Bond car. This stunning automobile was designed by Carrozzeria Touring Superleggera and manufactured from 1963 to 1965.

The 'DB' in DB5 pays homage to David Brown, the visionary who bought Aston Martin in 1947. The DB5 is powered by an aluminium 4-liter engine with three carburettors, and a five-speed manual transmission. That was enough to deliver an impressive 282 hp, allowing the DB5 to reach a maximum speed of 145 mph and accelerate from 0 to 60 mph in just eight seconds.

In 2020, in a remarkable move, Aston Martin embarked on a Goldfinger Continuation program, constructing 28 brand-new Goldfinger DB5s. These are faithful reproductions equipped with most of the gadgets featured in the Bond films, although some of them are simulated for safety and practicality. For instance, while the guns concealed behind the indicators may look convincing, they don't function and the oil trail that the car can supposedly leave behind consists of water. These exquisite replicas were priced at $3.6 million each and are not authorized for use on public roads.

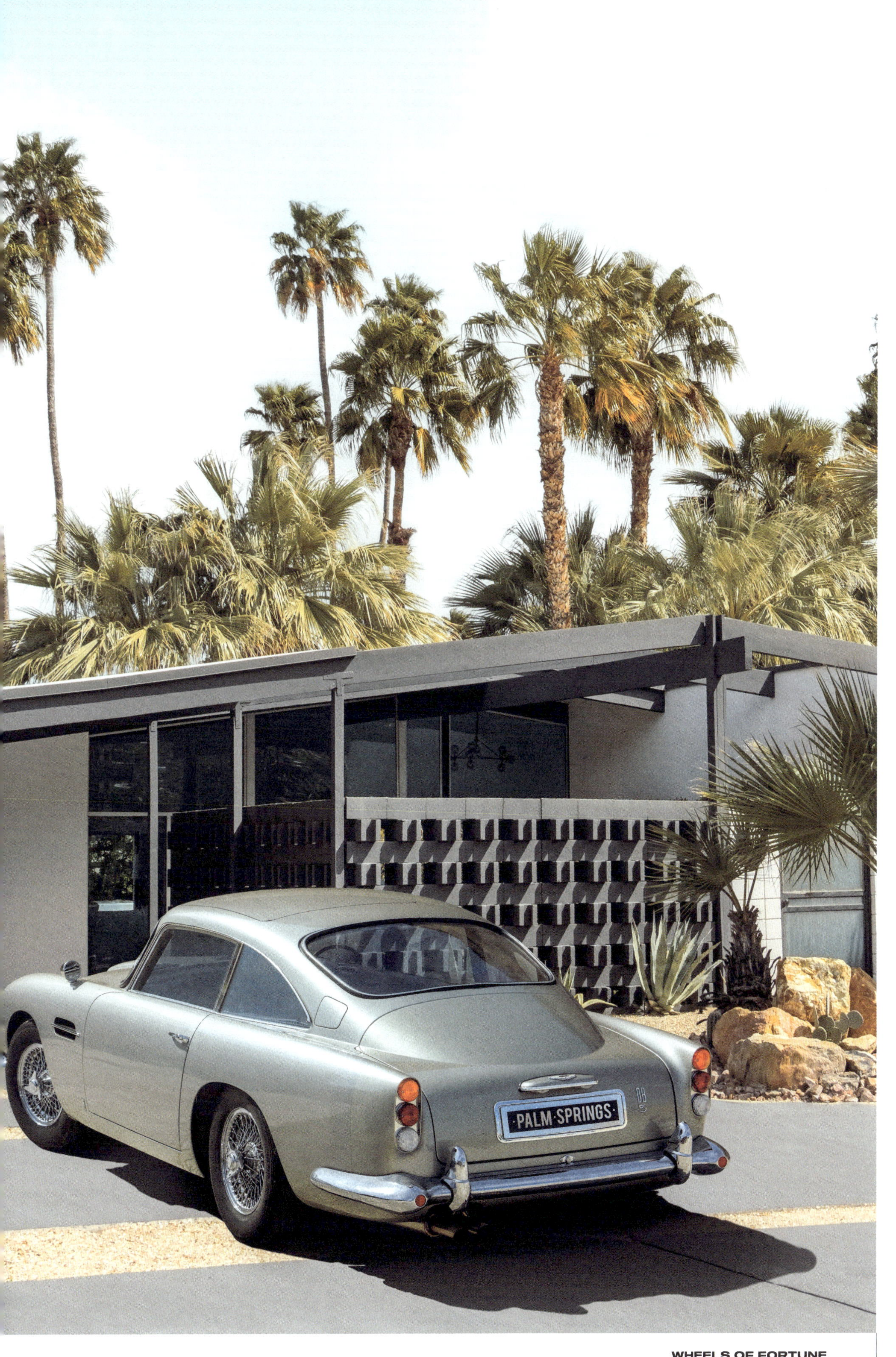
PALM·SPRINGS

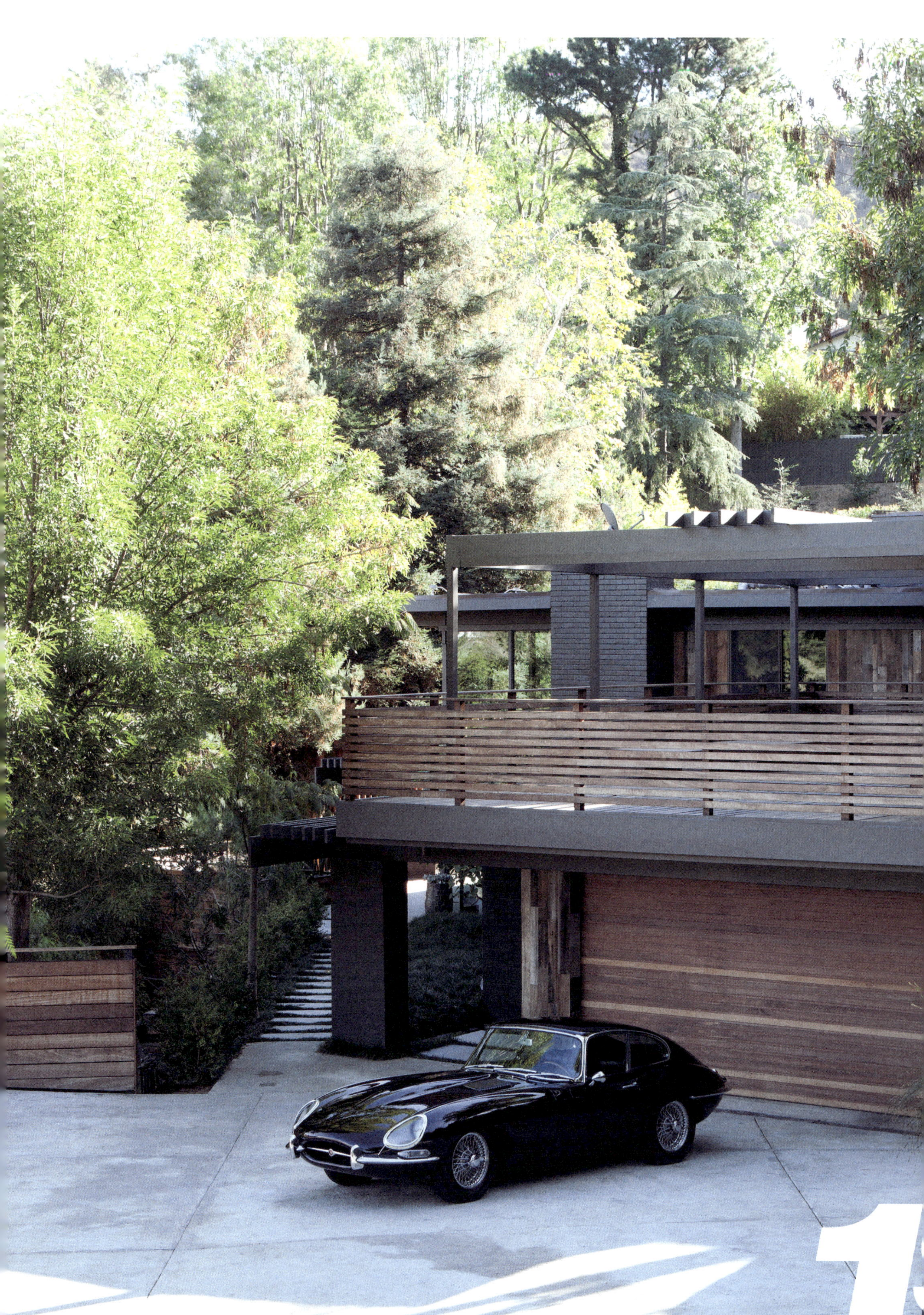

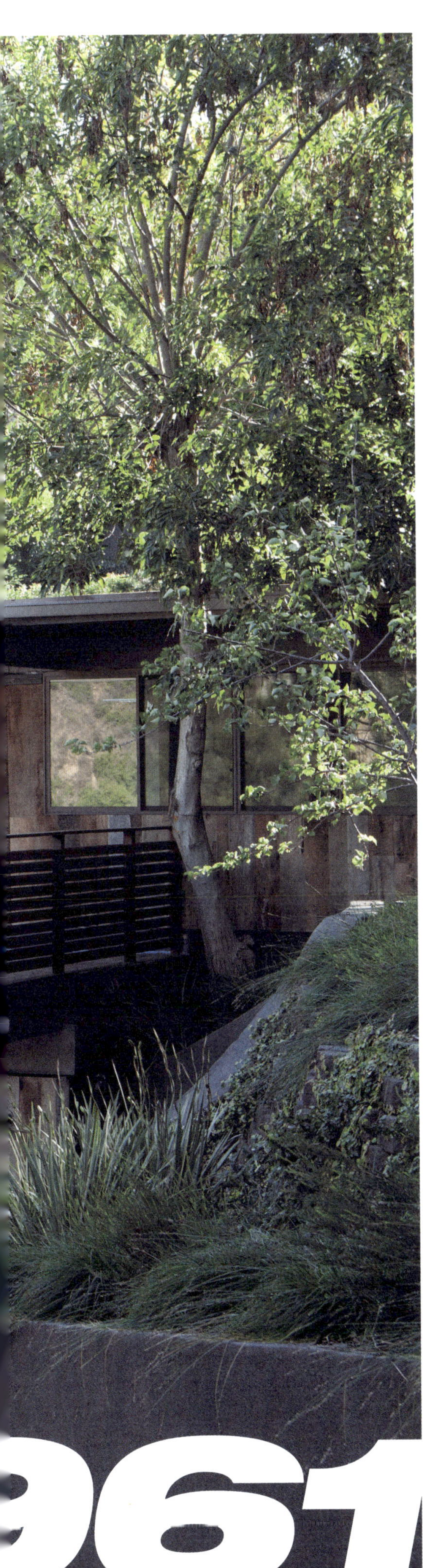

Jaguar E-Type Series 1 Coupé

ARCHITECTURE In 2020, the Ajioka House nestled in the Hollywood Hills, sold for a substantial price tag of $6.7 million. This sum not only secured a luxurious residence but also a piece of architectural history. Originally designed by the architectural firm Buff & Hensman, the house, located on Nichols Canyon Road, dates back to the 1960s, and was commissioned by Dewey Daisaku Ajioka and his wife Sugita Ajioka.

While the house has been thoroughly remodeled by the Los Angeles-based firm Commune, vestiges of Buff & Hensman's influence are still discernible in the façade. These influences draw from a range of inspirations including traditional Japanese ryokans and the modernist designs of architects Richard Neutra and Rudolph Schindler. Neutra was a good friend of the Ajioka family, having designed a garage for the Buffs early in his career. Buff & Hensman boasted a prestigious clientele that included actor Steve McQueen, actress Anne Baxter, graphic designer Saul Bass, and actor Laurence Harvey of Lithuanian-British descent. Conrad Hensman, one of the architects, and Laurence Harvey developed a close friendship over time. The architect even owed many clients to Harvey. However, their initial contact was far from smooth. When Harvey first contacted the Buff & Hensman office and politely introduced himself with his heavy accent, Hensman quipped, "And I'm Walt Disney," before abruptly hanging up.

CAR The Jaguar XK-E, the American name for what was called the E-Type in Europe, was produced in three series between 1961 and 1974, of which we see here the earliest coupé variant. Enzo Ferrari is said to have called the XK-E the most beautiful car in the world. It was also progressive: four disc brakes, an independent suspension with telescopic dampers at the rear, 'inboard' brakes against the rear differential, a self-supporting bodywork, an engine with double overhead camshafts, and so on. Moreover, it was much cheaper than its competitors, selling more than 70,000 units. When Jaguar increased cylinder capacity from 3.8 to 4.2 liters in 1964, power dropped from 265 to barely 170 hp: new emissions standards in California required new carburettors. Power increased again with the introduction of a V12 in the Series 3, although that series is now the least sought-after among collectors.

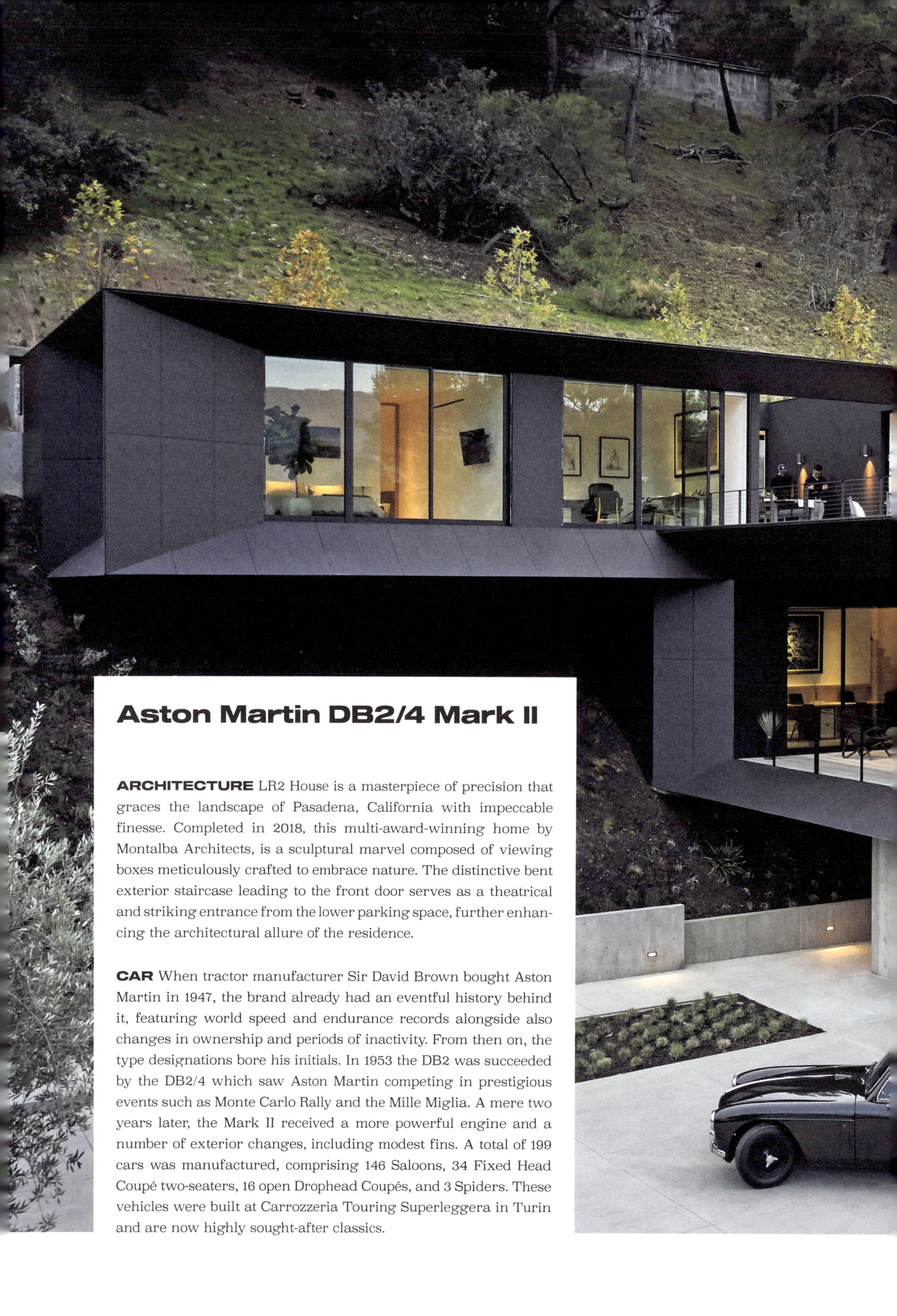

Aston Martin DB2/4 Mark II

ARCHITECTURE LR2 House is a masterpiece of precision that graces the landscape of Pasadena, California with impeccable finesse. Completed in 2018, this multi-award-winning home by Montalba Architects, is a sculptural marvel composed of viewing boxes meticulously crafted to embrace nature. The distinctive bent exterior staircase leading to the front door serves as a theatrical and striking entrance from the lower parking space, further enhancing the architectural allure of the residence.

CAR When tractor manufacturer Sir David Brown bought Aston Martin in 1947, the brand already had an eventful history behind it, featuring world speed and endurance records alongside also changes in ownership and periods of inactivity. From then on, the type designations bore his initials. In 1953 the DB2 was succeeded by the DB2/4 which saw Aston Martin competing in prestigious events such as Monte Carlo Rally and the Mille Miglia. A mere two years later, the Mark II received a more powerful engine and a number of exterior changes, including modest fins. A total of 199 cars was manufactured, comprising 146 Saloons, 34 Fixed Head Coupé two-seaters, 16 open Drophead Coupés, and 3 Spiders. These vehicles were built at Carrozzeria Touring Superleggera in Turin and are now highly sought-after classics.

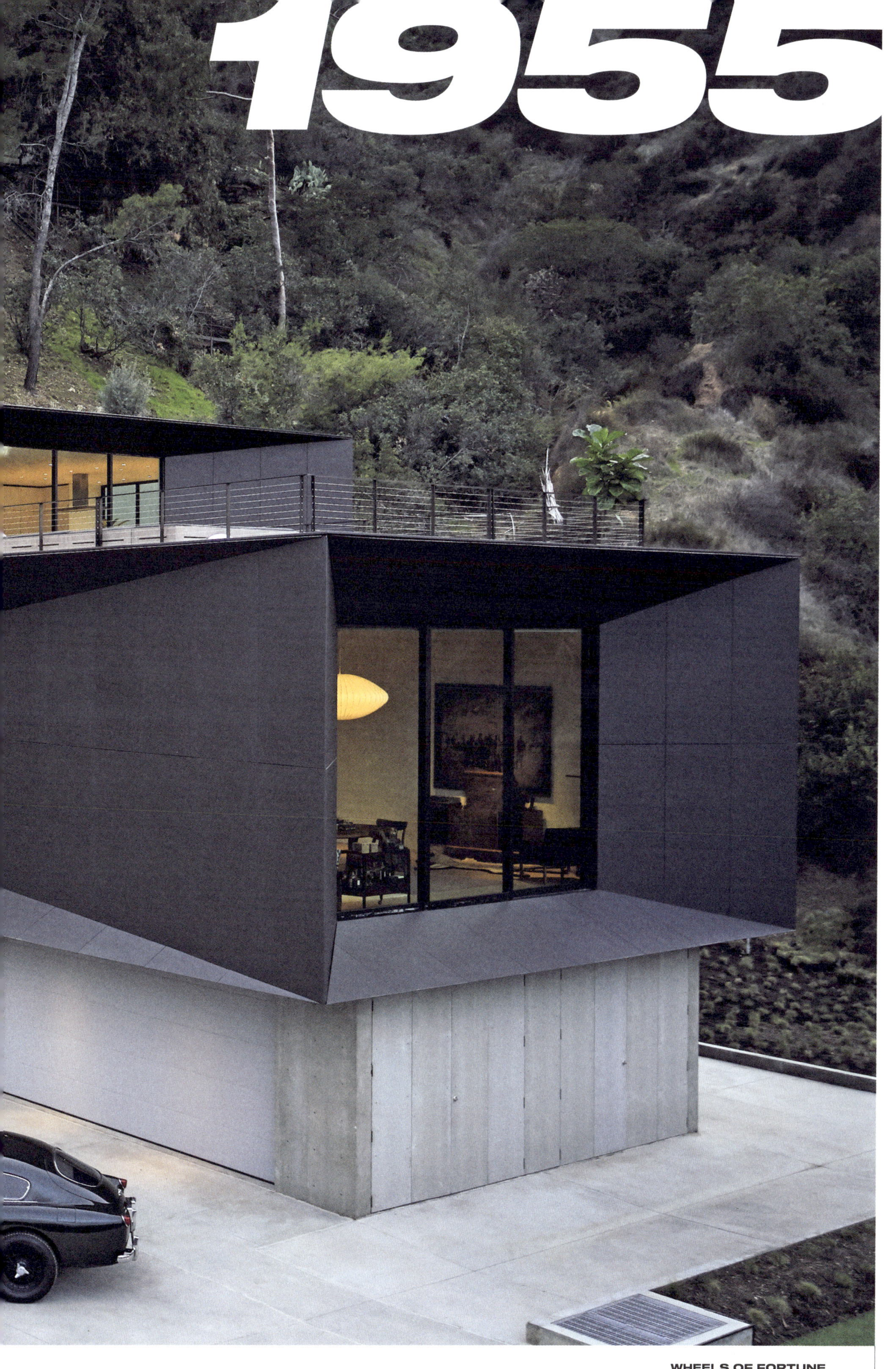
1955

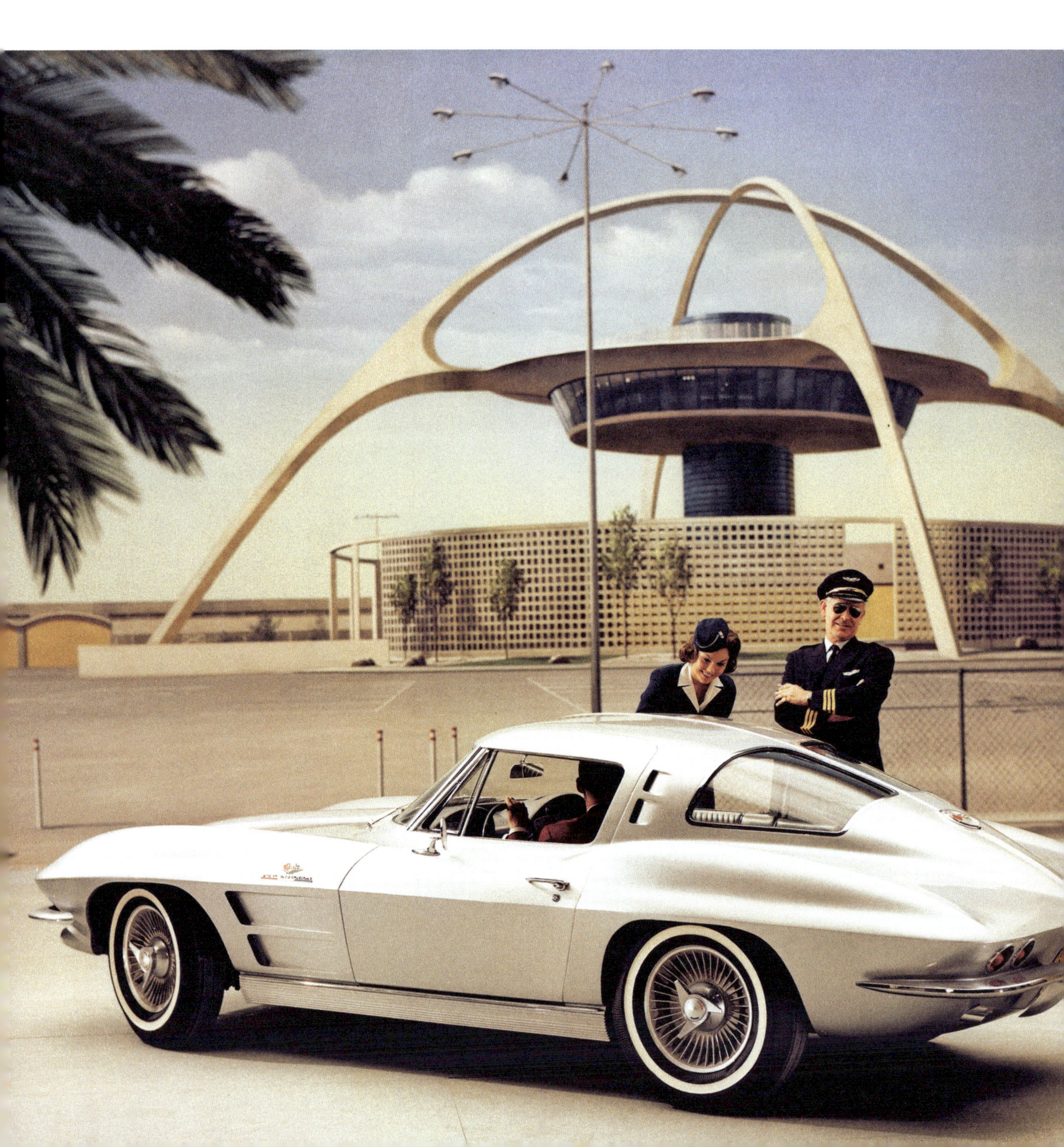

Chevrolet Corvette Sting Ray 289

ARCHITECTURE Resembling a flying saucer on four elongated legs, the Theme Building at Los Angeles Airport (LAX) is instantly recognizable. This unique structure represents the pinnacle of Googie architecture, a futuristic post-war architectural style characterized by a very distinctive Space Age aesthetic, often referred to as Populuxe or Doo Wop. The term 'Googie' takes its name from Googie's Coffee Shop in Hollywood, a creation by the renowned American architect John Lautner (1911–1994).
LAX's Theme Building was not designed by Lautner, but by the architectural firm Pereira & Luckman. When this Space Age landmark was realized from 1957 to 1961, Paul R. Williams was working for that firm. Williams, a name that may ring a bell, was the first African-American architect to be licensed in the United States. He graced the cityscape of Los Angeles with some 3,000 buildings, including prestigious villas for Frank Sinatra and Lucille Ball. The Beverly Hills Hotel, an iconic Hollywood establishment, displays William's legacy in a literal sense: the hotel sign bears his distinctive handwriting.

CAR After World War II, Americans were crazy about European sports cars. So much so that the urge to build their own took hold, adapted to their own circumstances. In January 1953, Chevrolet presented the Corvette at Motorama, GM's mobile car show that toured major cities with new models and prototypes at the beginning of each year. That year, the event took place in the lobby of the Waldorf Astoria Hotel in New York. The public was wild about the car and GM started production that same year. That Corvette was a design by Harley Earl with an innovative body made of fiberglass. Here we see the second generation (1963–1967), designed by Larry Shinoda. The 'Mako Shark' display model was inspired by the eponymous shark, brough to mind by the typical optical break line across the entire side and the sharply sloping roof. The coupé version of the final model was named Sting Ray, later Stingray. The car had fuel injection, which was exceptional in the US. The experimental split rear windshield tells us that the car in this image is of the model year 1963. Together with the grilles in the hood, it makes these versions highly desirable. There have been eight generations of the Corvette, designated C1 to C8.

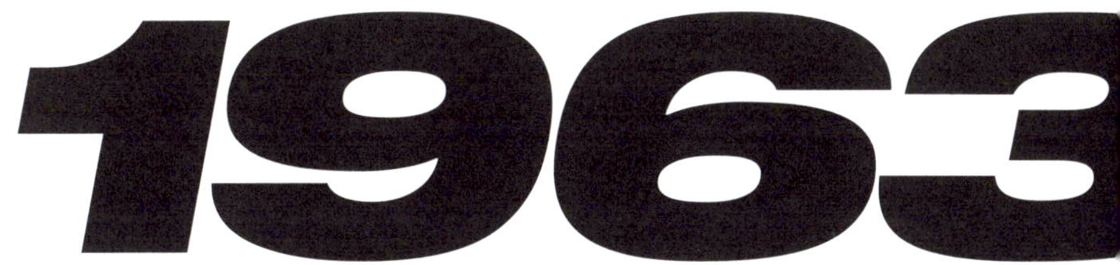

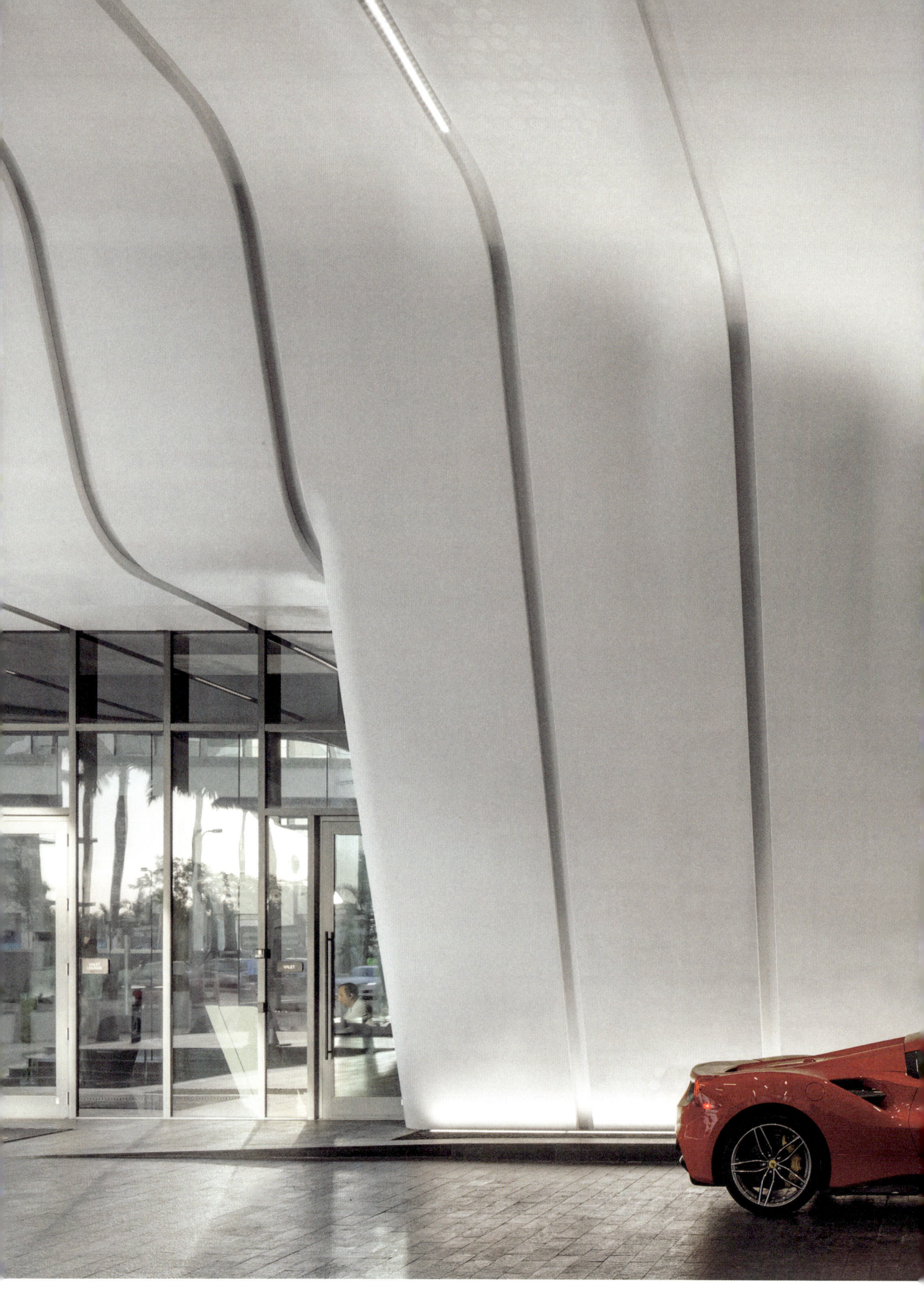
VALET

Ferrari 488 Spider

ARCHITECTURE Many architects harbor a silent dream of one day designing a car. Zaha Hadid was one of those who turned this dream into reality. Unlike Frank Lloyd Wright and Le Corbusier, who never ventured into car design, the Iraqi-British architect accomplished this feat. With her firm, she designed in 2006–2007 the Z-car I and II, a revolutionary concept for compact city cars powered by rechargeable lithium batteries.
Hadid's architectural prowess also extended to the automotive industry. Between 2002 and 2005 she designed the BMW Central Building in Leipzig, Germany, leaving her mark on the world of automotive architecture.
At the time of Hadid's premature death in 2016, her major residential project in Miami, One Thousand Museum had not quite been completed. The curvy 62-story residential tower faces Museum Park, hence its misleading name. The tower's organic exoskeleton design not only enhances the building's aesthetic appeal but also ensures that the interior spaces boast flowing lines, devoid of cumbersome load-bearing pillars. Perfect for showcasing beautiful cars.

CAR In 2015 the Ferrari 488 succeeded the 458, which had been nothing short of a quantum leap for Ferrari. Here we see the Spider variant with retractable roof. And it wasn't just a facelift: much had also changed under the hood. It had been since the F40 (1987–1992) that Ferrari had launched a mid-engine car. A V8 biturbo engine too, in this case with a capacity of 3.9 liters and the fastest-responding turbo engine in the world. As in its predecessors, that explosive heart is visible under glass and produces 670 hp at 8,000 rpm, to which the later Pista version added an extra 50 hp. When it appeared, the seven-speed gearbox was also one of the fastest shifting on the planet.

2015

The Man who Shaped America

What is the connection between Ian Fleming, Frank Sinatra, Shirley Bassey and Alice Cooper? Surprisingly, they all drove a Studebaker. And what is the connection between Studebaker, the Shell logo and the Lucky Strike cigarette pack? They were all designed by prolific French-American designer Raymond Loewy (1893–1986). The numerous successful products (and logos) he designed made him one of the great influencers of America's post-war consumer culture, earning him the epithet 'The Man who Shaped America.' Given his extensive portfolio, Loewy is sometimes likened to Philippe Starck, hailed as 'the man who has designed everything,' but he could similarly be labeled 'the Jony Ive of his time.' Ive is the brilliant designer responsible for creating Apple's iconic products from 1997 to 2019 using clean minimalist lines. Half a century earlier, 'cleanlining' was also Loewy's credo. He consistently sought to omit superfluous design elements, retaining only the essence. This was one of the great secrets of his commercial success.

REFRIGERATORS FOR ESKIMOS

Raymond Loewy's career isn't only an exemplar for product designers; it also serves as a comprehensive case study in PR, branding and communication. With his distinctive personality, Loewy possessed an unparaleled understanding of how to play the media. His main purpose was to draw attention to the products he had meticulously designed.

Loewy had a knack for the proverbial task of 'selling refrigerators to Eskimos,' a testament to his prowess in salesmanship. His personal touch graced Sears Coldspot refrigerators, which sold like hotcakes, with a staggering increase in sales from 15,000 to 275,000 units within five years. This incredible success was not attributed to their superior cooling properties, but rather to their sheer aesthetic allure. For the French-American designer, the look and feel of consumer goods were as important as their technical composition. His philosophy was straightforward: "When faced with two products equal in price, function and quality, the one with a more attractive exterior will win."

STREAMLINED BULLET TRAIN

Does this same principle extend to the cars, buses and trains Loewy designed? Did his work in transportation surpass the level of the vacuum cleaners and refrigerators he designed? Were his car designs primarily focused on the bodywork, with little attention to the mechanics under the hood? Did he approach car design with the same philosophy as he would an American kitchen or a Coca-Cola bottle?

Undoubtedly, Loewy's impact on the transportation sector was as substantial as his impact on the consumer goods market. His role as a designer at prestigious entities, such as car manufacturer Studebaker, bus company Greyhound and Pennsylvania Railroad, underscored the extent of his influence. It must have been quite something when, at the 1939 World's Fair in New York, Loewy presented the Pennsylvania Railroad (PRR) S1 class steam locomotive. A streamlined bullet train, this model was so different from any other that it effortlessly stole the spotlight. To this day bullet trains traverse the globe bearing the mark of his iconic design. The locomotive's distinctive nose even served as inspiration for Loewy's own Studebaker car models of the early 1950s.

ARCHITECTURAL CAR CONCEPT

Studebaker was not the first car brand for whom Loewy worked. His first venture into the US automotive sector was in the early 1930s, when he was commissioned by the Hupp Motor Car Company in 1932 to work on the Hupp Cyclefender, a flashy update of the rather stiff Hupmobile. Despite its impressive specs, sales were disappointing. The same goes for Loewy's next car design, the 1934 Hupp Aerodynamic. Fortunately for Loewy, when Hupp Motor Car Company went out of business in 1940, this didn't put an end to his automotive adventure. Since 1936 he had been working as a freelance design consultant for Studebaker, founded in 1852. This fruitful collaboration would last until 1962. Loewy had already redesigned the logo in the 1930s and made updates to some existing models, achieving success along the way. Notably, his 1938 Studebaker President earned the title of 'best-looking car of the year.'

Following the war, from 1946, Loewy increasingly left his mark on Studebaker's vehicle lineup, including his masterpiece Commander. As Bruno Sacco writes in his book *Raymond Loewy: Pioneer of American Industrial Design*:

> ***Here was something totally new: where the shape of the car had hitherto been largely determined by functional components such as fenders and hood, there was now an overall architectural concept of the automobile.***

In the 1950s Loewy's influence on the car industry continued to grow. He recognized that with Studebaker, unlike industry giants such as General Motors, Chrysler or Ford, he had the opportunity to forge a historic legacy by introducing something entirely new. Reflecting on this, he remarked, "I was given the opportunity to design cars liberated from most of Detroit's atavistic influence. No more inbred, incestuous designs. Instead, a fresh, new approach for a century-old respectable firm was demanded."

CAR HISTORY

Loewy was specifically seeking innovation in terms of weight and handling. This drive for innovation is precisely why his 1953 Studebaker Starliner was a huge success, especially in comparison to the releases of other major US carmakers at the time. The Starliner's popularity was so great that it appeared on the cover of *Time* magazine in February 1953 with a caption that read: 'For a sports-car era, a long, low whistle-stopper.' The revolutionary model etched its name into American car history. According to Loewy's biographer John Wall, "Car designers would not make a similar great leap forward until Ford redesigned the Thunderbird and Taunus in the 1980s."

In 1954 Studebaker merged with Packard, leading to a slight decline in innovation. In 1962 Loewy made another substantial impact with the long-awaited Studebaker Avanti, which became an instant classic. "The fiberglass-bodied sports car featured razor-like fenders sweeping into a raised rear end, a wedge-shaped front end, and safety features including a roll bar, disc brakes and a padded interior. The interior, a direct steal from airliners, featured an overhead console and controls that resembled jet throttles. The overall effect was a startling silhouette, unequalled to this day," writes John Wall, author of *Streamliner: Raymond Loewy and Image-making in the Age of American Industrial Design*. The designer himself said of his Studebaker Avanti: "If I were to redesign it, I would keep it much the same."

AN EARLY INFLUENCER

Raymond Loewy is a fine example of an entrepreneur who achieved his American dream. Raised in Paris, he moved to the US with his brother in 1919, after the death of their parents. The story goes that he entered a sketch in a talent contest aboard the ship en route to New York, catching the attention of Henry Armstrong, the British consul in New York, who also happened to be on board. Through Armstrong's contacts, Loewy was afforded his first opportunities in the world of illustration and design. Initially, he made a career as a fashion illustrator and designer of travel ads in the art deco style. Although he was making a good living, he grew tired of the industry around 1930, increasingly critical of the ugly designs that surrounded him. This dissatisfaction prompted him to establish his own design studio.

With his American sense of entrepreneurship and European sense of style, he successfully garnered an eclectic array of clients, ranging from American Tobacco to Exxon, from Air Force One to NASA's Skylab. His design studio thrived, riding the promotional wave that Loewy himself had become. As an early influencer, he diligently marketed himself and turned every product launch into a media event. He made sure he attended the right events and he socialized extensively in elite circles. His conspicuous presence was further accentuated by custom-designed cars that stole the limelight.

Even Loewy's homes served as vehicles for self-promotion. While he lived in a classy flat in New York, he partnered with architect Albert Frey to build a remarkable house in Palm Springs between 1946 and 1947. His neighbor was Edgar J. Kaufmann, renowned foe commissioning Richard Neutra's legendary

Kaufmann House in Palm Springs, as well as Frank Lloyd Wright's masterpiece, Fallingwater, in Pennsylvania. Surprisingly modest for a celebrity who graced the cover of *Time* magazine in 1949, Loewy's house framed the captivating landscape of Palm Springs through its glass structure. A standout feature, however, was the illuminated swimming pool, which, in Loewy's words, "resembles a blue lagoon in a desert oasis." Regrettably, the Loewy family no longer owns this private residence. Nonetheless, if the current owner ever contemplates venturing into carchitecture, embellishing this iconic house with the perfect car will be as easy as pie. Unquestionably, a 1962 Studebaker Avanti would do the trick.

"A car has all the ingredients of architecture, except it's mobile. It moves, it relocates, it traverses. But otherwise, it's answering so many of the requirements of architecture."

Sir Norman Foster, architect

CARCHITECTURE NOW

Ford Bronco

ARCHITECTURE This elegant three-story contemporary home was designed by Brett Rhode, founder of the Austin-based architecture firm Rhode Partners. It is nestled in the sought-after Boudlin Creek neighborhood, in the green outskirts of Austin. Located on Dawson Road, both Dawson and Austin would have been perfect car pairings for this contemporary villa. None of both legendary brands rests under the spectacular carport. What we see here is a robust Ford Bronco, a legendary off-road vehicle that evokes the weathered Corten steel that envelops the home's foundation. This Bronco is proudly owned by Brett Rhode himself, who likes to tinker with it in his basement studio, alongside his restoration project of a small plane.

CAR This 'early' Ford Bronco was originally conceived as a compact Sports Utility Vehicle (SUV), even before the term was coined. Ford Motor Company wanted this car to compete with the Jeep CJ-5, the International Harvester Scout, and Land Rover and Toyota models. Product manager Donald N. Frey, who had previously overseen the development of the Mustang, spearheaded this project. In its inaugural year of 1966, the four-wheel off-road vehicle for civilian use was equipped with an inline 6-cylinder engine. Shortly after, it offered a V8 engine option. The Bronco was available in different versions, including Wagon, Pick-Up and Roadster. Over time, six generations of the Bronco were produced, although there is admittedly a 25-year gap between them, as the model was discontinued in 1996, before being revived in 2021.

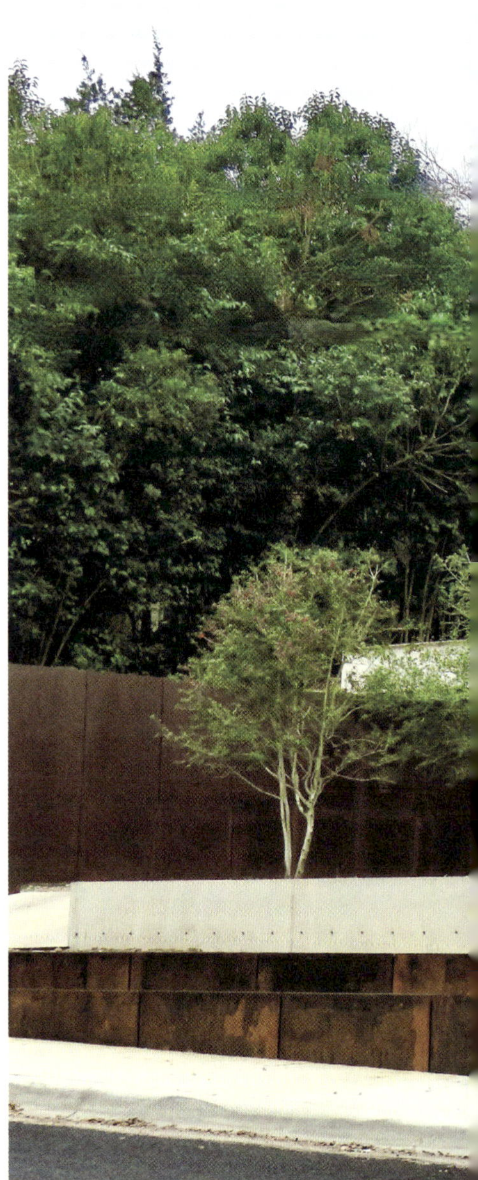

1966

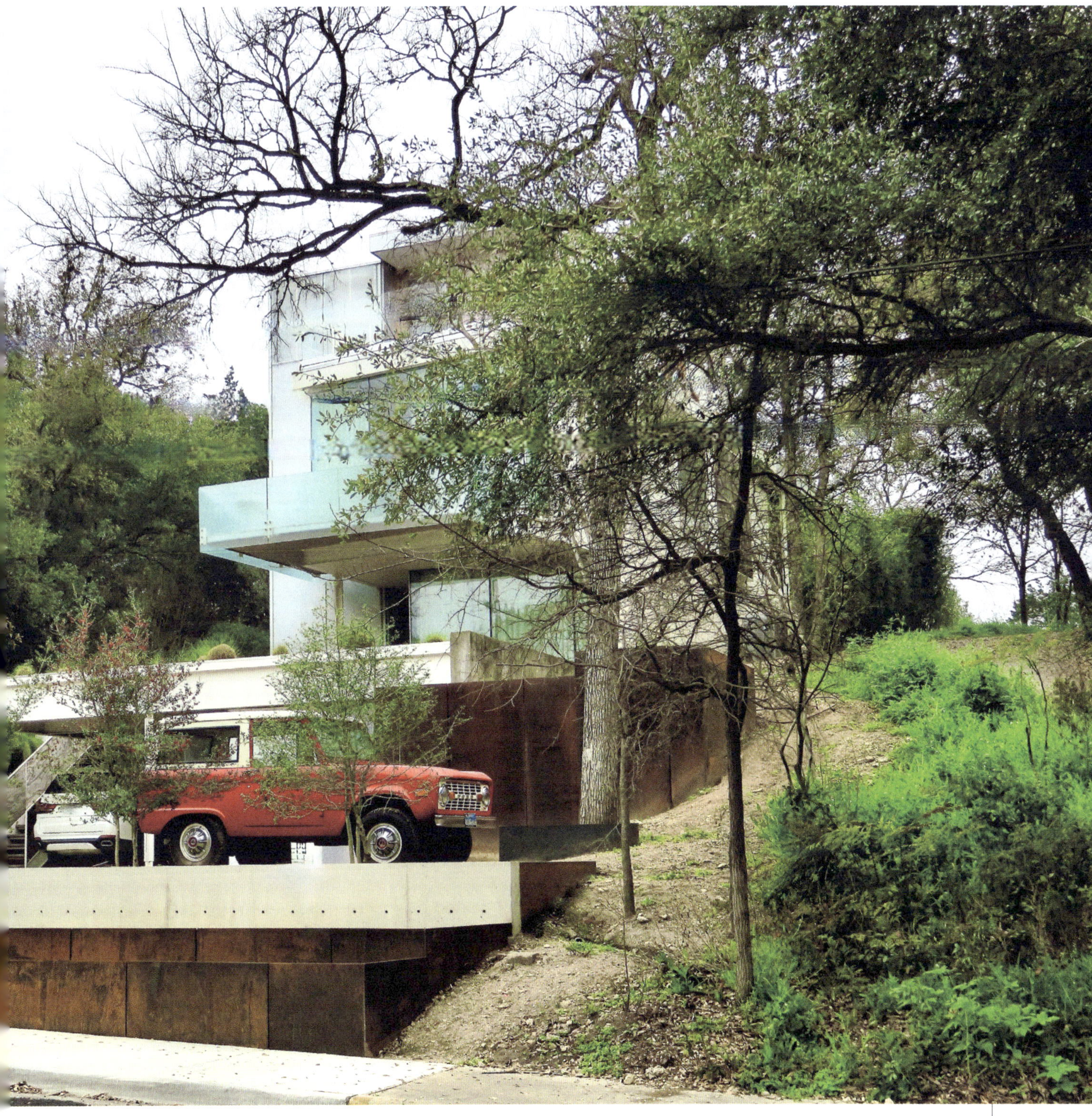

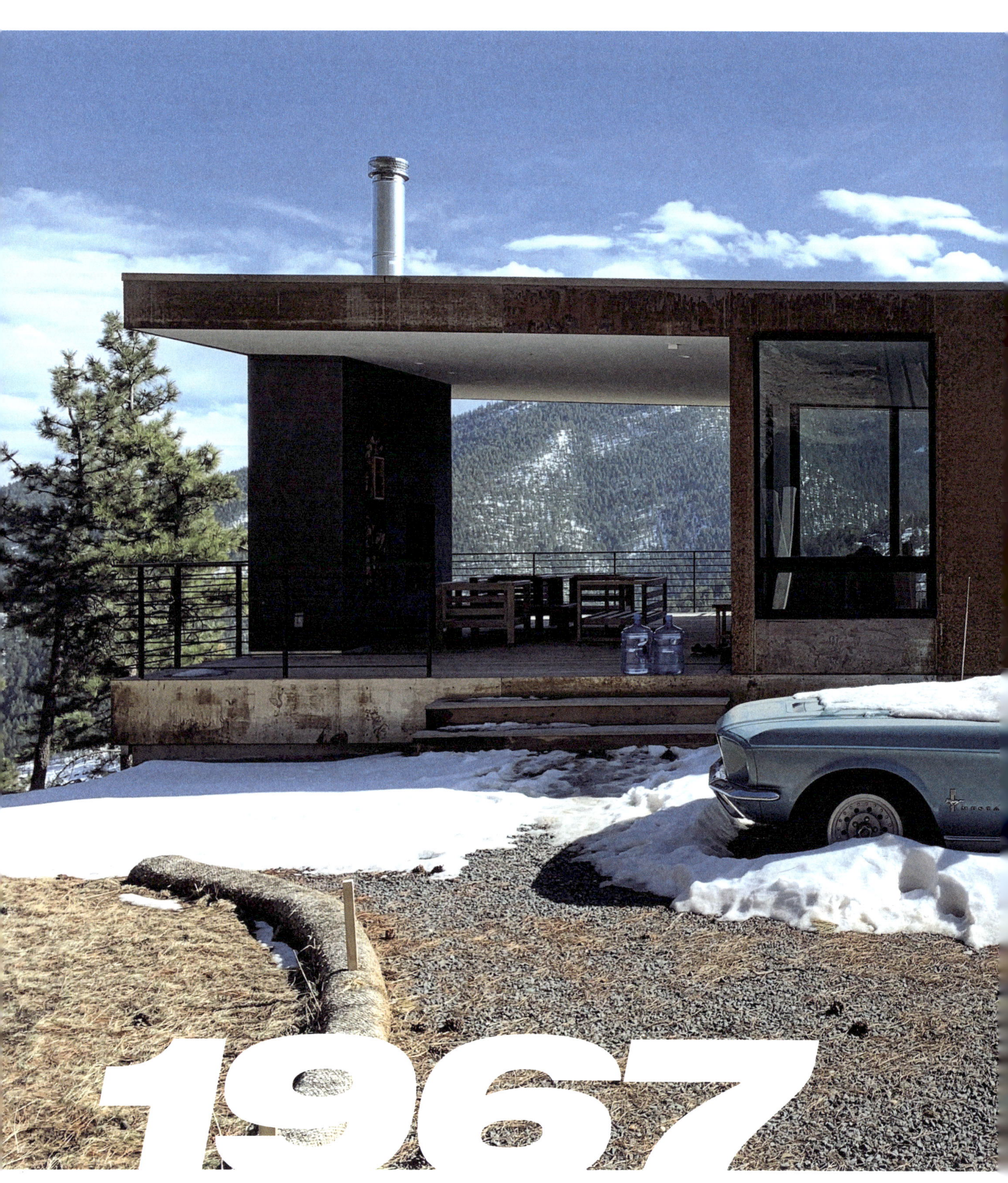
1967

Ford Mustang Hardtop Coupé

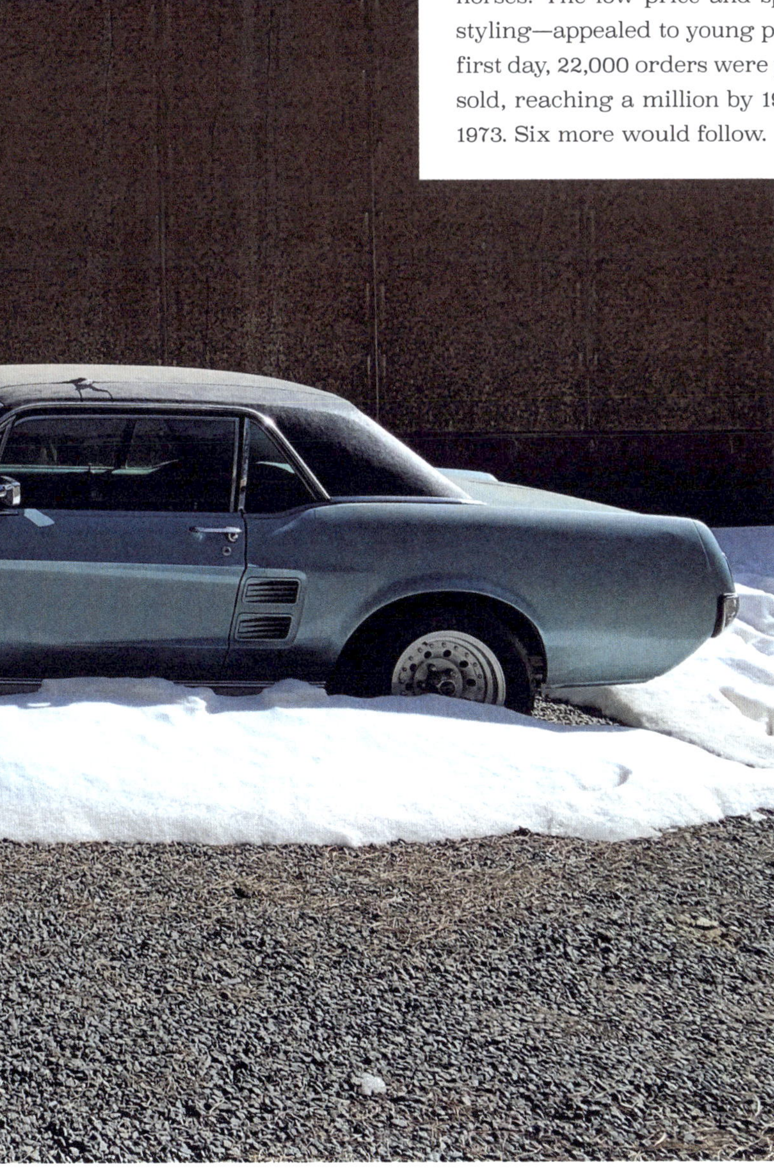

ARCHITECTURE The winding road leading to the 'Puma Run House' seems custom-made for the 1967 Ford Mustang parked in front. Situated amidst the picturesque landscapes of Denver, Colorado, this spectacular home, designed by Arch11, offers breathtaking views of the surrounding mountains. It is dubbed 'Puma Run House' due to its location between two mountains frequented by mountain lions (pumas), often spotted on their way to creeks where they look for food.

CAR "If on April 17, 1964 Martians had landed in downtown New York, no one would have noticed because everybody was at a Ford dealership." It is a legendary quote by then Ford executive Lee Lacocca. In its battle with the Chevrolet Corvair Monza, Ford showed the Mustang for the first time that day at the World's Fair in the Big Apple. The name of the model came about because stylist John Najjar was a fan of the eponymous fighter plane, the P-51 Mustang. But Henry Ford II didn't want an image associated with war, and so the name and logo were hung on the prairie and wild American horses. The low price and sporty look with long hood and short deck—Coke bottle styling—appealed to young people and made the Mustang an instant success. On that first day, 22,000 orders were placed. Four months later, 100,000 cars had already been sold, reaching a million by 1966. That first generation remained on the market until 1973. Six more would follow.

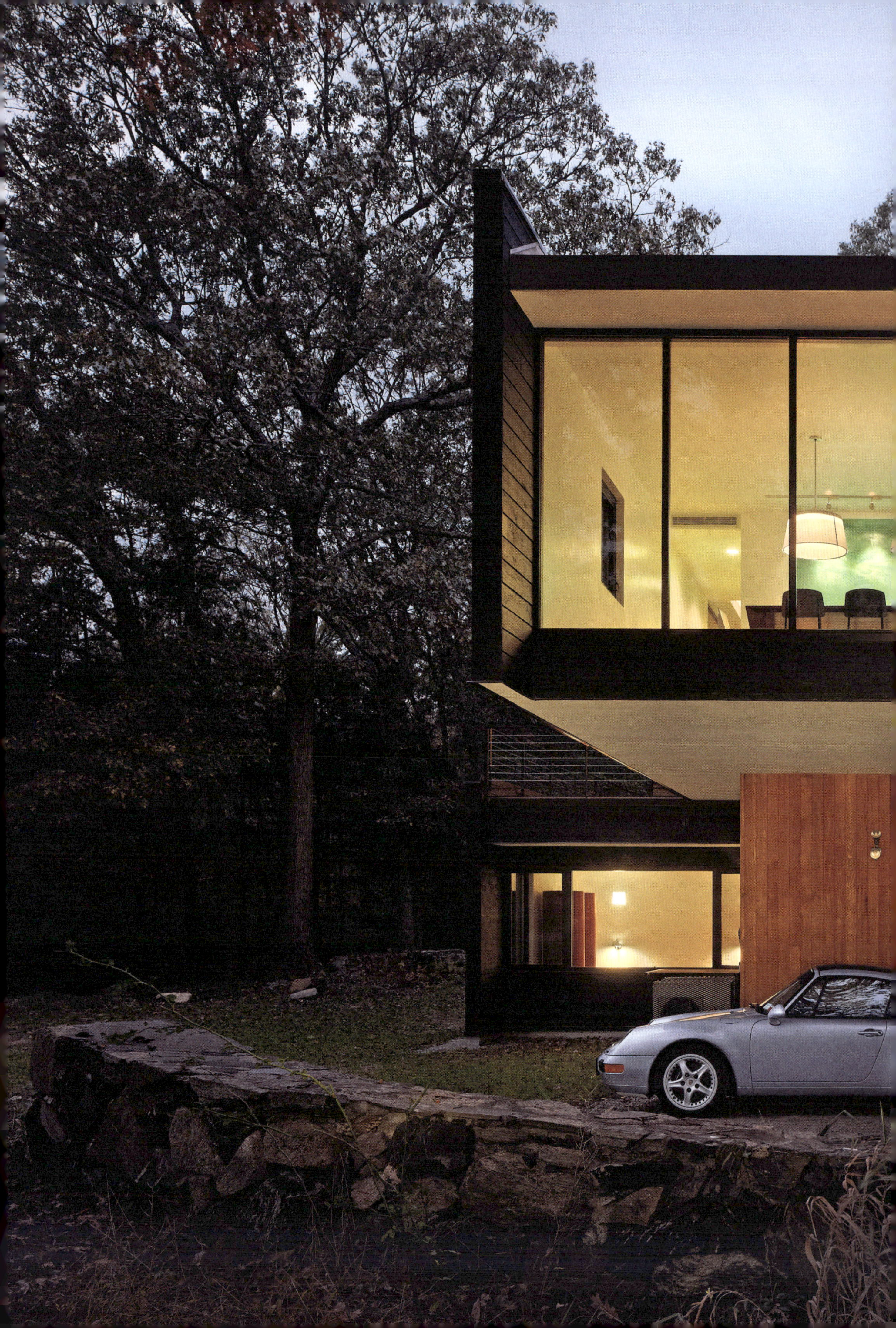

Porsche 993 Targa

ARCHITECTURE In this idyllic holiday home in Waccabuc, Westchester County, New York, you are greeted each morning with the scent of the woods. That was precisely the ambience that architect couple Chan-li Lin and Denise Ferris aimed to create when they demolished the old house on this wooded property. On the foundations, they built a new holiday home, complete with spectacular canopies spanning 10 feet (6 meters) on either side.
Their design was a reinterpretation of the Prairie School house, which provides impressive vistas of the natural surroundings and a perfect shelter beneath the canopies for a complementary car. Chan-li Lin worked for 22 years at Rafael Viñoly Architects, a renowned firm founded by Rafael Viñoly, an influential architect with Uruguayan roots who died in March 2023. Despite Viñoly's impressive body of work, his legacy also includes some controversial designs, such as the London Walkie Talkie tower in Fenchurch Street, whose windows generated enormous heat through reflection, reportedly causing car paint and plastic body parts on parked cars to melt, serving as an example of Carchitecture with unintended consequences.

CAR The Porsche 993 was produced from late 1993 to early 1998. It was the final and most evolved version of the air-cooled boxer engine 911 series, making it one of the most sought-after classic Porsches. In 1996 this Targa version entered the market, featuring a large, electrically operated sunroof made of tinted, laminated glass, a departure from the earlier removable soft top. This design change meant the omission of the distinctive rollbar, altering the car's appearance and causing some to question its authenticity as a Targa. Subsequent 991 models reintroduced the 'real' Targa.

1996

1997

Porsche 996

ARCHITECTURE In 2015, the Petersen Automotive Museum in California underwent a substantial facelift. Rather than demolishing the unremarkable existing structure, Kohn Pedersen Fox Associates (KPF) decided to envelop the former department store in a striking 'gift wrap.' This transformation featured elegant stainless steel 'ribbons' that dynamically draped around the once sterile tower block. The project required a staggering 100 tons of steel and 140,000 screws.
Inspired by the automotive world, the stainless-steel wrapping bears a striking resemblance to an abstract racing circuit. The design concept aimed "to express constant motion, suggesting speed, aerodynamics and the movement of air," as explained by KPF's Eugene Kohn. Visitors to the Petersen Automotive Museum are greeted with an equally ambitious interior. The museum offers an immersive experience, allowing visitors to explore the rich history of automobiles, racing and film. The collection includes iconic cars such as Elvis Presley's De Tomaso Pantera, and a Jaguar XKSS owned by Steve McQueen.

CAR Few car aficionados were happy when Porsche introduced the 996 in 1997, so different from the classic 911 with its air-cooled boxer engine and thrilling sound that had made the car an icon since 1964. Its front-end design and dashboard layout, plucked straight from the much cheaper Boxster, were thorns in their side. Yet despite the often-heard critique, the 996 became a commercial success, selling 175,000 units. Today, the car can be purchased relatively cheaply, and opinions are quietly evolving, with some now considering it a genuine 911 and good value for money.

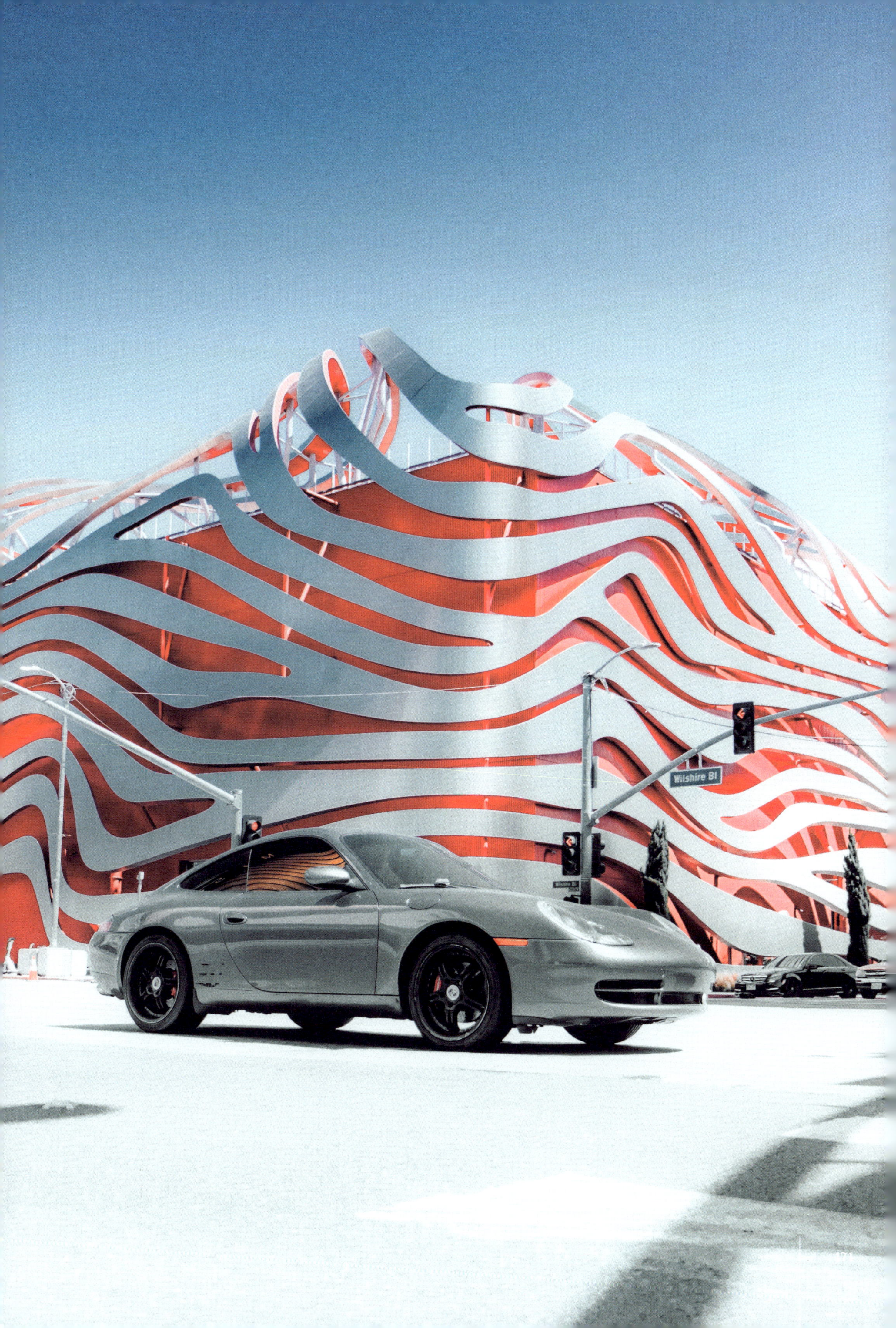
Wilshire Bl

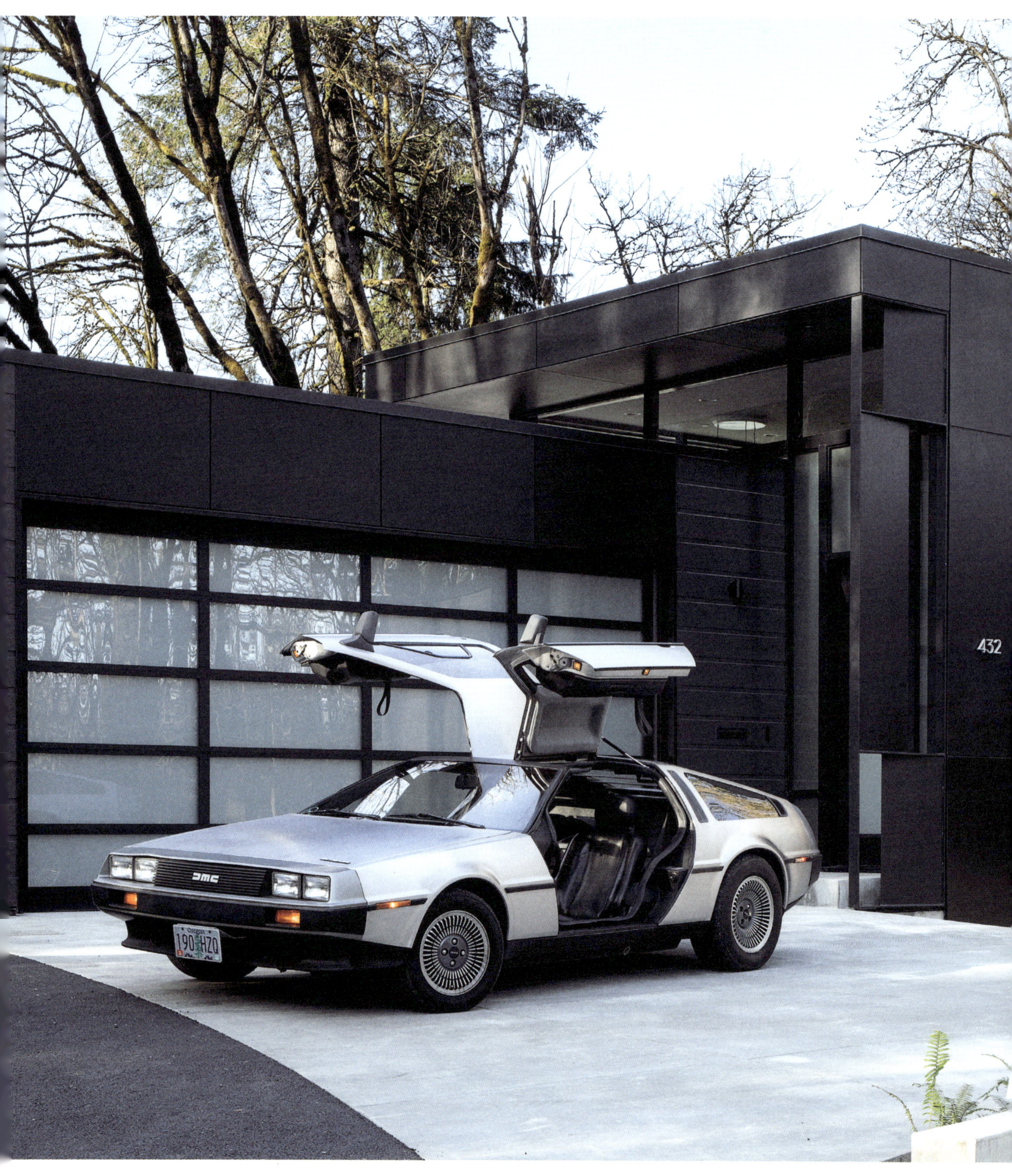
432
DMC

Delorean DMC-12

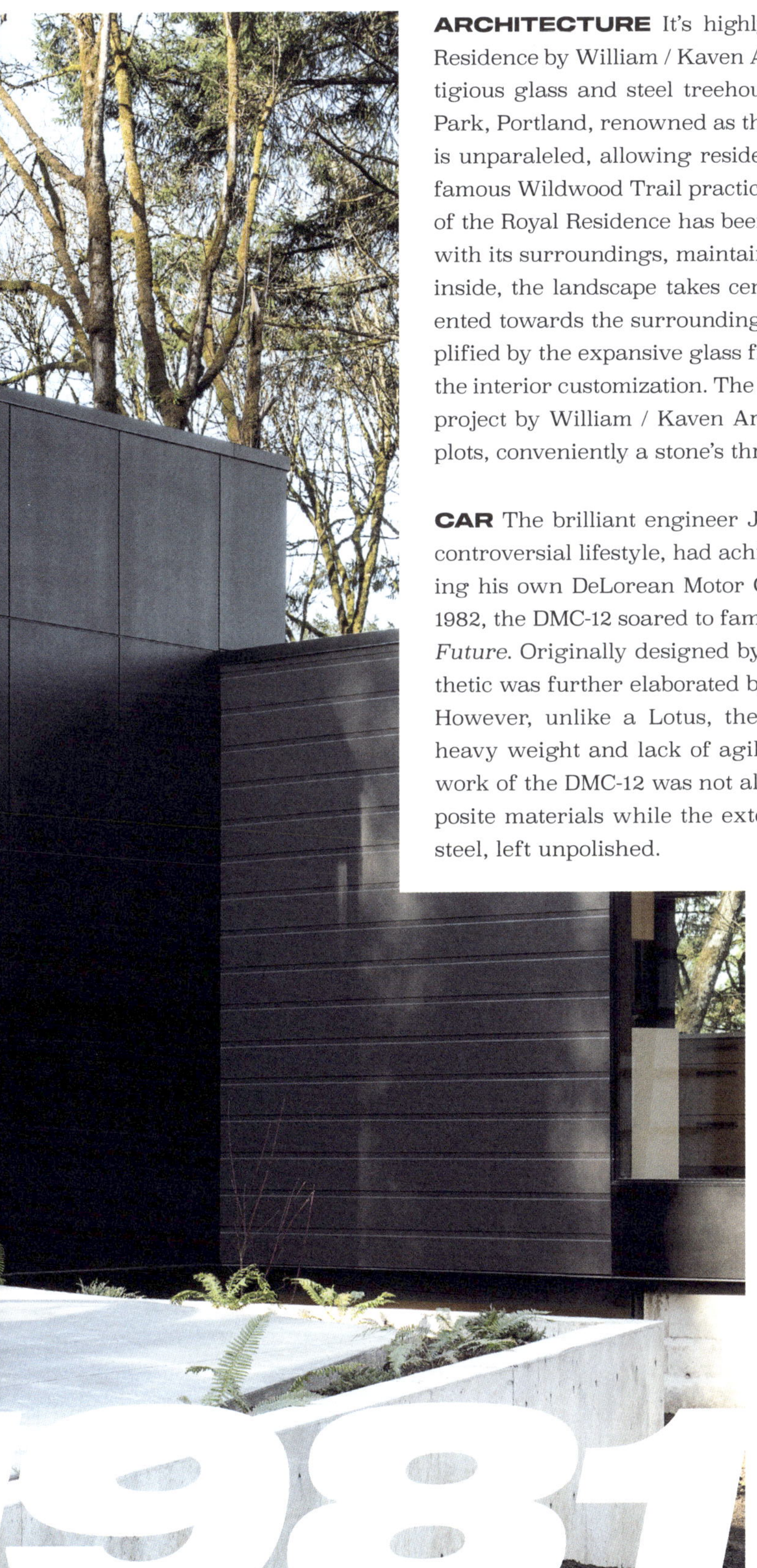

ARCHITECTURE It's highly unlikely that you would pass by this Royal Residence by William / Kaven Architecture without being captivated. The prestigious glass and steel treehouse is situated along a winding road in Forest Park, Portland, renowned as the largest public park in any US city. Its location is unparaleled, allowing residents to immerse themselves in nature, with the famous Wildwood Trail practically at their doorstep. The exterior architecture of the Royal Residence has been meticulously designed to blend harmoniously with its surroundings, maintaining a discreet presence amidst the trees. Once inside, the landscape takes center stage, with the residence thoughtfully oriented towards the surrounding wilderness. The international design is exemplified by the expansive glass front and the generous use of oak and walnut in the interior customization. The Royal Residence is part of a larger development project by William / Kaven Architecture and Kaven + Co, and is one of nine plots, conveniently a stone's throw away from downtown Portland.

CAR The brilliant engineer John DeLorean, known for his flamboyant and controversial lifestyle, had achieved success at Pontiac of GM before establishing his own DeLorean Motor Company. Manufactured in Belfast in 1981 and 1982, the DMC-12 soared to fame as the time machine in the movie *Back to the Future*. Originally designed by Giorgeto Giugiaro, the car's flat, angular aesthetic was further elaborated by Lotus founder Colin Chapman.
However, unlike a Lotus, the DeLorean DMC-12 was characterized by its heavy weight and lack of agility. Despite popular misconceptions, the bodywork of the DMC-12 was not aluminum: its inner structure was made of composite materials while the exterior was constructed of sandblasted stainless steel, left unpolished.

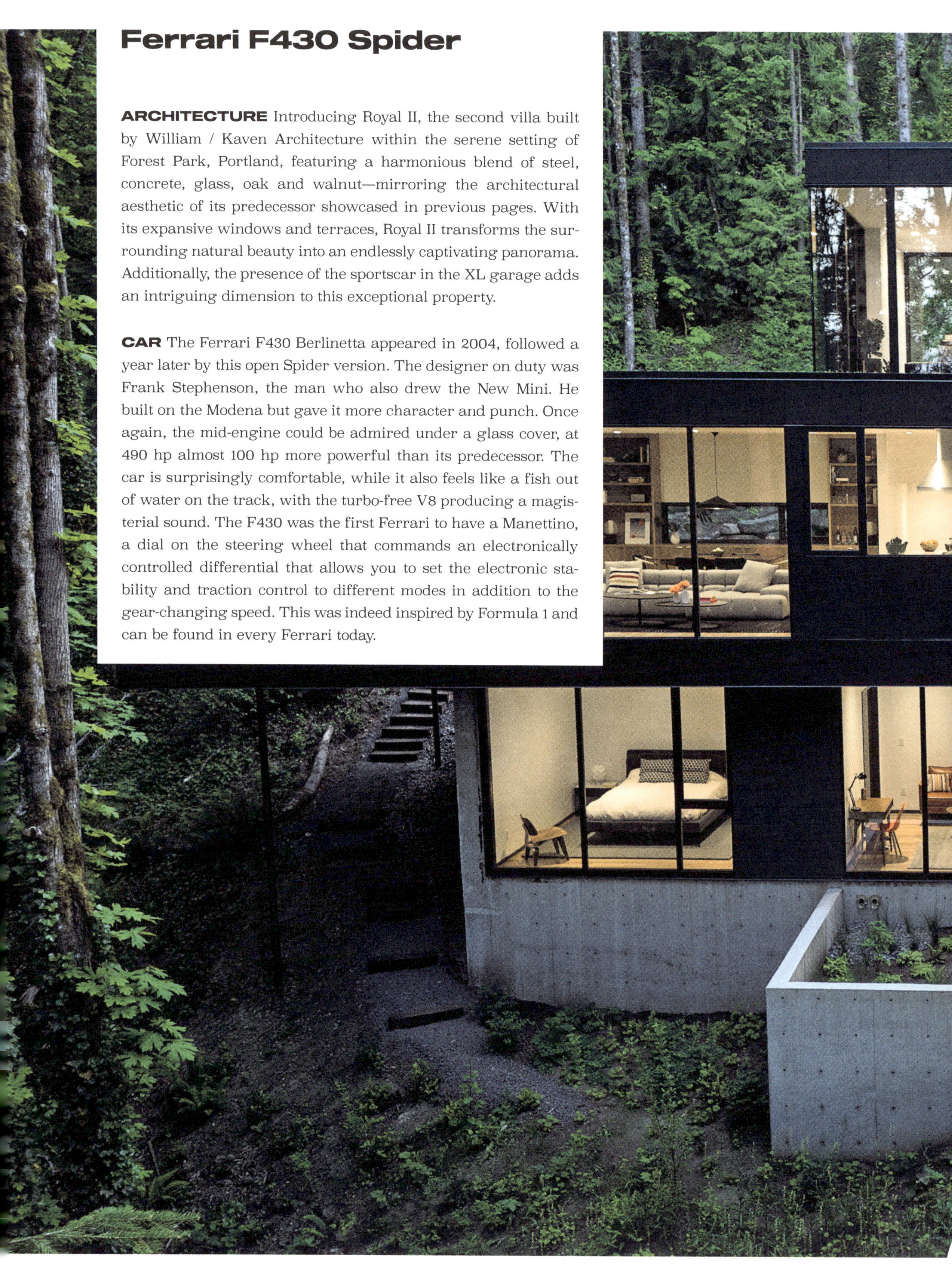

Ferrari F430 Spider

ARCHITECTURE Introducing Royal II, the second villa built by William / Kaven Architecture within the serene setting of Forest Park, Portland, featuring a harmonious blend of steel, concrete, glass, oak and walnut—mirroring the architectural aesthetic of its predecessor showcased in previous pages. With its expansive windows and terraces, Royal II transforms the surrounding natural beauty into an endlessly captivating panorama. Additionally, the presence of the sportscar in the XL garage adds an intriguing dimension to this exceptional property.

CAR The Ferrari F430 Berlinetta appeared in 2004, followed a year later by this open Spider version. The designer on duty was Frank Stephenson, the man who also drew the New Mini. He built on the Modena but gave it more character and punch. Once again, the mid-engine could be admired under a glass cover, at 490 hp almost 100 hp more powerful than its predecessor. The car is surprisingly comfortable, while it also feels like a fish out of water on the track, with the turbo-free V8 producing a magisterial sound. The F430 was the first Ferrari to have a Manettino, a dial on the steering wheel that commands an electronically controlled differential that allows you to set the electronic stability and traction control to different modes in addition to the gear-changing speed. This was indeed inspired by Formula 1 and can be found in every Ferrari today.

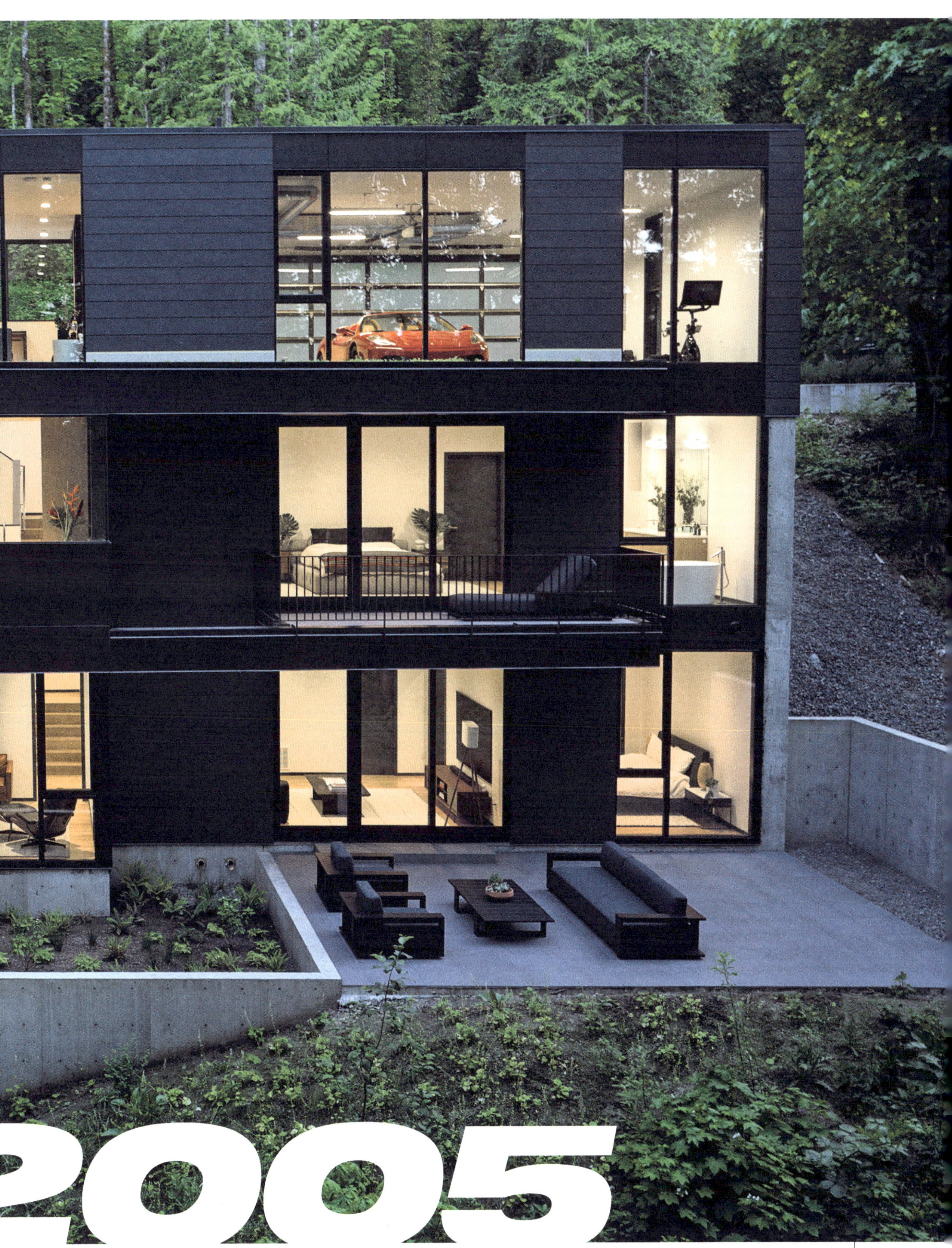
2005

1967

Volkswagen T2

ARCHITECTURE For Caleb Johnson, building with wood is as instinctive as manufacturing a car in steel. The Portland-based architect and founder of the Woodhull firm was commissioned by a Boston couple to design an energy-efficient home that would gracefully mature over time. The exterior of this contemporary barn in Maine is lined with cedar, while the interior is finished with hemlock and ash. This architectural gem is an example of a design that draws inspiration from classical aesthetics, yet possesses the qualities to withstand the test of time, much like the enduring appeal of a Volkswagen van.

CAR In 1947 Dutch Volkswagen importer Ben Pon laid the foundations for the VW van, internally known as T2 (the Beetle, on which it was based, was called T1). Production commenced in 1950, and there have been seven generations from T1 to T7. Until the arrival of the T4 in 1990, the engine was located in the rear, much like the Beetle. The model shown here is a T2, the first version with a panoramic windscreen without a central bar, and produced from 1967 to 1979, although production in Brazil continued until the end of 2013.

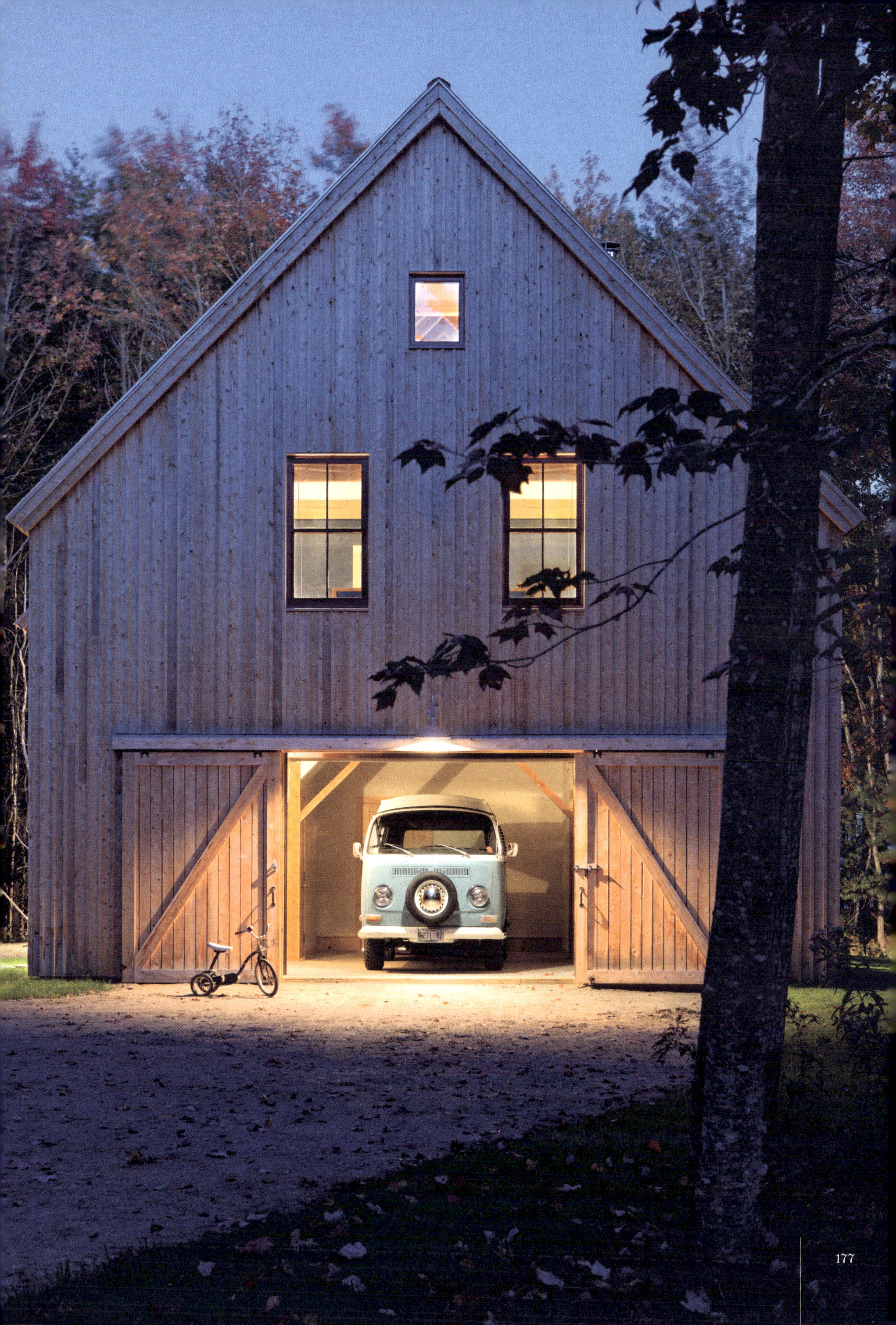

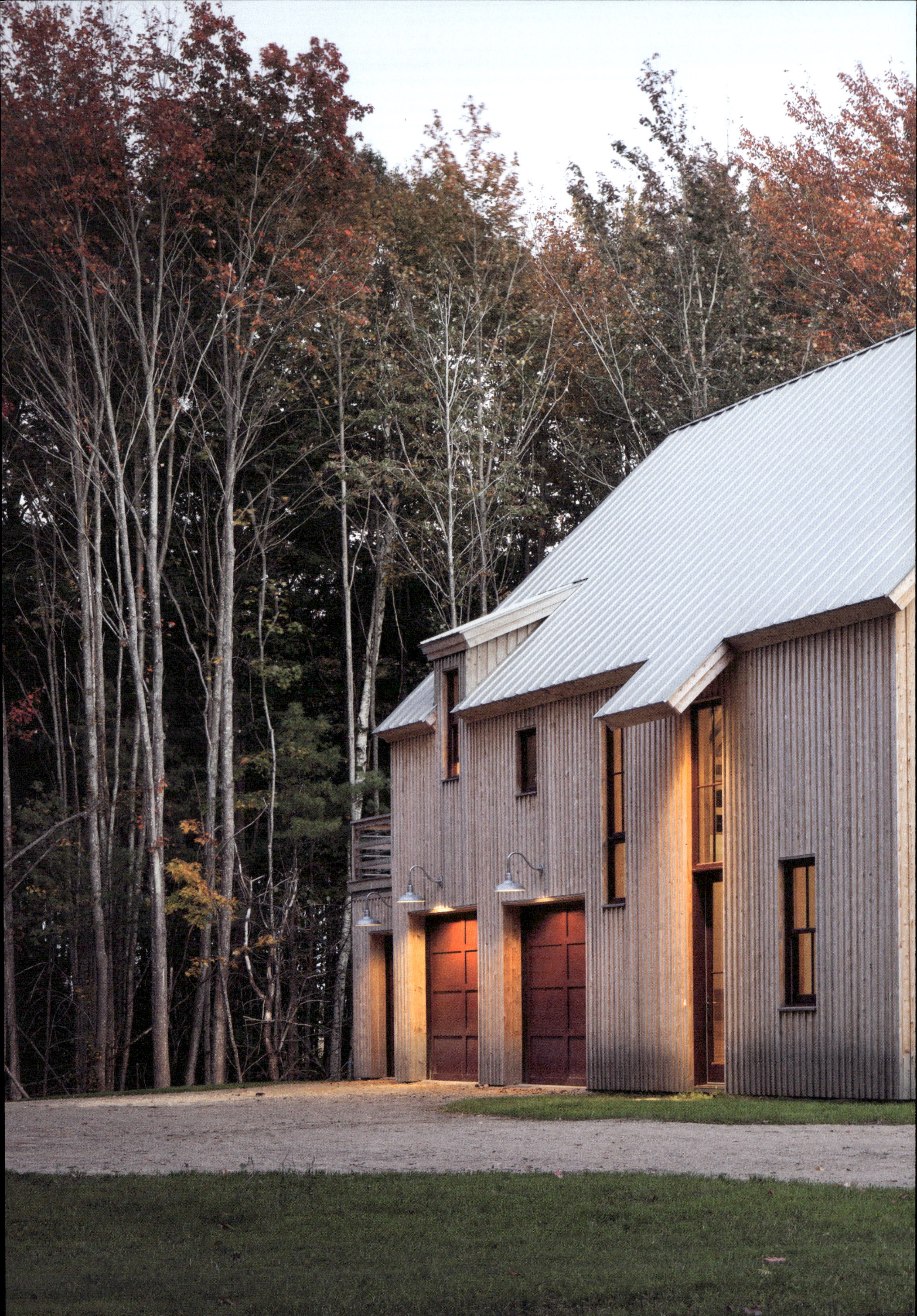

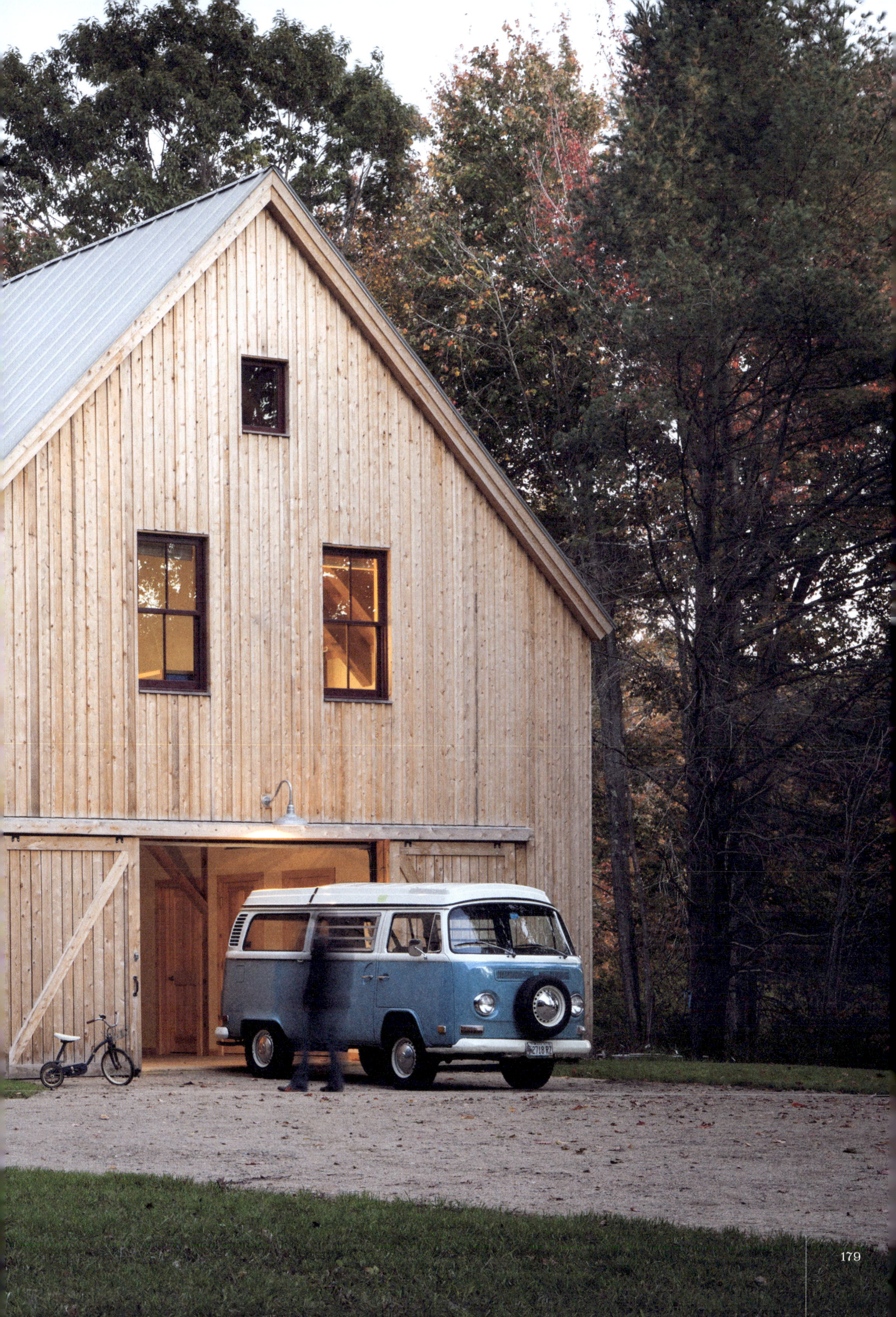

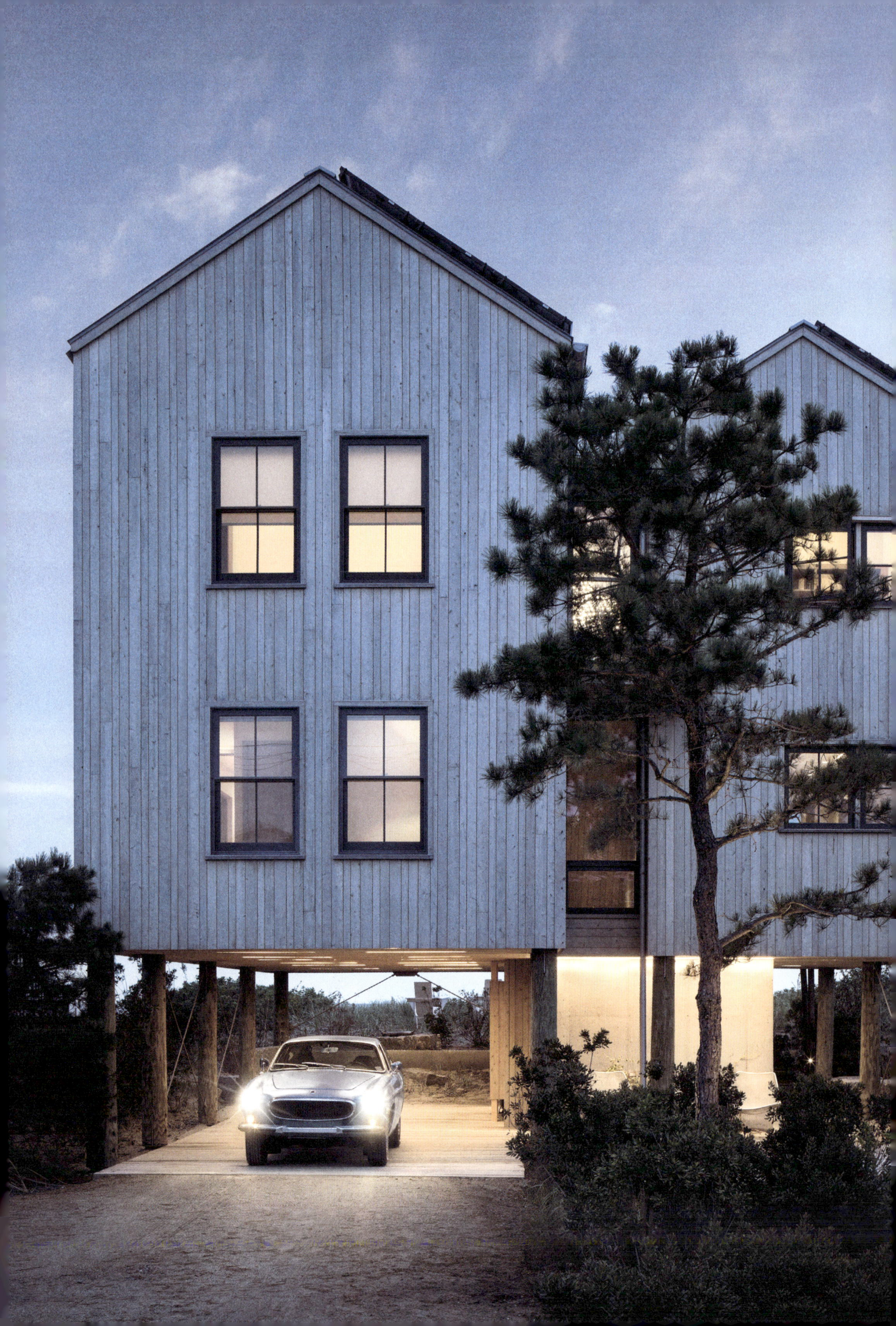

Volvo 1800 ES

ARCHITECTURE Perched amidst the dunes of Moody Beach in Maine, this private residence appears as if it were a house on stilts, rising gracefully from its surroundings. The design for this coastal retreat was created by Woodhull, the Portland-based architectural firm of Caleb Johnson. Wood remains the central theme throughout this project. Douglas fir and American white oak imbue the interior with a natural and inviting atmosphere, while cedar envelops the exterior. The house harmoniously blends with the spectacular landscape, so magnificent that the architecture itself takes a backseat. By elevating the structure above ground level, Johnson ingeniously opens up impressive vistas that capture the untamed beauty of the coastline and the hinterland. The elevated structure also provides an ideal and photogenic shelter for a car.

CAR The Volvo 1800 ES, derived from the P1800, is considered by many to be one of the most beautiful Volvos of all time. The design was inspired by Pietro Frua's 'Rocket' concept car, which was deemed too futuristic. Ultimately, Norwegian Jan Wilsgaard, chief designer at Volvo Car Corporation from 1950 to 1990, was responsible for its design. Just over 8,000 cars were built in 1972 and 1973, primarily finding customers in the United States. The car earned the nickname 'Snow White's coffin' on account of its elongated 'shooting brake' bodywork, large side windows, all-glass trunk lid and high load floor. While not a full-blooded sports car, the 1800 ES packed a punch for its time, with 135 hp and weighing about 2,650 lb (1,200 kg), Its timeless design is evident in the rears of the Volvo 480 ES (1986) and the C30 (2006) which feature clearly recognizable elements from the 1800 ES.

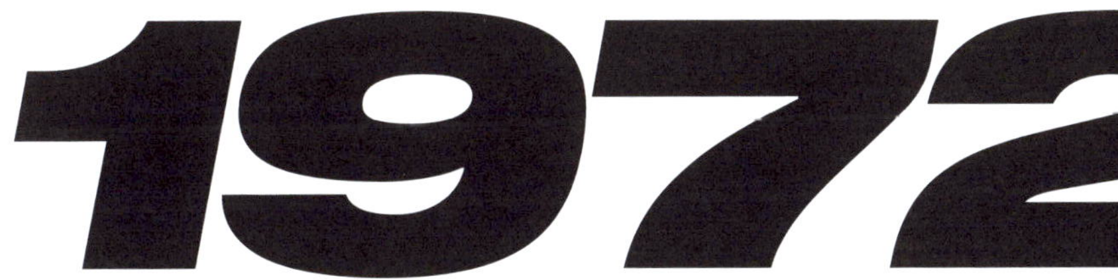

How EVs are Reshaping our Buildings

The rise of electric cars is significantly impacting architecture on several fronts. Energy infrastructure, spatial planning and the design of public and private buildings now require creative solutions from architects. Bidirectional charging, in particular, has the potential to be a gamechanger, as electric vehicles, charged by solar panels, can serve as a home battery for extended periods.

The transition to electric cars aligns with the broader trend towards sustainability and environmentally friendly design, focusing on energy-efficient materials and practices to minimize ecological footprints in both car and building design and construction.

Architects are faced with the challenges of seamlessly integrating car-charging infrastructure into various environments, including public spaces, commercial buildings and private residences, in both rural and urban settings. The evolving needs of electric cars, which often require longer parking time for recharging, may necessitate the creation of additional parking spaces, while integrating charging stations into the aesthetic and functional aspects of buildings and public areas.

Additionally, changes in parking needs brought about by electric cars and the potential transition to autonomous vehicles could led to the repurposing of existing parking facilities for other uses. Moreover, the quieter operation of electric vehicles compared to conventional combustion engines could influence traffic patterns and allow for the development of public spaces and buildings closer to busy roads.

The most significant impact of electric cars on architecture is expected to be felt in residential spaces, particularly in terms of energy storage and management. Electric cars are increasingly being viewed as mobile energy storage units with bidirectional capabilities. This means they can not only draw power from the grid but also feed surplus energy back into that grid (Vehicle-to-Grid, V2G) or supply it to buildings (Vehicle-to-House, V2H). Consequently, architects must consider how to effectively integrate these advanced energy management systems into the designs of individual buildings and public spaces.

THE CAR AS HOME BATTERY

Let's delve further into this concept. Did you know that electric cars can serve as both power sources for household tasks such as ironing and cooking, and as potential revenue generators by returning excess power to the grid? This emerging concept envisions electric cars as mobile home batteries, and several car manufacturers are already offering or developing bidirectional charging capabilities to make this a reality. The underlying idea is that our cars spend about 95 percent of their time idle, presenting a substantial untapped energy source.

To leverage this capability, your electric car must be capable of bidirectional charging, which holds particular appeal when combined with solar panels. When your solar panels generate surplus energy that your home doesn't immediately consume, you can store that excess power in your electric car's battery. Later, during the evening, when electricity rates are higher, you can use this stored energy to power your electric household appliances effectively while implementing smart energy management strategies. The potential benefits of this setup are greater than you might imagine.

Consider that the battery in a typical electric car has a capacity ranging from 50 to 80 kWh, while the average daily consumption of a household in the United States is about 29 kWh. Consequently, a fully charged electric car can cover two to three days of household electricity consumption. In some European countries a single battery charge from your car can potentially last an entire workweek. This flexibility is also reassuring in the sense that you won't deplete your car's driving range if it's actively assisting with household energy needs.

However, it's important to note that plugging your electric car into a standard garage socket won't suffice for bidirectional charging. You'll need a specialized bidirectional charging station or a wallbox, equipped with a converter. This is necessary since a car's battery operates on direct current, while a house typically requires alternating current. Additionally, modern wallboxes often feature data connectivity, allowing then to manage charging times, consider peak and off-peak electricity tariffs, and even transfer excess or low-cost power back to the grid when demand is high. As a result, you may be compensated for contributing power to the grid during peak periods, adding a potential source of income from your electric car's bidirectional capabilities.

TESLA: STANDARD BY 2025

The capability of electric cars, trucks and buses to feed energy back into the grid can be particularly valuable during times of high electricity demand, or in more critical scenarios during power outages. A noteworthy example occurred during the historic ten-day heatwave in the summer of 2022 in California, when the state faced the risk of a brownout due to grid overloading. To help mitigate this issue, a school in San Diego County took an innovative approach by utilizing electricity from its electric school buses and injecting it back into the grid. The seven buses provided enough energy to power up to 452 homes daily throughout the heatwave. Notably, the buses were charged during non-peak hours, further optimizing the use of available resources.

This successful initiative with bidirectional buses and the school's accompanying infrastructure is part of a broader pilot project, and many experts consider it a potential gamechanger. Such technology could play a pivotal role in expanding the electric car fleet, promoting emission-free solar energy utilization, and enhancing the stability of power grids. In light of these advantages, the state of California is currently assessing legislation that would mandate bidirectional charging for all new electric vehicles sold in the state from 2030. This would effectively transform California's rapidly growing fleet of electric vehicles into a substantial backup power resource. A designated working group is expected to be set up, tasked with submitting a report to the governor and legislature by January 1, 2026. Furthermore, it is increasingly likely that cars will be equipped with bidirectional charging technology by 2030, given the ongoing efforts of various car manufacturers in this regard. Currently, only a handful of electric models, such as the Hyundai Ioniq 5 and Ioniq 6, the Kia EV6, the Nissan Leaf and the Ford F-150 Lightning (which can store up to 131 kWh), support bidirectional charging, but more and more brands are actively working on implementing this technology. In fact, Tesla announced its plans to provide bidirectional charging as standard equipment by 2026.

While enabling electric cars to function as home, batteries holds great promise in enhancing energy independence, there are notable challenges and drawbacks to consider. For instance, it takes a relatively long time for solar panels to charge a car's battery pack. Additionally, the purchase cost of an electric car remains high, and even the installation of a smart wallbox can be expensive, with costs starting at a minimum of $5,000, excluding installation charges. Individuals who use their car daily may benefit less from bidirectional charging, and those living in terraced houses may find it challenging to install a charging box. However, such challenges can present exciting opportunities for visionary architects and engineers to develop innovative solutions. Furthermore, utility companies are still figuring out a way to compensate taxpayers for selling excess power. Denmark has already adopted this practice, where selling excess power yields the average family $3,000 a year per vehicle. This could potentially reduce the overall cost of owning an electric car by about 40 percent. On the flip side, the implementation of bidirectional charging technology could increase the price of a car by around $3,700, according to the Alliance for Automotive Innovation, which represents major car companies such as General Motors and Ford. As a result, there are ongoing discussions within the industry about whether customers who do not utilize this technology should be required to pay more for their vehicles.

“Any customer can have a car painted any color that he wants, as long as it’s black.”

Henry Ford, founder of Ford Motor Company

CREDITS

pp.10-11	Architecture: John Lautner / Photography: © Lisa Romerein/OTTO (Special acknowledgment to The John Lautner Foundation and the John Lautner Archives at the Getty Research Insitute ©2024 The John Lautner Foundation — for their ongoing support in the publishing of Lautner's iconic work.)
pp.12-13	Architecture: Craig Ellwood / Photography: © Mads Mogensen
p.14	Architecture: Albert Frey / Photography: © Daniel Chavkin
pp.16-17	Architecture: Tivadar Balogh / Photography: © Amy Claeys
p.19	Architecture: Craig Ellwood / Photography: © Pressrender
pp.20-21	Architecture: Robert Wolfson / Photography: © Amy Claeys
pp.22-25	Architecture: Louis DesRosiers / Photography: © Amy Claeys
p.26	Architecture: Mies van der Rohe, © SABAM Belgium 2024 / Photography: © James Haefner
pp.28-29	Architecture: E. Stewart Williams / Photography: © Steven Separovich
pp.30-31	Architecture: John Lautner / Photography: © Paul Jasmin (Special acknowledgment to The John Lautner Foundation and the John Lautner Archives at the Getty Research Insitute ©2024 The John Lautner Foundation — for their ongoing support in the publishing of Lautner's iconic work.)
pp.32-35	Architecture: Irving Tobocman / Photography: © Amy Claeys
pp.42-43	Architecture: Palmer & Krisel / Photography: © Demetrius Romanos
pp.44-45	Architecture: William Krisel / Photography: © Demetrius Romanos
pp.46-49	Architecture: E. Stewart Williams / Photography: © Tom Blachford
p.50	Architecture: Charles Du Bois / Photography: © Tom Blachford
pp.52-53	Architecture: William Krisel / Photography: © Tom Blachford
pp.54-55	Architecture: E. Stewart Williams / Photography: © Tom Blachford
p.56	Architecture: William Francis Cody / Photography: © Daniel Chavkin
p.58	Photography: © Daniel Chavkin
p.61	Architecture: Palmer & Krisel / Photography: © Daniel Chavkin
pp.62-63	Architecture: A. Quincy Jones / Photography : © Daniel Chavkin
pp.64-65	Photography: © Christine Barrett (@atomictravel)
p.66	Architecture: William Krisel / Photography: © Paul Fuentes
p.69	Architecture: Jack and Bernie Meiselman / Photography: © Paul Fuentes
pp.70-71	Photography: © Ludwig Favre
p.73	Photography: © Ludwig Favre
p.74	Architecture: Palmer & Krisel / Photography: © Ludwig Favre
p.77	Architecture: Palmer & Krisel / Photography: © Vincent Pelletier-Wassmer
pp.78-81	Photography: © Tom Ferguson
pp.82-85	Architecture: Palmer & Krisel / Photography: © Tom Ferguson
pp.86-87	Architecture: William Krisel / Photography: © Tom Ferguson
p.95	Architecture: Arthur Brown, Jr. / Photography: © Vivienne Scholl
pp.96-97	Architecture: Louis Armet and Eldon Davis / Photography: © Charles Phoenix
p.98	Photography: © Paul Fuentes
p.101	Architecture: Thomas W. Lamb / Photography: © Paul Fuentes
pp.102-105	Architecture: Steve Curry / Photography: © Benjamin Hill
pp.106-107	Architecture: John Portman / Photography: © Raymond Arondoski
pp.108-109	Architecture: Belford Shoumate / Photography: © Stephen Kent Johnson/OTTO
p.112	Architecture: Frederick Emmons and Claude Oakland / Photography: © Demetrius Romanos
p.114	Photography: © Jeffrey Czum
p.117	Photography: © Vivienne Scholl
pp.118-119	Photography: © Ludwig Favre
pp.120-127	Photography: © Rachel Michael (rachelmichaelmichaelrachel.com)
pp.129-130	Photography: © Vivienne Scholl
pp.132-133	Architecture: Charles Bobo / Photography: © Laura Serrato
pp.140-141	Architecture: Daniel Dworsky / Photography: © James Haefner
pp.142-143	Architecture: Frank Lloyd Wright, © F.L.C. / SABAM Belgium 2024 / Photography: © James Haefner
pp.144-147	Architecture: Pierre Koenig / Photography: © Evan Klein
p.149	Architecture: William Krisel / Photography: © Paul Fuentes
pp.150-151	Architecture: Buff & Hensman, Commune / Photography: © Roger Davies/OTTO
pp.152-153	Architecture: Montalba Architects / Photography: © Kevin Scott
p.154	Architecture: Pereira & Luckman / Photography: © General Motors
pp.156-157	Architecture: Zaha Hadid Architects / Photography: © Brad Feinknopf/OTTO
pp.164-165	Architecture: Brett Rhode / Photography: © Ken Altes
pp.166-167	Architecture and photography: © Arch11
pp.168-169	Architecture: © Chan-li Lin, AIA and Denise Ferris, AIA / Photography: © Brad Feinknopf
p.171	Architecture: Kohn Pedersen Fox Associates / Photography: © Vincent Pelletier-Wassmer
pp.172-175	Architecture: © William / Kaven Architecture / Photography: © Jeremy Bittermann / JBSA
p.177-180	Architecture: Caleb Johnson / Photography: Trent Bell
Front cover:	Photography: © Jeffrey Czum
Back cover:	left: Photography: © Paul Fuentes
	right top: Architecture: Pierre Koenig / Photography: © Evan Klein
	right below: Architecture: Steve Curry / Photography: © Benjamin Hill

Texts & Image Selection
Thijs Demeulemeester
Bert Voet

Translation
Patrick Lennon

Copy-editing
Melanie Schapiro

Book design
Thomas De Bruyne

Typesetting
Keppie & Keppie

If you have any questions or comments about the material in this book, please do not hesitate to contact our editorial team: art@lannoo.com

ISBN: 9789401489492
D/2024/45/285 - Thema: AJ, AM, WGC
www.lannoo.com

“Automobiles have interior spaces corresponding to an outer form, like buildings, but the designer’s aesthetic purpose is to enclose the functioning parts of an automobile, as well as its passengers, in a package suggesting directed movement along the ground.”

Arthur Drexler, architect